GENDERED VIOLENCE

Jewish Women in the
Pogroms of 1917 to 1921

Jews of Russia & Eastern Europe and Their Legacy

Series Editor
MAXIM D. SHRAYER (Boston College)

ACADEMIC
STUDIES
PRESS

GENDERED VIOLENCE

Jewish Women in the
Pogroms of 1917 to 1921

Irina Astashkevich

Boston
2018

Library of Congress Cataloging-in-Publication Data: the bibliographic record for this title is available from the Library of Congress.

ISBN 978-1-61811-999-5 (paperback)
ISBN 978-1-61811-617-8 (electronic)

Book design by Kryon Publishing Services (P) Ltd.
www.kryonpublishing.com

On the cover: "White City," by Alexandra Rozenman
(watercolor and white-out on paper); reproduced by the artist's permission.

Published by Academic Studies Press in 2018.
28 Montfern Avenue
Brighton, MA 02135, USA
P: (617)782-6290
F: (857)241-3149
press@academicstudiespress.com
www.academicstudiespress.com

An electronic version of this book is freely available, thanks to the support of libraries working with Knowledge Unlatched. KU is a collaborative initiative designed to make high quality books Open Access for the public good. The Open Access ISBN for this book is 978-1-61811-907-0. More information about the initiative and links to the Open Access version can be found at www.knowledgeunlatched.org.

To my mother and grandmother

Table of Contents

Acknowledgments

Without the advice and incredible support of many people, this volume would not have been possible. It took over a decade to write this book, but it took many more years of learning and searching to become capable of doing so. I am grateful to my teachers, mentors, colleagues, friends, and family, who guided and supported me on the journey that led me to write this book.

First and foremost, I would like to thank Project Judaica, a joint program between the Jewish Theological Seminary, YIVO Institute of Jewish Research, and the Russian State University of Humanities, founded and maintained by Professor David Fishman. In 1991, Project Judaica opened up opportunities for students in Moscow to study Jewish history, culture, and tradition. I am forever grateful to David Roskies, Zvi Gitelman, and Steven Zipperstein, whose lectures inspired me to continue into graduate research in the field of Jewish studies.

I want to thank my adviser, Antony Polonsky, who suggested that I explore the history of pogroms, and then saw this project through its initial stages with wisdom and patience. I am grateful to ChaeRan Freeze, who opened up for me the field of gender research and encouraged me to explore the history of gender violence. Her knowledge, rigor, and generosity guided me through the most difficult phases of this project, and helped me to find my own voice. Thank you for being my mentor, colleague, and friend. I am grateful to the Near Eastern and Judaic Studies Department at Brandeis University, and to all the amazing people who made it my true home and one place of empowerment. I want to thank the Tauber Institute for the Study of European Jewry at Brandeis University, and its executive director Sylvia Fuks Fried, for providing me with the best research environment and support, something for which is impossible to overstate my gratitude.

I don't know how to thank Anna Shternshis for her crucial contributions to the structure and theoretical basis of this book, and for her inexhaustible support and motivation, without which this project would have forever remained just a project. And, above all, thank you for the trust and friendship that sustained me on this journey. I am grateful to Maxim D. Shrayer, who believed in this project and helped to shape it at the most critical stages. I am honored that this book is included in his series at Academic Studies Press. I would like to thank the scholars whose comments on different chapters of this book broadened my views and enriched my research. I am indebted to Elissa Bemporad and Jeffrey Veidlinger, who shared with me their work in progress, offered precious comments, and responded to my queries. Thank you for the much needed challenge and support. I want to thank Glenn Dynner for discussing with me the most crucial issues of secularism and modernity, and for invaluable suggestions and comments that have made me a better writer. I want to thank Simon Rabinovitch for many insights into Russian Jewish politics as well as invigorating discussions about it. I would also like to thank David Shneer, Eugene Sheppard, John-Paul Himka, Jonathan Dekel-Chen, Mihaly Kalman, Debra Bergoffen, Ilana Szobel, Laura Jockusch, Polly Zavadivker, Nathan Meir, Eugene Avrutin, Vassili Schedrin, and many others, who answered my questions, discussed difficult issues, and offered solutions. I would also like to thank Daniel Czitrom,who generously offered much needed help at the very last yet crucial moment.

This project was generously supported by the Jewish Memorial Foundation, Hadassah-Brandeis Institute, the Tauber Institute for the Study of European Jewry at Brandeis University, and the Genesis Foundation. Awarded grants made my extensive archival research possible.

I am ever grateful to the archive of the YIVO Institute of Jewish Research, where I conducted my research for over a decade. I want to express my gratitude to the exceptional group of people who welcomed and accommodated me during my time at the Center for Jewish History, among them Fruma Mohrer, Lyudmila Sholokhova, and Gunnar Berg. I want to thank Marek Web, who taught me about Jewish archives back in Moscow and advised me during my research in YIVO, and Leo Greenbaum, who helped me to struggle with particularly difficult Yiddish handwriting. Also, I would like to express my gratitude to Lidia Miljakova, chief editor of the "Book of Pogroms" collection of documents from the Russian State Archive, who responded to my questions. I appreciate the services provided by the Judaica Department of Harvard Widener Library when I worked with the Poalei Zion Party Archival Collection.

My very special and sincere thanks go to LeeAnn Dance and the crew of "My Dear Children," the first documentary about pogroms. I am proud to be part of this amazing project that led me into much deeper exploration of the personal narratives of the pogrom survivors. The days spent with LeeAnn Dance, Cliff Hackel, Catherine Zimmerman and Rick Patterson doing research and filming led me to explore new lines of inquiry and to write further. I owe a debt of gratitude and appreciation to the incredible Judy Favish, who had the courage to embark on the painful and difficult journey into an exploration of her grandmother's life, which was warped by pogroms. Thank you for sharing with me Feiga Shamis's memoir and the story of her life—an absolutely unique and precious piece of evidence that considerably enriched my research.

I want to thank Academic Studies Press and its director, Igor Nemirovsky, for publishing my work. I feel privileged that my book is published as part of series entitled Jews of Russia & Eastern Europe and Their Legacy. I am grateful to my editors Oleh Kotsyuba and Gregg Stern for their immense patience and generous assistance, and to my anonymous reader for useful insight and suggestions. Thanks to Glenn Dynner and Elissa Bemporad, a modified version of the last chapter will be published in the forthcoming spatial edition of East European Jewish History.

I want to express my gratitude to a vast group of individuals who supported my work in many different ways. I thank Vardit Ringvald, who patiently guided me to undertake this project and believed that I would succeed. I want to thank my New York City friends—particularly Tonya Lifshits, Boris Reizis, and Luba and Michael Roitman—whose couches I occupied while conducting research at YIVO. I want to thank my dearly missed friend, Natalia Smoliarova, z"l, to whom I am indebted in more ways than I can express. I want to thank Yuri Machkasov and Diane Covert, who painstakingly proofread parts of this manuscript and made me believe that I could write.

I want to thank my parents, Boris Astashkevich and Yulia Bentsianova, who taught me to work hard and to think critically, who believed that I would write this book, and who helped to take care of my children while I was writing. My sister Natalia is my source of power and strength, and I am blessed to have her by my side. I thank my husband, Dmitri Pal, who enabled me to find my true calling and to follow it. My children Nikita and Elizabeth grew up unable to casually discuss, or even to understand, what exactly was the topic of their mother's research, but they were always proud of me notwithstanding. I learned a lot from my children while raising them, and I feel grateful and blessed.

My grandmother Susanna had to walk her daughter, my mother Yulia, to school daily to protect her and her brothers from antisemitic slander. My grandparents wanted to live a normal life; instead, they faced wars, hunger, evacuations, later antisemitism, and all the other big and small hardships that constituted life in the Soviet Union. Neither of them wanted it, but they survived it. Their unconditional love and their evident and hidden experiences made me who I am today. My grandmother, Susanna Nagy, never talked about anything Jewish in attempt to shield me. My mother, Yulia, encouraged me to study Jewish history. With respect for the most important women in my life, I dedicate this book to my mother and to the loving memory of my grandmother.

Introduction

A POGROM IS A POGROM!

Growing up in Moscow in the 1970s and 1980s, we, the last Soviet generation, learned and told a lot of jokes. One of the jokes that I remember from my childhood appears to still be popular today in Russia:[1]

There's a pogrom going on in a shtetl. The gang of hoodlums rush into a Jewish home and start to loot, plunder, and smash anything they do not grab. The owner, an old Jew, begs the assailants: "Take anything you want, just spare my daughter!" The old Jew's daughter hears this and comes out into the room, saying, "No, Dad! A pogrom is a pogrom!"

This joke was considered funny, like many other "Jewish jokes" that were very common and unexceptional. No one judged it to be offensive or humiliating; after all, no foul language was used. I cannot recall having been disturbed by the word "pogrom" either, because I did not feel that it applied to me in any way: no one in my family had ever discussed being Jewish; neither the implication of rape as an inextricable part of a pogrom nor the suggestion of Jewish girls having elevated sexual appetites were considered offensive or degrading.

What I did not know, and what my family never wanted me to know, was that my grandmother had been born in a small town near Balta in 1920, about a year after a wave of anti-Jewish violence had swept through the town and its vicinity, leaving hundreds dead and many more women raped. My grandmother was always uneasy talking about being Jewish, and she urged me not to show or tell anybody that I was Jewish too. She was very concerned that my looks might betray me as a Jewish girl.

---

1   Judging from how frequently it appears on many Internet pages. For example: http://anekdotov.me/evrei/55412-nachalo-veka-v-mestechke-evrejskij-pogrom.html.

Every joke, as the colloquial wisdom has it, is only "partly a joke," which illustrates how Soviet popular humor helped people "cope with uncertainties" of life.[2] Notwithstanding the sophisticated undertones and therapeutic effect of many Soviet jokes, this particular one is problematic for a number of reasons. Looking back at this exceedingly derogatory joke, I can clearly see now that it trivializes the phenomenon of potentially deadly ethnic violence, which integrated into itself the mass rape of Jewish women as a symbolic feature. Rape culture that prevailed and still prevails today in Russia suggested that offensive remarks about sexually assaulting women could and should be laughed at.

Astoundingly, this short anecdote accounts for the crucial and symbolic features of pogrom rape at the time of the Civil War in Ukraine in 1917–21: pogroms were violent, vast numbers of women were raped, and they were raped by groups of assailants, often publicly. What shocked me when I started my research into pogroms, besides the realization of my childish ignorance of the problem, is that over half a century later an enormous tragedy, which left many tens if not hundreds of thousands of Jews dead and an even larger number of women raped, had been turned in the public culture into a dirty joke.

A number of questions guided my research when I first started to work on pogrom history: Why did raping Jewish women become an integral part of a pogrom? Why did pogrom perpetrators so often perform the rapes in groups? How did the Jewish community of Ukraine respond to rape? Why are insulting jokes and crude songs seemingly the only traces of the mass rape of Jewish women left in the public culture? Are jokes and crude songs the only way to deal with trauma? I endeavored to find answers, but sometimes found only more questions, and so the research of the pogrom history evolved into this first-of-its-kind research of the mass rape of Jewish women. This book is the result of more than a decade of studying the phenomenon of gender violence during pogroms in Ukraine at the time of the Civil War of 1917–21.[3] It aspires to establish a new line of inquiry into the strategic employment of rape

---

2 Anna Shternshis, "Humor and Russian Jewish Identity," in *A Club of Their Own: Jewish Humorists and the Contemporary World*, ed. Eli Lederhendler and Gabriel N. Finder (Oxford: Oxford University Press, 2016), 1010–112.

3 The series of military conflicts on the territory of modern Ukraine that ensued during the First World War and the Russian Revolutions of 1917 are commonly known in historiography as the Civil War, the Soviet Ukrainian War, or the Ukrainian War for Independence. In 1921, the military conflict resulted in the victory of the Bolsheviks and the establishment of the Ukrainian Soviet Republic. See Chapter 1.

during pogroms, and the repercussions of mass rape for Russian Jewish history throughout the twentieth century and beyond.

The Civil War on the territory of Ukraine had started amid the First World War and continued through 1921, when Bolsheviks established a Soviet republic in Ukraine.[4] It was a time of absolute chaos, as numerous armies, guerrilla forces, and armed gangs fought one another all over Ukraine. The belligerents—which included the Ukrainian National Army, the former Russian imperial officers united into the Volunteer Army, the Bolsheviks, and a number of guerrilla militant groups—perpetrated anti-Jewish violence and utilized the systematic rape of Jewish women as a strategic weapon to convey that they were superior and to dehumanize the Jewish victims. No definite rape statistics are available, because rape was stigmatized as shameful. However, an estimate based on thorough study of various sources suggests that the mass rape of Jewish women occurred in at least two-thirds of pogroms and often involved the majority of the Jewish female population in the victimized communities. These cautious estimates suggest that tens if not hundreds of thousands of Ukrainian Jewish women were victims of sexual violence and many more Jewish men and women witnessed it. After 1922, when Ukraine became part of the Soviet Union and the violence subsided, the problem of mass rape during the pogroms was never specifically addressed or recognized by either the Soviet government or the Jewish population. The Jewish community in its traditional form ceased to exist, while many Jews, especially those who were young and educated, moved to larger cities outside of former Pale of Settlement. The impact of unresolved and unspoken trauma of mass rape in Ukraine on what has now become known as the post-Soviet Jewry is yet to be evaluated.[5]

The territories where violent pogroms took place in 1917–22 lay in "the border areas between the Russian and Polish heartlands—present-day Ukraine and Belarus."[6] Just as it is difficult to determine the exact number of the military and social conflicts that constituted the Civil War, it is also hard to make geographic distinctions. However, my research is primarily based on the materials on pogroms that occurred on the territory of Ukraine and will be focused

---

4   Some violent outbreaks, however, continued on the territory of Ukraine in 1922.

5   The role of the pogroms in the making of Soviet Jewry is discussed at length by Elissa Bemporad in the first chapter of her book forthcoming from Oxford University Press in May 2019: *Legacy of Blood: Jews, Pogroms and Ritual Murder in the Lands of the Soviets*.

6   David Engel, *The Assassination of Symon Petliura and the Trial of Scholem Schwarzbard 1926–1927: A Selection of Documents* (Gottingen: Vandenhoeck & Ruprecht GmbH & Co, 2016), 59.

on anti-Jewish violence that happened in Ukraine. I had to exclude from my research the pogroms on the territory of modern Belarus and on some Polish territories that occurred at approximately the same time but under somewhat different circumstances.

The anti-Jewish violence during pogroms, which took lives of approximately tens or even hundreds of thousands of Jews[7] in over a thousand pogroms in about five hundred localities, constitutes genocide.[8] The impact of this assertion on the research of pogrom violence, and particularly gender violence, is crucial, as it transfers the previously understudied history of pogroms in Ukraine into the realm of genocide studies. At the same time, it also furthers those studies that have already been actively redefining their methods, while the range of research has grown geographically and chronologically. The genocidal violence during the pogroms can thus be treated as a precursor to the Holocaust, and until recently the latter overshadowed the significance of pogrom violence and research regarding it in the East European Jewish historiography. Similarly, the mass rape of Jewish women during pogroms has never been considered as a subject for in-depth research, because it was never considered within the framework of genocidal rape, a flourishing field of study of gender violence as a strategic weapon of war and genocide.

Existing historiography of the pogroms in Ukraine during the Civil War, while rich and extensive,[9] has so far been missing two key elements. On the one hand, the pogroms during Civil War were either subsumed into the historiography of the previous pogrom waves of 1881–82, or of the Kishinev pogrom of 1903; or were discussed as a backdrop to the dramatic events of the Civil War in Ukraine and the First World War. Scholarship on the pogroms has never broached the subject of gendered experience of violence and rape as an

---

7   All casualty estimates are based on a number of various sources, but no confirmed data exists. Since the number of casualties is employed for illustrative purposes, I chose the median number. For in-depth assessment of the accounts for victims of pogroms see Engel, *The Assassination of Symon Petliura*, 59–60.

8   See Jeffrey Veidlinger's upcoming book and also his public presentations. For example, video record of Jeffrey Veidlinger, "A Forgotten Genocide: The Pogroms in Ukraine, 1918–19," program of YIVO Institute for Jewish Research (2016), organized by Elissa Bemporad.

9   The most acknowledged works on the subject include John Klier and Shlomo Lambroza, *Pogroms: Anti-Jewish Violence in Modern Russian History* (Cambridge: Cambridge University Press, 1992); Jonathan L. Dekel-Chen, *Anti-Jewish Violence: Rethinking the Pogrom in East European History* (Bloomington: Indiana University Press, 2011); Henry Abramson, *A Prayer for the Government: Ukrainians and Jews in Revolutionary Times, 1917–1920* (Cambridge, MA: Harvard University Press, 1999).

independent line of inquiry. My book is the first study to evaluate the traumatic impact of rape on both Jewish women and men through scrupulous analysis of the gendered narrative of pogrom rape. This gendered form of violence shaped the experience of the victims and the narration of the events, which largely followed normative gendered scripts and but also deviated from them in important ways.

The bulk of the sources for this research originates in the archival collection of Elias Tcherikower (YIVO Institute of Jewish Research in New York).[10] A renowned historian, Tcherikower came to Kiev (Kyiv) from the United States in order to participate in Jewish politics, which blossomed after the democratic reforms of the Ukrainian parliament. Little did he know that he would become a witness of the enormous humanitarian tragedy of the Jewish people. After pogroms surged, Tcherikower with his collaborators established the Editorial Board that began to assemble documents about anti-Jewish violence, and also sent out a call for Jews to contribute to the project. The Editorial Board interviewed the refugees and victims when assessing the damage inflicted by the pogroms. After the material was collected, it was sorted, cataloged and summarized by Tcherikower and his wife Rivka. Laura Jockusch placed this massive effort within the framework of *Khurbn-Forshung*[11]—a tradition of history writing, as fitting the Jewish response to catastrophe. Tcherikower's and his collaborators' efforts toward creating an inclusive collection of documents that would explicitly describe pogroms in Ukraine resulted in a vast archive that contains unique documents as well as materials from various relief organizations that provided help for victims of pogroms and conducted their own research. Tcherikower moved his archive to Berlin in the early twenties, where he began to publish a series of books about pogroms, and later to Paris, where Tcherikower used the archival materials for the defense of S. Shwarzbard, who assassinated General Petliura[12]—the man admittedly responsible for the pogroms.

Some copies of the documents from Tcherikower's archive have been published as part of the Russian State Archive volume on pogroms,[13] but not all of the materials in the archival collections were identical to each other, and the volume contains some unique archival material. Other collections utilized

---

10 YIVO Archive, Elias Tcherikower Archive 1903–63, Rg 80–89 (Mk 470).

11 Laura Jockusch, *Collect and Record! Jewish Holocaust Documentation in Early Postwar Europe* (Oxford: Oxford University Press, 2012), 28–30.

12 Leader of the Ukrainian Government–Directory in 1919.

13 L. V. Miljakova, ed., *Kniga Pogromov: Pogromy na Ukraine, v Belorussii i Evropejskoj Chasti Rossii v Period Grazhdanskoj Vojny 1918–1922 gg.; Sbornik Dokumentov* (ROSSPĖN, 2007).

for the purposes of this research include the Kiev Regional Archive[14] and the archive of Poalei Zion Party.[15] The source base was supplemented with variously assembled secondary sources and a number of memoirs.

THE MORAL ECONOMY OF THE POGROM AND ITS SCRIPT

"The dam of inhibition broke,"[16] wrote Helmut Smith, describing the changing pattern of the anti-Jewish violence in modern history. "In incidence and intensity, the anti-Jewish violence was something new, even if in form it represented an archaic form of protest,"[17] Smith continued, describing the murderous turn of the new violence in the late nineteenth to the early twentieth century that was no longer curbed by the state and army, and often employed by them. Smith based his observations primarily on the pogrom waves in Russia that occurred in 1881–83 and in 1903–6, which, compared to the relatively undisturbed existence of European and Russian Jews in the previous century or centuries, appeared to represent a significant surge of anti-Jewish violence. The following pogrom wave of 1917–21 surpassed any violence previously experienced by Jews anywhere, and yet retained the name and the form of pogrom.

Searching for the exhaustive definition of pogrom, David Engel asks the crucial question: What is gained by defining a multitude of violent ethnic, usually urban, riots as pogroms?[18] Or, in other words, what distinguishes pogrom violence from any other forms of ethnic violence, considering that notion of pogrom is more and more applied to the events outside of the Jewish realm?[19] In response to his own question, Engel identifies the necessary conditions that lead to pogroms.[20] First, victims are easily identified as a group, religious or ethnic, which is considered lower in stature than the group of perpetrators

---

14 Jewish Pogroms in Ukraine, 1918–24. Documents of the Kiev Oblast' Commission for Relief to Victims of Pogroms (Obshetskom) (Fond 3050), years covered by document are 1918–21.

15 World Socialist Union of Jewish Workers—Poalei, Zion (Rossiiskii tsentr khraneniia i izucheniia dokumentov noveishei, istorii: [Poalei Zion archive] : [on microfiche] IDC, Harvard Library, 1998).

16 Ibid., 117.

17 Ibid.

18 David Engel, "What's in a Pogrom? European Jews in the Age of Violence," in Anti-Jewish Violence: Rethinking the Pogrom in East European History, ed. Jonathan Dekel-Chen (Bloomington: Indiana University Press, 2010), 21.

19 For example, see Parvis Ghassem-Fachandi, Pogrom in Gujarat: Hindu Nationalism and Anti-Muslim Violence in India (Princeton, NJ: Princeton University Press, 2012).

20 Engel, "What's in a Pogrom?," 24.

of violence. Secondly, the offending group claims collective injury or offense committed by the victimized group. The proclaimed offense or injury can be righted and the "injured" high-ranking group can be made whole only through immediate application of violence against the victimized group. "In the perpetrators' hierarchy of values the transgressions of the lower-ranking group were of such magnitude that the legitimate order of things could be restored only when either they themselves took the law into their own hands or— as in Pinsk in 1919, Ukraine during the Russian Civil War, Kristallnacht, or Iaqi in 1941— instruments of the state or claimants to state power bypassed normal political and legal channels in favor of direct action against the offenders."[21] The process of restoration of corrupt social norms through violence, according to Edward Thompson, represented the "moral economy" of the crowd.[22]

The act of restoring the right and punishing the wrong is a symbolic one, and is exercised best through ritualized violent theater, not unlike Foucauldian "public punishment."[23] The pogrom, as a social ritual, utilized a combination of specific semantically laden patterns and rites played by the rioters, and to a certain extent by their victims. This performance brought not only symbolic restoration of justice, but moral satisfaction to the aggressive crowd. As a result the violent theater of pogrom played out over and over coalesced into a recognizable pattern or pogrom script.

Pogrom as a form of repair of broken social norms has permeated Jewish history. David Nirenberg has applied this concept to medieval Jewish history and classified such violent outbreaks as systematic violence,[24] the purpose of which was to punish the Jews and emphasize their inferior position in the society. By the beginning of the twentieth century not only the pogrom phenomenon became an unexceptional part of life,[25] but also the pogrom script itself became part of everyday reality. The increase of anti-Jewish violence was facilitated by the growing "visibility" of Jews in relation to European society and a weakening of state power at the same time.[26] The latter is unanimously recognized as a necessary condition that promotes pogrom violence.

---

21 Ibid.
22 Edward P. Thompson, "The Moral Economy of the English Crowd in the Eighteenth Century," *Past & present*, no. 50 (1971).
23 Michel Foucault, *Discipline and Punish: The Birth of the Prison* (New York: Vintage, 1995).
24 David Nirenberg, *Communities of Violence: Persecution of Minorities in the Middle Ages* (Princeton, NJ: Princeton University Press, 1998).
25 Klier and Lambroza, *Pogroms: Anti-Jewish Violence*, 33.
26 Engel, "What's in a Pogrom?," 30–31.

The unprecedented surge of violence during the Civil War in Ukraine, when the country was in a "state of collapse,"[27] was truly catastrophic, per Nirenberg's classification, but was expressed through an archaic form of pogrom and retained its meaning as a social ritual. The case-by-case analysis of approximately five hundred pogroms at the time of the Civil War in Ukraine suggested that during this period of time the pogrom script had been adapted to a new purpose. The grotesque and ferocious pogrom script precipitated the "carnival of violence,"[28] as aptly defined by Hagen, for the purpose of ultimate "restoration of justice"—a genocide. The anti-Jewish violence during the Civil War in Ukraine began as widespread but isolated incidents of pogroms and changed into a massive genocidal wave that devastated the Jewish population of Ukraine caught amid both Civil War and revolutionary changes.

Juxtaposing genocidal violence in the form of pogroms with the common perception of genocide as a killing machine, Jeffrey Kopstein calls it an intimate genocide: "ultimately the intimate violence [was] perpetrated by people well known to the victims."[29] Intimate genocidal violence aimed to destroy victimized community beyond extermination. For the pogrom perpetrators, the intimate involvement with genocide allowed them to "teach Jews a lesson," to punish them, and at the same time to dehumanize the Jews, to exclude them from the world of *Homo sapiens*, and to ultimately justify the genocide. Among the atrocities committed by the pogrom perpetrators the mass rape of Jewish women foregrounds as not only gruesome torture but also a unique semantically laden tool of destruction that causes maximum suffering. Rape had been previously employed in the pogrom script, as was humiliation and torture. However, the genocidal character of the pogrom violence during the Civil War changed the way in which mass rape of Jewish women was employed.

GENOCIDAL RAPE

In order to understand rape in the context of the pogroms, it is essential to observe it from an even more distant perspective of contemporary philosophical, gender, social, and legal studies of genocides of the twentieth century. As pogroms of the Ukrainian Civil War were tragically overshadowed in common

---

27 Jeffrey S. Kopstein and Jason Wittenberg, "Intimate Violence: Anti-Jewish Pogroms in the Shadow of the Holocaust," unpublished version (2013): 6–23.

28 William W. Hagen, "The Moral Economy of Ethnic Violence: The Pogrom in Lwow, November 1918," *Geschichte und Gesellschaft* 31, no. 2 (2005): 204.

29 Kopstein and Wittenberg, "Intimate Violence: Anti-Jewish Pogroms," 20.

cognizance by the Holocaust, so the history of mass rape of the Jewish women during pogroms has all but vanished from collective memory and scholarship alike. Otherwise, it would have been widely recognized as one of the first violent conflicts of the twentieth century to which the term "genocidal rape" could and should be applied. The research of wartime rape yielded a number of theories, the most compelling of which is the "strategic rape theory" based on the classic work of Susan Brownmiller.[30] This theory interprets wartime mass rape as a weapon of war strategically employed and systematically used. The term "genocidal rape" was coined only in 1996 by Beverly Allen in her ethnographic research of rape during the genocide in former Yugoslavia,[31] where she makes a clear distinction between wartime rape and genocidal rape, because "the horrible difference genocidal rape makes" is in the "particular suffering it causes."[32] The rape became the versatile weapon of genocide due to its pervasive damaging qualities.

The concept of genocide, as it was defined by Raphael Lemkin in 1944, leaves room for interpretation and debate, currently ongoing from scholastic, legal, and philosophical perspectives. Debra Bergoffen, who researches genocidal rape from the perspective of contemporary politics, notes that the United Nations' interpretation of genocide reversed Lemkin's definition, focusing on physical extermination, while "Lemkin's definition does not make physical destruction of [a] targeted group essential to the crime of genocide."[33] The continuing study of the Holocaust as the most prominent example of genocide and other cases of genocidal violence of the twentieth century[34] required systematic philosophical reevaluation of the concept.

Philosopher Claudia Card contends that social death is utterly central to the evil of genocide. According to Card, the shared cultural identity of a group is vital to the individual identity of its members, and genocidal practices target the destruction of the social vitality of the victimized group, not necessarily through mass physical extermination. Loss of social vitality implies that the collective identity of the particular group, based in shared history, culture, practices, and

---

30 Susan Brownmiller, *Against Our Will: Men, Women, and Rape* (New York: Simon and Schuster, 1975).

31 Beverly Allen, *Rape Warfare: The Hidden Genocide in Bosnia-Herzegovina and Croatia* (Minneapolis: University of Minnesota Press, 1996).

32 Ibid., 39.

33 Debra B. Bergoffen, *Contesting the Politics of Genocidal Rape: Affirming the Dignity of the Vulnerable Body* (London: Routledge, 2013), 19.

34 Reevaluation of some ancient history extrapolates the concept of genocide. See, for example, John K. Roth, *Genocide and Human Rights* (New York: Springer, 2005), 241.

language, is shattered or dramatically altered. The social death of the targeted group will negatively impact its surviving members,[35] and "is not necessarily less extreme than ... physical death," but may aggravate the physical death by making it indecent, stripped of dignity and respect.[36]

Card concludes her line of thought by arguing that by no means is social death accidental to the aim of genocide, but it is central to it, and the intent of genocide is to achieve social death for the murdered and surviving victims alike.[37] Card, who has also written extensively on wartime rape, explicitly placed it within the framework of genocide: "There is more than one way to commit genocide. One way is mass murder, killing individual members of a national, political, or cultural group. Another is to destroy a group's identity by decimating cultural and social bonds. Martial rape does both."[38]

Mass rape became the crucial factor in the Jewish genocide during the pogroms in Ukraine, and it was not a unique occurrence, but part of an emerging global pattern. Two genocides took place at the time of the First World War: the Armenian genocide of 1915 in the Ottoman Empire and the pogroms in Ukraine during the Civil War in 1917–21. Gender violence was utilized as a weapon of genocide in both cases, and its tactics were similar, as well as with the much better-documented and studied genocidal rapes in Bosnia and Herzegovina, Rwanda, etc.[39] Mass rape practices throughout the twentieth century aimed to extend the damaging impact of rape onto the whole community through making rape public, and provide for a greater traumatic impact of rape through its own social and psychological attributes. The physical impact of rape is magnified tremendously due to the shame, guilt, and humiliation associated with it. Shame associated with rape effectively silenced its victims and observers—on one hand, forcing the traumatic experience deep inside victims and victimized communities, and, on the other hand, leading to the concealment of rape evidence.

---

35 Claudia Card, "Genocide and Social Death," *Hypatia* 18, no. 1 (2003): 64–65.
36 Ibid., 73.
37 Ibid., 77–78.
38 Claudia Card, "Rape as a Weapon of War," *Hypatia* 11, no. 4 (1996): 8.
39 Marion Faber and Alexandra Stiglmayer, *Mass Rape: The War against Women in Bosnia-Herzegovina* (Lincoln: University of Nebraska Press, 1994); Louise du Toit, *A Philosophical Investigation of Rape: The Making and Unmaking of the Feminine Self* (London: Routledge, 2009); Iris Chang, *The Rape of Nanking: The Forgotten Holocaust of World War II* (New York: Basic Books, 2012); Catharine A. MacKinnon, "Rape, Genocide, and Women's Human Rights," *Harv. Women's LJ* 17 (1994).

The study of rape as a weapon of genocidal violence during pogroms in Ukraine in 1917–21 falls into several lines of inquiry and requires a systematic approach that will define the structure of this book. The historical background and discussion of the pogrom script place rape within the framework of the pogrom history and integrate it into the ritualized performance of pogrom violence. Genocidal rape is a versatile instrument that is employed to harm victims in many ways and on many levels, and also to produce a powerful internal and external communication from the group of offenders. Therefore, it is essential to begin discussion of genocidal rape by discerning its internal mechanisms and forms. The form of public spectacle augmented the impact of genocidal rape and transformed it into a weapon of mass destruction.

There are two major sides to gendered violence: victims and perpetrators. From the perspective of rape perpetrators, I distinguish broadly two major issues: rape as internal communication or tool, and rape as public communication and weapon. The discussion of rapists dwells on their motives and on how and why the mass rape of Jewish women fit their purposes. For a diverse groups of belligerents during Civil War in Ukraine, mass rape of Jewish women became a weapon of choice and a resource to resolve specific internal issues.

The experience of rape by the Jewish community of Ukraine falls into three categories: the immediate, physical ordeal and its aftermath, the gendered narrative of rape, and individual emotional responses to rape. The trauma of rape devastated Jewish communities by epidemics of venereal diseases and a surge of unwanted pregnancies, and simultaneously silenced female victims of rape and male witnesses, who were both shamed and degraded by their experience and struggled to narrate it.

NOTE ON TRANSLITERATION

The absolute majority of the sources used in this book utilize Russian versions of geographic locations, names, and titles. I will use the names of locations and persons as they appear in the sources with the modern Ukrainian version indicated in parentheses, whenever possible. For Russian transliteration, I use the Library of Congress system, unless there is a universally acknowledged alternate version of transcription. For Yiddish, I use the YIVO system of transliteration.

CHAPTER 1

Chaos in Ukraine: Defining the Context of Anti-Jewish Violence

" I don't know how to begin, because I have lived through so much. . . . I have survived the following pogroms: Petliura's, Denikin's, Sokolovsky's, and so many more."[1] Roza Rozenvasser, the twelve-year-old girl born in Vasilkov, found herself unable to account for all the violence that she had witnessed from February to November 1919, when she was questioned by the representatives of the Central Committee for Relief to the Pogrom Survivors. Roza's memory betrayed her, because the outbreaks of anti-Jewish violence followed one another continuously as various armed forces from formal regiments of different armies to armed bands of locals captured Vasilkov or passed through.

By 1919, Vasilkov (Vasylkiv), a town to the southwest of Kiev, was home to over five thousand Jews that constituted over forty percent of the population. The destiny of Vasilkov's Jewish community is emblematic of the dynamic of anti-Jewish violence as it unfolded and engulfed the territory of Ukraine. In the beginning of February, when the pogrom by the "Petliura's soldiers," as Ukrainian National Army soldiers were commonly referred to, devastated the shtetl, it left many Jews dead and Jewish property plundered and ruined. The exact number of pogroms that followed the first one is very hard to pin down, as the witness accounts contradict each other,[2] because the pogroms continued for weeks on end, and regiments and armed bands[3] followed one another. At least two pogroms were perpetrated by the armed bands led by infamous atamans—Sokolovsky and Zelenyi—who continued to torture and

---

1   Miljakova, *Kniga Pogromov*, 320.
2   Ibid., 366–80.
3   The Russian word "banda," a band, is unanimously used by contemporaries to identify armed gang of (usually) uprooted natives led by a commander—an ataman.

murder the Jewish population, rob their property, and extort money. The sixth pogrom, as related by some survivors,[4] happened in July, when the Bolsheviks fought the Volunteer (White) Army. Volunteer Army soldiers started a pogrom in Vasilkov, which lasted for approximately four weeks, while the unfortunate town was captured and recaptured again. Little did Roza Rozenvasser know in November 1919 that in May 1920 yet another pogrom would be perpetrated by the soldiers of the Polish armed forces.

Continuous pogroms, multiple armed forces passing through town, and gangs of locals who formed their own armed bands and roved the land were all too common characteristics that defined the life of shtetls and towns all over Ukraine. The disastrous continuous anti-Jewish violence in Vasilkov unfolded in 1919 amid the Civil War that ensued following the First World War and the Revolutions.

Chaos would be the most concise yet accurate description of the historical situation in Ukraine from the beginning of the First World War in 1914 until the official declaration creating the Ukrainian Soviet Socialist Republic in 1922. Those were the years when rapidly shifting war fronts, hostile invasions, brutal battles of the Civil War, and prowling warlord armies—combined with two Russian revolutions and erratic succession of various governments—inundated Ukraine, which was already being torn from within by the deteriorating economy and the unresolved ethnic hostilities, and turned it into a pandemonium of violence and disorder. The Jewish question[5] was at the center of this complex situation, and defined the politics and actions of the major belligerents engaged in the conflict that included the Ukrainian National Army, former Russian imperial officers united into the Volunteer Army, the Bolsheviks, and a number of guerrilla militant groups. The outbreak of the First World War and the engagement of the Russian army on the Eastern Fronts brought the war violence literally home and became the turning point in the history of anti-Jewish violence.[6]

---

4   YIVO Archive, file 165, 14022.
5   Oleg Budnitskii has explored in depth in his research how "the Jewish question" (a commonly used euphemism to describe the complex of problems and all degrees of anti-Jewish opinions in public discourse) has been interpreted and utilized by various belligerents in the Civil War. Oleg Budnitskii, *Rossijskie Evrei Mezhdu Krasnymi i Belymi (1917–1920)* (ROSSPÈN, 2005), 496.
6   For further research on the topic, see Eric Lohr, "The Russian Army and the Jews: Mass Deportation, Hostages, and Violence during World War I," *The Russian Review* 60, no. 3 (2001); and Eric Lohr, *Nationalizing the Russian Empire: The Campaign against Enemy Aliens during World War I*, vol. 94 (Cambridge, MA: Harvard University Press, 2003)—as well as

The First World War exacerbated the turbulent situation in the country and imposed many adversities on the Jews of the Russian Empire. The Russian government's policies after the beginning of the First World War intentionally victimized and punished its Jewish population that remained deprived of civil rights and confined to the Pale of Settlement, the territory where the Jewish population could legally reside. The Russian Command branded the Jewish civilian population as traitors and spies, and ordered deportation of Jewish residents from the areas close to the front lines, which included vast areas in Ukraine and Belarus. According to the latest estimates,[7] deportations affected about half a million Jews in the border communities. In some localities the evacuations, although still looming as a threat, were eventually replaced by the heinous practice of taking hostages among the local Jewish population in an attempt to prevent sabotage and espionage. The result of the expulsions and the violent hostage policies was a massive refugee crisis: large numbers of Jews found themselves in need of immediate relief and resettlement. Jewish communal and philanthropic organizations responded to the crisis and provided aid and support to the uprooted Jewish population.

On the eve of the first Russian Revolution in February 1917, the Ukrainian countryside swelled with a vast number of Jewish refugees, who, while being branded as enemies on the one hand, were driven to seek a new economic niche and settlement and, on the other hand, had all their movable possessions with them and received humanitarian aid. Those combined factors distinguished the Jewish population as an obvious target of racial violence and fomented the rise of the pogrom wave that devastated the Jewish community of Ukraine during the Civil War and became "a genocidal killing spree that left over one hundred thousand Jews dead in its wake and hundreds of thousands of refugees and orphans."[8]

The First World War was a time of crisis for the Jews of the Russian Empire and European Jewry, because the Jews became the scapegoats blamed for all misfortunes and were placed in an extremely vulnerable situation. This

---

Semion Goldin, "Deportation of Jews by the Russian Military Command, 1914–1915," *Jews in Eastern Europe* 41, no. 1 (2000): 40–73.

7   Lohr and Goldin share the same estimate.

8   Jeffrey Veidlinger, from the unpublished manuscript of his forthcoming book on pogroms, by author's permission. The First World War as a point of origin of the pogroms in Ukraine has been recently discussed and supported by many historians. See also Oleg Budnitskii, "Shots in the Back: On the Origin of the Anti-Jewish Pogroms of 1918–1921," in *Jews in the East European Borderlands. Essays in Honor of John D. Klier* (Boston: Academic Studies Press, 2012), 187–201.

continuous crisis not only paved the way for the anti-Jewish violence but also "became an opening for transformative communal change."[9] The need for organized relief effort, according to Simon Rabinovitch, promoted the combined effort of Jewish communal organizations locally and internationally and gave an impulse to the Jewish struggle for the national rights,[10] which would forever transform Jewish politics in the world.[11]

The First World War and the ensuing dramatic revolutionary changes in Europe had the most direct impact on Jewish political activity in Ukraine. The fall of the Russian Empire in 1917 promised positive changes for the Jewish population, gave hope of success to Jewish politics, and evoked powerful positive dispositions and enthusiasm[12] among Jewish activists and the general population. The Revolution in February 1917, which abolished discriminatory class-based, religious, and ethnic legislation, initiated the process of revolutionary change in Ukraine. The Central Rada (Parliament) was constituted in April 1917 in Kiev and, following the agreement with the Provisional Government in Petrograd, three national minorities, the Russians, the Jews, and the Poles, were shortly called to join its ranks. The majority in the Ukrainian parliament pressed for greater independence of Ukraine, and in July 1917 the Central Rada declared autonomy within the Russian Federation and established the Ukrainian government in the form of the General Secretariat, which consisted of fourteen branch secretariats. The National Secretariat, a branch of the General Secretariat, had three national minority divisions headed by the vice-secretaries. Later, the secretariats would be renamed into ministries, and each national division would become a separate ministry. The first secretary, and later minister of Jewish affairs, was Moshe Zilberfarb, member of a Zionist party and a fervent autonomist.[13] The key issue on the agenda of the Jewish

---

9   Simon Rabinovitch, *Jewish Rights, National Rites: Nationalism and Autonomy in Late Imperial and Revolutionary Russia* (Stanford, CA: Stanford University Press, 2014), 170.

10 Ibid., 168–69.

11 For detailed analysis of Jewish politics at the time, see Simon Rabinovitch's research (Rabinovitch, *Jewish Rights*) and also David Engel's analysis of the Jewish politics on the eve of Schwarzbard's trial (Engel, *The Assassination of Symon Petliura*).

12 Many Jewish political activists had been inspired by the initiatives of the young Ukrainian democracy. More on Jewish politics and particularly on Tcherikower's attitude toward changes, see Joshua M. Karlip, *The Tragedy of a Generation* (Cambridge, MA: Harvard University Press, 2013).

13 For more on Zilberfarb, see Jonathan Frankel, "The Dilemmas of Jewish National Autonomism: The Case of Ukraine 1917–1920," *Ukrainian-Jewish Relations in Historical Perspective* (1990): 265; Abramson, *A Prayer for the Government*, 55.

Secretariat/Ministry was the Jewish national autonomy, and in January 1918 the Central Rada passed into law the Bill of National Personal Autonomy that was celebrated as a significant victory for the Jewish minority. The recognition of the rights of minorities invigorated Jewish politics despite the rise of anti-Jewish violence and rapid deterioration of the economic situation. The short-lived democracy in Ukraine established the unique precedent of the national minorities' representation in the parliament and the government, described as a "noble experiment in human rights."[14] The period of active Jewish participation in the Ukrainian government was far from insignificant, although it lasted only briefly from its glorious beginnings in the summer of 1917 until its ignoble demise in spring of 1918,[15] when the rising wave of pogroms caused the Jewish support to be withdrawn from the Ukrainian government that itself did not survive beyond 1920.[16]

JEWISH POLITICS IN UKRAINE: GREAT EXPECTATIONS

The relationship of the Ukrainian government and the minorities, which historically represented the majority of the urban population, and particularly with the Jewish community, was a very intricate and multidimensional affair. On the one hand, the Ukrainian government was in dire need of support from the major national minorities—Russians, Poles and Jews; on the other hand, the attitude toward the Jewish community was ambivalent at the very least. Due to the long history of anti-Jewish antagonism, Ukrainian politicians were suspicious of the Jewish allegiances, but in 1917 and in early 1918 Jewish support was much needed by the Ukrainian parliament. Considering this imperative, historians argue that the Central Rada vied to attract Jewish support and succeeded by its consistent devotion to the idea of national autonomy and its declared desire to preserve unity with Russia.[17]

It is also true that Jewish political activists were just as much interested in participating in the Ukrainian parliament and the institutionalization of Jewish national autonomy, prompted by the fast development of the Ukrainian state.[18] Ukrainian Jews did not want to risk missing this unique historical opportunity.

---

14 Abramson, *A Prayer for the Government*, 163.
15 Formally, the Jewish representation in the Ukrainian government lasted for two more years.
16 Serhy Yekelchyk, *Ukraine: Birth of a Modern Nation* (Oxford: Oxford University Press, 2007), 83.
17 Abramson, *A Prayer for the Government*, 66.
18 Frankel, "The Dilemmas of Jewish National Autonomism," 265.

This sense of urgency was sharpened by the example of other national minorities' struggles for their rights and even independence, and encouraged similar activism among some groups of Jewish politicians. Rabinovitch concludes that "the fact that most of Russia's Jews lived among other national groups vying for territorial independence or autonomy within a federal state bolstered the determination of Jewish autonomists to secure similar rights for Jews."[19] The autonomous national rights fit the agenda of almost all Jewish political parties and groups that otherwise were bitterly divided.

Jewish participation in Ukrainian democracy was a mutually beneficial if fragile deal: just as the new Ukrainian state needed the support of ethnic minorities, the Jewish community cooperated with the Ukrainian government seeking national minority rights. The major discrepancy that lay in the basis of this union was the question of the Ukrainian independence, as it was not favored by most Jewish political parties and movements that had their headquarters in the Russian capital and were actively preparing for participation in elections to the All-Russian Jewish Congress. The reserved support of the Ukrainian cause among the Jewish political leaders became one of the factors that precipitated further fragmentation of the Jewish faction in the Central Rada. Although Jewish parties in the government almost unanimously supported the Central Rada against the Bolsheviks and the Red Army,[20] the finale of the experiment of national autonomy was ultimately inevitable.

At the same time, the rising pogrom wave presented new challenges for the Jewish representatives in the government, as Jewish communities all over Ukraine forwarded their reports of the pogroms to the Ministry of Jewish Affairs, seeking protection and justice. There is documented evidence of pogroms in seventy-nine locations that took place in the period from October 1917 to July 1918. This rate of pogroms per year is comparable to that of 1881–82,[21] when the first wave of pogroms shocked and terrified Russian and international society and forever embedded the pogroms in Russian Jewish history. Not forty years later this level of anti-Jewish violence deeply alarmed the

---

19 Rabinovitch, *Jewish Rights*, 206.
20 The problem of allegiancies of the Jewish fractions in the Central Rada became the focus of intense discussions by the historians and contemporaries alike. Tcherikower argued this point to contradict the proliferation of the popular canard of Judeo-Bolshevism (Di Ukrainer Pogromen) and for some politicians, like A. Revutsky of Poalei Zion, their participation in the Ukrainian government became a sore point in his negotiations with Soviet Russia. See more in Rabinovitch, *Jewish Rights*.
21 Klier and Lambroza, *Pogroms: Anti-Jewish Violence*, 39–43.

Jewish community and its leaders, and was considered catastrophic, though not exceptional. The language of the anti-pogrom proclamations issued jointly by the Vice-Secretariat for the Jewish Affairs, the National Secretariat, the Military Secretariat, Secretariat of the Internal Affairs, and the General Secretariat of Ukraine in October and November 1917 is indicative of how "incidents" of anti-Jewish violence, as they were commonly referred at the time, became a routine occurrence. The proclamation against pogroms and other forms of anti-Jewish violence reads as follows:

> From all over Ukraine we receive unfortunate reports that *in addition to the usual looting, arson etc.,*[22] some attempts to organize Jewish pogroms and loot Jewish property have also been noted. Felonious instigators are exploiting the ignorance of the citizen masses. . . . It is a duty of all conscientious Ukrainians . . . to assist the Secretariat General in the fight against this abomination inherited from the Tsarist regime.
>
> We were oppressed, but we must never become oppressors. . . . If we allow national enmity to develop and Jewish pogroms to fester, we shall have alienated an entire people. We shall have allowed a dark blemish on our collective consciousness. . . .[23]

Anti-pogrom politics originally was not among the major goals and objectives of the Ministry of Jewish Affairs, but as anti-Jewish violence increased, the work on stopping and preventing the pogroms became the ministry's daily agenda and necessitated an active involvement of both the Ukrainian government and the Central Rada in order to respond to the violence and curtail it. The Ministries (Secretariats) of the Military Affairs and Internal Affairs cooperated with the Ministry of Jewish Affairs, although the chaotic situation in the country, the ongoing war, and the weakness of the new government considerably undermined the efforts.

The Jewish community of the town of Makarov (Makariv), located about thirty miles west of Kiev, sent a formal letter to the Jewish representative in the Ukrainian government on October 21, 1917, concerning the head of the militia (the name for the local police force). Jewish citizens addressed their complaint, written in Yiddish, to the head of the Jewish Secretariat, applying to him as "Great Master" and "Enlightened of Israel," and requested a different chief of

---

22 Emphasis is mine.
23 YIVO Archive, file 123, 9406–16.

the militia: the current one took bribes ten times higher than before and was therefore very costly, so they asked to send them "a cheaper one."[24] This letter in a subtle way reflects three chief sociopolitical aspects that determined the plight of the Jewish community in 1917–18: the relationship with the Ukrainian authorities, the relationship with the Jewish representatives in the government, and the rising anti-Jewish violence. The Jewish community of Makarov tried to ensure protection from growing incidents of anti-Jewish violence, but the local militia chief requested bribes to execute his direct responsibilities and to calm civil unrest. The distress caused in the Jewish community by police abuse was a matter all too common, and the community leaders were not complaining about corruption as such, only about its rapid increase, seeking to curb the amount of bribes paid to the authorities. The most uncommon feature of this appeal is that it is written in Yiddish and addressed to the government structure that is designed to protect the rights of the Jewish population—both options that did not previously exist. The Jewish community leaders of Makarov had no recent precedent in communication with the Jewish representatives in the government, which explains the confused and convoluted style of the address. In response to the complaint, the Jewish Secretariat did follow through and forwarded an official inquiry to Ministries of the Internal and Military Affairs to resolve the problem, and the Kiev prosecutor's office conducted the investigation that by the end of December 1917 resulted in an official reprimand sent to the head of the militia in Makarov.

The Ukrainian government did take measures to stop and prevent anti-Jewish violence and contributed not only by undertaking administrative measures, like in Makarov, but also by dispatching regular troops to the pogrom locations. However, the Ukrainian government distanced itself from the cause of the pogrom and strictly opposed the attempts of the Jewish representatives to organize centralized Jewish self-defense, to institute anti-pogrom units within the Ukrainian army,[25] or any other form of organized civic response to the pogroms. The Rada and the government did not engage in developing a consistent policy to systematically prevent pogrom violence. It was not a priority for the Ukrainian government especially since the position of the Jewish

---

24 I. M. Cherikover, *Antisemitizm un Pogromen in Ukraine, 1917–1918: Tsu der Geshikhte fun Ukrainish-Yidishe Batsihungen*, ed. Archiv Ostjüdisches historisches, Geshikhte fun der Pogrom-Bayegung in Ukraine, 1917–1921 (Berlin: Mizreḥ-Yidishn historishn arkhiv, 1923), 96.

25 Mihaly Kalman, "A Pogromless City: Jewish Paramilitaries in Civil War Odessa" (paper presented at New Directions in Russian Jewish Studies, Brandeis University, April 3, 2016).

fraction in the parliament was weakening fast and the apparent lack of Jewish support for Ukrainian independence undermined it even further.

In the beginning of 1918, Ukraine finally proclaimed its independence from Russia. At the same time, following much deliberation, the Law of National-Personal Autonomy had been promulgated, ostensibly opening new perspectives for Jewish politics. What appeared to be the victorious commencement of the Jewish politics in Ukraine was in fact the beginning of its rapid demise. While denying its allegiance to Bolshevism, the deeply divided Jewish fraction decided against following the Rada into exile and remained in Kiev. Equating Jews with Bolsheviks became the most commonly and frequently employed rationale for the anti-Jewish violence in 1919. For the belligerent armies, as well as for numerous military gangs that loosely associated with Ukrainian National Army, the anti-Jewish violence became the focus of their rhetoric, and acquired a redeeming quality, as all the Jews were branded as Bolsheviks.

The origin of the Judeo-Bolshevik canard, which will be discussed from a different prospective in the course of this research, has been traced by the scholars at least as far as the First World War.[26] During the Civil War in Ukraine, this slander was consistently employed by soldiers of the Ukrainian National Army,[27] various independent military groups, and the White Army as well.[28] The pogrom perpetrators placed the rationale for anti-Jewish violence strictly on the fervently unquestionable argument that all Jews were Bolsheviks and were responsible for the Revolution, the Civil War, the fall of the Russian Empire, and the decline of the independent Ukrainian republic, and "none entertained the idea that Ukrainians could be Bolsheviks, even though this was undoubtedly the case."[29] This allegations apparently stemmed from the visual overrepresentation of the Jews among revolutionaries in general and Bolsheviks in particular. Also, it appeared that Jews benefited from the Revolution more than any other minority, as the restrictions against them were lifted. In fact, the Bolshevik command did not treat Jews favorably, considered them to be capitalists, and exploited the Jewish population frequently through expropriations and forced labor. Nevertheless, the popular opinion

---

26 Simon Rabinovitch, *Jewish Rights*, 170–73.
27 Christopher Gilley, "Beyond Petliura: The Ukrainian National Movement and the 1919 Pogroms," *East European Jewish Affairs* 47, no. 1 (2017): 45–61.
28 Budnitskii, "Shots in the Back," 87–201.
29 Gilley, "Beyond Petliura," 48.

was firmly set in the belief that Jews were Bolsheviks, and this conviction has never been fully eradicated.

Tcherikower and his contemporaries considered those accusations to be the fundamental reason for the ultimate failure of Jewish politics in Ukraine and the major reason for anti-Jewish violence, and proving these claims false became the major theme of Tcherikower's writings on pogroms.[30] As Ukraine started to sink into the abyss of the Civil War, Jewish politics crumbled alongside Ukrainian democracy, growing increasingly detached from the turmoil of war and lawlessness that devastated the country. Despite the continued fervent political, cultural, and philanthropic activity of various Jewish parties and organizations in Ukraine, the experiment of the Jewish national-personal autonomy in Ukraine was over by spring 1918.

THE BOLSHEVIKS, THE GERMAN PROTECTORATE, AND THE DIRECTORY

Following the Bolshevik coup in Petrograd in November 1917 and the establishment of the Russian Soviet Republic, the Bolsheviks of Ukraine proclaimed the Ukrainian Soviet Republic at the end of December 1917. The Bolshevik government in Russia supported the new Ukrainian Soviet Republic with troops, and the Bolshevik army began an immediate advance on the Ukrainian capital. At the beginning of February 1918, the Red Army captured Kiev for the first time in the course of the Civil War. Five weeks later, Kiev was liberated by the German Army, supported by the government of the Ukrainian republic. However, the German Army had its own agenda, seeking the end of hostilities on the Eastern Front. The German government made a pact with the Bolsheviks in March 1918, according to which Russia unilaterally withdrew from the World War and the Triple Entente coalition with France and Great Britain, and Germany assumed control over Ukraine. Following this agreement in April 1918, German command took power in Kiev and established the regime of protectorate under the leadership of their protégé Hetman (Commander) Skoropadsky, who formally dispersed the Ukrainian government. The Central Rada continued its work in exile and plotted its restoration.

---

30 See I. Cherikover, "Antisemitizm i Pogromy na Ukraine, 1917–1918 gg.," *K istorii ukrainsko-evreiskikh otnoshenii* (1923); I. M. Cherikover, *Di Ukrainer Pogramen*, Pogroms in the Ukraine in 1919 (New York: Yidisher Visnshaftlekher Institut, 1965).

German and Austro-Hungarian military forces that backed up the puppet regime of Hetman Skoropadsky effectively curbed anti-Jewish violence along with other forms of unrest throughout most of 1918. The Central Powers, who received a "breathing space" as a result of the Brest Peace, required of Ukraine the resources to continue the war, and a ceasefire on the Eastern Front to serve the same objective. Any kind of disturbance in Ukraine was dangerous for the Central Powers, and the pogrom violence wound down for almost a year.

The regime of Hetman Skoropadsky began to deteriorate by the end of 1918, following the withdrawal of German and Austro-Hungarian forces from Ukraine after their defeat in the First World War. Concurrently, Ukrainian political activity in exile was on the rise. The Ukrainian opposition contemplated the return to power and had established a five-member committee, a Directory, to coordinate the uprising. Symon Petliura,[31] the former minister of war of the Ukrainian republic, and a journalist and a playwright by profession, was initially one of five members of the Directory. Following the successful uprising, Petliura arrogated to himself the absolute power of the Directory within the first months of recapturing Kiev and did not reinstate the Rada. The Directory proclaimed unification with Western Ukraine, which had been occupied first by Austro-Hungarian and later by Polish troops. However, before any decisions could be implemented, the Directory had to abandon Kiev to Bolsheviks in early March 1919. From that moment on, Petliura's government constantly moved away from the shifting front lines to the west and south of Kiev, while plotting the counteroffensive. The Ukrainian National Army finally managed to recapture Kiev on the last day of August 1919, but retreated on the same day, abandoning the Ukrainian capital to the advancing Volunteer Army. August 31, 1919, symbolically marks the end of the short "Petliura's 1919," and although Petliura still made attempts to regain control over Ukraine, his movement lost momentum, leaving the territory of Ukraine as a battlefield for the Civil War between the Reds and the Whites.[32]

---

31 Symon Petliura is a very controversial historical figure forever linked to the pogroms in Ukraine. In the course of this book, I will not discuss Symon Petliura and his personal responsibility or lack thereof for the pogrom, and in the course of this and the following chapters I will make arguments for this position. This point of view is supported by a number of modern historians; see, for example, Christopher Gilley, "Beyond Petliura," 45–61. Notwithstanding the irrelevance of the discussion of Symon Petliura to this book, I would like to point out several significant works, the most recent and thorough of which is Engel, *The Assassination of Symon Petliura*.

32 Yekelchyk, *Ukraine: Birth of a Modern Nation*, 79.

The general scope of events in the first half of 1919 is best described as disarray and anarchy. Petliura's government was too weak to have any impact on the internal affairs or even to maintain its own regular operations. With no allies and no support, the Directory metamorphosed into military headquarters for the army on the march. From the very beginning, the Directory found itself in a very difficult political and military situation, caught between several belligerents. One side was represented by the Bolsheviks, who sent an entire army to Ukraine. Some members of the Directory and the Rada were ready to negotiate with Soviets with the goal of concluding a pact with them, but this undertaking failed even before it began, and by mid-January 1918 Ukraine and the Soviet Republic were already at war, with the Red Army advancing from the north. At the same time, the Polish army was holding onto western provinces of Ukraine, vying to maintain a buffer territory there to separate itself from the Soviets. In the southeastern regions, the former Russian officers, in coalition with the Cossack military unions, plotted an offensive against Bolsheviks and organized into the Volunteer Army, also known as the Whites. The Whites considered Ukraine to be a province within the Russian Empire, and used the name "Southern Russia" or "Lesser Russia" instead of "Ukraine." They had no interest in an alliance with the Directory. The Entente Coalition, former allies of Tsarist Russia, sent their troops to Ukraine in an attempt to support the Volunteer Army in their bid to overthrow the Bolsheviks, restore the Russian Empire, and regain control of their former ally, especially since Bolsheviks took control over the army, disrupted the war alliance, and refused to recognize any debts of the Tsarist government. French troops landed in Odessa and other port cities, backing the Whites from the south.

THE UKRAINIAN NATIONAL ARMY AND ANTI-JEWISH VIOLENCE

The first half of 1919 saw an enormous surge of anti-Jewish violence committed by Petliura's army. Locked in the midst of the intertwining front lines, the Ukrainian National Army became the most prominent functioning body of Petliura's government, and in many respects constituted the entirety of the government. The military action unfolded across most of the Ukrainian territory, as Ukrainian troops advanced from the western provinces of Ukraine and engaged in warfare with the Reds and Whites in the southeastern provinces along the Dnieper River and in the central regions. Everywhere the Ukrainian army moved, anti-Jewish pogroms took place, starting with the pogrom in Kiev that began the moment Petliura's army entered the town. The statistics are scarce, and the estimates vary; for example, the Russian Red Cross Committee to Assist Pogrom Victims reported 391 pogroms perpetrated under Directory rule,[33] and this number appears to represent the most probable number of pogroms that took place during the first six months of 1919. Even the most cautious estimates attribute at least forty percent of all the pogroms to the Directory.[34] The Ukrainian army, for the entire time of its existence called "insurgents" by the Jews and local population alike, was not a homogeneous structure, but rather a patchwork of various detachments of different origin and levels of training and experience that shared little in common except the general commitment to the Directory cause—to fight against Bolsheviks.

The insurgent nature of the Petliura's army was defined by its lack of structure and cohesion.[35] The army of the Ukrainian republic consisted of about fifteen thousand "Free Cossacks" and volunteers, who were for the most part peasants. Only some of the troops had seen previous engagement as part of the Tsarist army. Before Petliura's uprising, several elite battalions known as Sich Riflemen, formed in Galicia during the First World War and trained under German command, defected to the Directory side. The Ukrainian army had no uniform organization or consistent rank system, and many detachments were under the sole command of various officers or "atamans," while numerous independent bands and gangs almost indistinguishable from the regular insurgent army prowled various regions of Ukraine. In the Ukrainian army, what an ataman was varied from ranking officer who was subordinate to the high command, to chieftain or warlord who fought independently alongside or sometimes against the poorly organized Ukrainian army.

Though Petliura had over little control over his army, his name and the fight against the Reds and Whites became the common denominator that ostensibly united the diverse array of the armed units in Ukraine in the first half of 1919. That is why most of the atamans, whether they were leading a small guerilla band or commanding a large battalion, associated themselves with Directory cause and Petliura's name. Ataman Palienko, whose "Battalion of Death" perpetrated bloody pogroms in Berdichev (Berdychiv) and Zhitomir (Zhytomyr), and ataman Semesenko, who masterminded and carried out the

---

33 YIVO Archive, file 49, 4034–37.
34 Yekelchyk, *Ukraine: Birth of a Modern Nation*, 80.
35 For further discussion of Ukrainian army soldiers and their motives for anti-Jewish violence, see Chapter 4 of this book.

infamous Proskurov (now Khmelnytskyi)[36] pogrom, both acted as heads of divisions of the Ukrainian army.

Although the sparse documentary evidence does not account for every insurgent band and every warlord, the combination of direct and circumstantial evidence suggests that most of the numerous atamans roving Ukraine with their bands either allied with the Ukrainian army at some point or supported it. Notorious atamans Kozyr-Zyrka, Angel, and Zelenyi, who operated in the northern and central parts of Ukraine, arguably started as Ukrainian officers,[37] and others, like Laznyuk and Struk, called themselves ones. Ataman Tyutyunik, whose dubious allegiances were rarely bestowed on anyone, wrote in his rather illiterate leaflet: "Trust Petliura and nobody else; the rumors of Bolshevik advance are all silly lies."[38] Even the vicious ataman Grigoriev, whose independent army terrorized and exterminated Jewish communities in the southeastern region of Cherkassy and Elisavetgrad, started his campaign on the side of the Directory. The only consistently anarchist army under the command of the peasant chieftain Nestor Makhno nevertheless fought against Reds, Whites, and Germans, just as Petliura's army did.

The loose and unstable structure of the Ukrainian army, its various allies, and fellow fighting countrymen resulted in the constant shifting of allegiances and changing sides as a distinctive form of warfare. Often, when the Bolsheviks were winning, and defeat became inevitable, Ukrainian army regiments and ataman armies would defect to the Bolshevik side—temporarily or permanently. Atamans like Grigoriev, Kozyr-Zyrka, Zelenyi, and many others, as well as regular Ukrainian army regiments, changed sides fairly easily, out of conviction or convenience. The same people became soldiers in various armies, and the Red Army readily accepted the new arrivals, needed to fight its true enemy—the Whites.

---

36 As in Berdichev and Zhitomir, the Proskurov pogrom occurred during the very first wave of the pogroms in early 1919. The Proskurov pogrom stands out because it was masterminded by the officer of the Ukrainian National Army ataman Semesenko, who organized the massacre of the Jews in Proskurov as a punitive expedition. The Proskurov pogrom is considered to be the most violent attack on Jews during the pogrom wave, taking lives of an estimated 800–1,500 Jews.

37 According to Tcherikower's own research: YIVO Archive, file 658, 55817–33.

38 Ibid., file 75, 5870.

THE WHITES

The Whites or the Volunteer Army is the common designation for the anti-Bolshevik forces that participated in the armed resistance to the new regime.[39] Following the Bolshevik coup in October 1917, groups of Russian officers that did not support the Revolution began to form organized resistance. When the Bolsheviks made temporary peace with Germany, Russia's former allies France and Great Britain fought the Bolshevik army on the front lines of the First World War and endorsed the internal military resistance to the Soviets. The Entente provided financial and military support for the White movement until its defeat in the Civil War against the Reds. The White movement was loosely organized and lacked centralized command and strategic planning; its armies were dispersed widely along the Civil War fronts from Siberia and Urals to Caucasus and Crimea. The major challenge of the Volunteer Army was the lack of fighting force; there were not enough soldiers. Bolsheviks had successfully targeted the backward, amorphous, and undersupplied Russian army with their propaganda, and the recruited soldiers and sailors became the basis of the Soviet army and major supporters of the Soviet state. The officers, robbed of their privileges and property by the Revolution, controlled only a small number of devoted elite regiments. During 1918 the Volunteer Army in South Russia sought to obtain manpower by uniting with the Cossacks of the Kuban and Don regions near the Black Sea and Caucasus.

The Cossacks were members of long-established militarized communities and served directly under the tsars' command as their private guards and elite units, retaining their privileges and land ownership. The negotiations between the elected governments of several Cossack communities and the White Army command proved to be extremely involved. Peter Kenez has thoroughly researched the alliance between Cossacks and the White movement, and concluded that this temporary union remained fragile since both sides never truly shared the same goals and ideology.[40] As Kenez persuasively argued, antisemitism became the center of the White movement doctrine,[41] while for the Cossack communities anti-Jewish violence presented a lucrative incentive.

---

39 For further discussion of White Army soldiers and their motives for anti-Jewish violence, see Chapter 4 of this book.
40 Peter Kenez, *Civil War in South Russia, 1918: The First Year of the Volunteer Army* (Berkeley: University of California Press, 1971), 138–64.
41 Peter Kenez, "Pogroms and White Ideology in the Russian Civil War," *Pogroms: Anti-Jewish Violence in Modern Russian History* 311 (1992), and also Peter Kenez, "The Ideology of the White Movement," *Europe-Asia Studies* 32, no. 1 (1980): 58–83.

And as the prospective of anti-Jewish violence surfaced as a unifying factor, the White Army gained much needed manpower through an alliance with the most powerful Cossack hosts in the southern regions and Caucasus—Kuban, Don, and Terek.

In spring 1918, General Anton Denikin consolidated the White movement on the southern front and assumed command of the various units of the Volunteer Army under the name Armed Forces of the South of Russia. Neither the White Army command nor General Denikin personally recognized Ukraine as a sovereign state or as federal unit, never considered a union with any of the Ukrainian governments, and never used the word Ukraine, calling it only "South Russia." The focus of the White movement advance was Moscow, and Ukrainian territory became a strategic and economic foothold in the war with Bolsheviks.

In the first half of 1919, while Petliura's army was heavily engaged in the war with Bolsheviks in the territory of Ukraine, Denikin consolidated his forces, gained control of the Caucasus and Southern Russian Provinces, entered Eastern Ukraine, and began to advance in the direction of Moscow. In early July 1919, Denikin's army started its victorious offensive in the territory of Ukraine, capturing Odessa and Kiev, and in early September turned to the north and almost reached Moscow. The Bolsheviks seriously considered surrendering the old capital and were getting ready to go underground by forming a clandestine organization of the Bolshevik Party. However, the White forces in the south were overstretched. The Reds, who made a great effort to consolidate their forces in order to push back against Denikin, started to advance, aiming to cut the Volunteer Army in two. The final attempts of the Whites to advance further weakened their position, and they had to start withdrawing from Ukraine and Russia, moving back towards the Kuban region.

The White Army swept through Ukraine twice in less than six months, during the swift attack and then the rapid retreat, and on both marches the White Army perpetrated exceedingly violent pogroms. While the pogroms of the first half of 1919 were widespread and were carried out by various groups allegiant or similar to the Ukrainian army, the pogroms by the hands of the White Army were confined more to eastern and central Ukraine, particularly the area alongside Dnieper River in the Cherkassy region. The White Army perpetrated fewer pogroms in fewer locations, although in many locations the pogroms happened at least twice. For a number of reasons to be thoroughly discussed later, the White Army pogroms are characterized by a much higher overall death toll, brutality, and torture.

In early January 1920, Denikin assumed the title of supreme governor of Russia that was conferred on him by the leader of the Siberian front—legendary general Kolchak. However, this was by then a desperate, symbolic gesture that could not prevent the coming defeat. The Cossacks deserted the White movement, and the remnants of the Volunteer Army retreated to Crimea by the end of March 1920. On April 4, 1920, General Denikin resigned from the post of the chief commander of the Armed Forces of the South of Russia and left Russia, handing the leadership of the White Army to Baron Wrangel, who continued to fight Bolsheviks until 1924.

The Reds continued to fight against the armed resistance of the remnants of the White Army and miscellaneous Ukrainian peasant bands that prowled various regions of the country after the Bolsheviks established their control of Ukraine in 1920. Violent clashes of armed forces and outbreaks of anti-Jewish pogroms continued for a couple of years longer, but the Bolsheviks remained firmly in power, and proceeded to oppose, prohibit, and punish anti-Jewish violence, as they did from the beginning of the Civil War on the grounds of internationalism. Bolsheviks had consistently curbed and denounced pogroms occasionally perpetrated by the Red Army and prosecuted the pogrom instigators. The Soviet and Bolshevik Party organizations joined with Jewish and international philanthropic organizations to provide aid for the victims of the pogroms. The Ukrainian Soviet Republic, although never truly independent from the Soviet Russia, formally entered the Union of the Soviet Socialist Republics when it was created at the end of 1922.

The anti-Jewish violence in the form of pogroms permeated the turbulent history of Ukraine at the time of Civil War from the scattered outbreaks in 1914–17 and through the two powerful waves of genocidal violence perpetrated by Petliura's army and the Whites in 1919. Already by 1917, systematic anti-Jewish violence, as classified by David Nirenberg[42] and extrapolated by Helmut Smith,[43] evolved into catastrophic violence that affected and threatened the existence of Jewish communities all over Ukraine, as a result of the war and Revolution. In 1919, pogrom violence reached previously unseen proportions and became, alongside the warfare of the Civil War, the central most vigorous and essential activity of the various belligerents. The genocidal violence against Jews was not just at the center of the Civil War; it became the Civil War.

---

42 Nirenberg, *Communities of Violence*.
43 Helmut Walser Smith, *The Continuities of German History: Nation, Religion, and Race across the Long Nineteenth Century* (Cambridge: Cambridge University Press, 2008), 117.

CHAPTER 2

Carnival of Violence: Development of the Pogrom Script

"I am sorry for you, Moishke, but there is nothing to be done,"[1] a Ukrainian man said to his Jewish neighbor around the first week of May 1919, when they were smoking together in the evening, sitting on the same bench. Ataman Grigoriev's regiments had captured several towns nearby and moved close to Dmitrovka, a small town in the Cherkassy region of Ukraine to the southeast of Kiev, where neighbors were now discussing the inevitable: a pogrom. The Christian neighbor probably felt pity if not sympathy for Moishke, who would be subjected to looting, humiliation, torture, and violence, but at the same time this likely meant a rather lucrative affair for a non-Jew, since he did have a choice in his actions, while his Jewish counterpart's options were severely limited.[2] By May 1919, anti-Jewish violence inundated Ukrainian cities and the countryside. As armed forces moved, pogroms and "excesses" happened: Jews were robbed in their homes and on railway stations, Jewish women were raped, and Jewish men were tortured and subsequently killed. Jewish self-defense units could not curb the violence and often became its first victims. By May 1919, both the Jews and the non-Jews knew that whenever armed men entered the town the pogrom would start, and everyone knew what to expect. In other

---

1   YIVO Archive, Elias Tcherikower Archive 1903–63, Rg 80–89 (Mk 470), file 167, 14222–25.

2   The Jews did not completely lack agency in response to pogrom violence, but the most immediate option was nearly exhausted in the first months of 1919—self-defense units were almost never able to protect the victimized communities for long. While a limited course of action was initially available to the Jewish population, on the eve of the inevitable pogrom in the shtetl it was mostly lacking. For detailed analysis of Jewish agency during genocide, see Evgeny Finkel, *Ordinary Jews: Choice and Survival during the Holocaust* (Princeton, NJ: Princeton University Press, 2017).

words, the anti-Jewish violence had become a common practice and unfolded according to an established script. The neighbors who shared a smoke on a warm evening were right in their premonitions about the events of the days and weeks to come: the pogrom lasted for ten days while town changed hands, and every time the ataman's regiment reentered town, the pogrom would start over with the most vigorous brutality: over thirty Jewish women were raped in one night, aged from ten to seventy. The Jewish population of Dmitrovka, reduced from 2,300 to fifty, left the town, and that was the end of this community.

Long before 1919, when over five hundred pogroms swept through Ukraine, "the pogrom phenomenon became a familiar and unexceptional part of Russian life,"[3] as John Klier noted in his introductory remarks regarding the pogrom paradigm in Russian history. The waves of pogroms in 1881–82 and in 1903–5 consolidated among the Jewish and non-Jewish population the perception of a pogrom as an outlet for the expression of civil unrest and anti-Jewish sentiment, as the two had been for a long time deeply intertwined in areas of Jewish settlement. The concept of a pogrom was commonly recognized by the Jewish and non-Jewish population as a sequence of actions on behalf of pogrom perpetrators from growing tensions and premonitions preceding the pogrom, through the outbreak of violence, ensuing looting, and infliction of various degrees of harm and humiliation onto a victimized community, followed by cessation of violence through the interference of civil or military power. In other words, a pogrom was understood as an organic whole composed of various elements, or as "an uninhibited script of robbery, sexual assault, beating, and murder, demanding these actions and delighting in them."[4]

During the last decades of the Russian Empire, the pogrom script became a concept that entered the domain of common knowledge not as a symbol but as a protocol to be employed when anti-Jewish violence broke out. Neighbors in Dmitrovka, like most people in Ukraine at the time, did not question the inevitability of the pogrom or its general scenario; the only uncertainty that remained was the extent of the brutality. Since the beginning of the First World War, pogrom violence had reemerged predominantly alongside the front line, and had not ceased until the end of the Civil War and the establishment of the Soviet power in Ukraine, when the last outbreaks of armed resistance and unrest

---

3   John D. Klier, "The Pogrom Paradigm in Russian History," in *Pogroms: Anti-Jewish Violence in Modern Russian History* (Cambridge: Cambridge University Press, 1992), 33.

4   John-Paul Himka, "The Lviv Pogrom of 1941: The Germans, Ukrainian Nationalists, and the Carnival Crowd," *Canadian Slavonic Papers* 53, nos. 2–4 (2011): 209–43.

were finally suppressed by the Bolshevik army. During this turbulent period, the nature of the anti-Jewish violence that spread through war and engulfed Ukraine changed dramatically: the pogroms became exceedingly brutal and vicious, and transformed into genocidal violence.

The exponential increase of murderous violence during the pogroms indicated significant alterations to the pogrom script that, while it retained its original outline, transformed to allow for mass murder and gruesome torture. Amid the chaos of the Civil War, the familiar and comprehensible pogrom pattern became free of the restraint of legal and social bonds, and fueled ethnic cleansing. The continuous escalation of violence during the Civil War, the "power vacuum"[5] in the land, and the escalation of anti-Jewish sentiment released pogrom perpetrators from inhibitions that previously curbed physical violence to a certain extent. The archaic pogrom script in fact proved to be the perfect vehicle of genocidal violence. The demonstrative nature of the pogrom violence, played out like a street theater performance, served the genocidal purpose in two crucial ways. On the one hand, it exacerbated existing violent rituals and accommodated the murder of Jews on an unprecedented scale. And on the other hand, the new pogrom script employed torture, humiliation, and gender violence as a strategy to publicly degrade and destroy Jews.

According to the latest scholarship,[6] the social death of the victimized community is no less essential to genocidal violence than physical extermination. Publicized violence in its various forms that include but are not limited to mass rape is a strategy to irreparably harm the social status of the victimized community, and thus fulfill the genocidal objective. The transformation of the pogrom script from its customary form into the vehicle of genocide is the focus of this chapter. Through in-depth analysis of the most iconic pogrom scripts, I aim to both establish the continuity of violent rites and determine the specific points of transformation of the script in order to subsequently place gender violence within the existing framework for pogroms.

Anti-Jewish violence was on the rise in Ukraine in 1917 and in the beginning of 1918. The unstable political situation in Ukraine at the time and the

---

5 Gilley, "Beyond Petliura," 46.
6 Card, "Genocide and Social Death," 63–79; Frank Chalk, "Redefining Genocide," in *Genocide: Conceptual and Historical Dimensions*, ed. George J. Andreopoulos (Philadelphia: University of Pennsylvania Press, 1994), 47–63; Lisa Marie Cacho, *Social Death: Racialized Rightlessness and the Criminalization of the Unprotected* (New York: New York University Press, 2012); Damien Short, *Redefining Genocide: Settler Colonialism, Social Death and Ecocide* (London: Zed Books Ltd., 2016).

growing civil unrest and deterioration of the economy inevitably instigated the escalation of pogroms. Compared to hundreds of pogroms in 1919, several dozen[7] pogroms in 1917 appear to be "low grade violence," although this rate is similar to the pogroms of 1881–83, when over two hundred pogroms occurred in the course of about three years. The pogroms of 1917–18 claimed only a few casualties and targeted primarily Jewish property, and while the Jews were often beaten and humiliated, reports of rape during this period are very rare. The early pogroms resembled the pogroms of 1881–83 in pattern and reflected a commonly recognized script. The early pogroms were alarming and were treated as such by the Ministry of Jewish Affairs; however, the positive bias generated by the fall of the Russian Empire and the new prospect of Jewish politics did not forebode the forthcoming tragedy.

The pogrom that took place in the town of Kanev (Kaniv) can serve as an example of a typical pogrom scenario in 1917–18. Kanev has always been an important port town at the bend of the Dnieper River to the south of Kiev. Jews settled in the area from the early eighteenth century, and by the beginning of the First World War the Jewish community, numbering over two and a half thousand members, constituted about 30 percent of Kanev's population. Jews constituted 90 percent of Kanev's entrepreneurs and owned most of the shops in town, as well as hotels, pharmacies, and other businesses, big and small. The Jewish community anticipated the pogrom and endeavored to prevent it by organizing a self-defense unit that survived until the end of the Civil War and had thirty members in 1922,[8] and by petitioning the Jewish Secretariat in order to procure protection by Ukrainian government forces. On the morning of November 6, 1917, the crowd of locals started to ransack and loot Jewish shops and properties. The town's militia arrested the most prominent miscreants, but the agitated crowd freed their ringleaders, while members of the police force either left the town or joined in the pogrom.[9] The pogrom continued for about

7 There are seventy-nine instances of pogroms in 1917–18 accounted for in the Tcherikower archive. This number is inaccurate, as most pogrom statistics are, but it draws a picture of the scope of anti-Jewish violence at the time. YIVO Archive, files 6–26.

8 Miljakova, *Kniga Pogromov*, 538. Self-defense units were organized in many places of Jewish settlement during the Civil War in Ukraine, and in some rare cases the self-defense was organized jointly with the non-Jewish population; however, these units were unable to impact the unfolding violence in any significant way. Destroyed during the first wave of the pogroms in 1919, Jewish self-defense units were often resurrected by the end of the Civil War, when the pogroms began to subside, to protect surviving communities from bandits in times of dire poverty and need.

9 YIVO Archive, file 18, 1078–98.

two weeks, during which outbreaks of plunder and looting devastated Jewish businesses and homes. *Pogromschiki*[10] disarmed the Jewish self-defense unit and the remaining local police. The government troops that arrived in Kanev did not interfere to stop the pogrom. No fatalities among the Jewish community were reported. On November 20, 1917, the prosecutor for the regional court, alerted by the Jewish Secretariat, intervened to establish whether or not any administration remained in Kanev, and if it had any authority.[11] Finally, by the end of November more troops arrived and the pogrom stopped. Eight pogrom instigators were arrested, but there is no conclusive evidence that those people were ever prosecuted. This was the first of many pogroms of the Civil War in Kanev, which culminated two years later in August 1919, when platoons of the White Army fought the armed gang of ataman Zelenyi, and the pogrom lasted for weeks, rekindling itself every time the shtetl changed hands.[12]

The key elements of the typical pogrom scenario, as seen in the Kanev pogrom, included active pogrom anticipation; looting and plunder dominating during the pogrom; low levels of physical violence and few Jewish victims, with rare fatalities; and the pogrom being perpetrated jointly by the local population and by the armed troops. In Kanev, the talk of the pogrom among local population started a significant time before the pogrom itself: in the port town the news about pogroms elsewhere circulated among the port workers. Since the economic situation was quickly deteriorating due to ongoing war and the revolutionary situation, the Jewish shops more than ever became a prominent target for the violent crowd, while the Jewish population, concentrated in the town, presented an easy and obvious mark. The local administration was rather weak, and the general uncertainty of the political situation in the former Russian Empire eased inhibitions, since the prospect of retribution was remote. The non-Jewish population was getting ready for the pogrom because pogroms were a commonly occurring event in a time of crisis.

The premonition of the pogrom became an essential stage of the violence, during which the Jewish population was emotionally terrorized by fear and apprehension of violence to come. The dynamic of polarizing collective emotions laid a foundation for intergroup conflicts and intergroup violence through emotion-focused rituals, as leading scholars of emotions argue.[13]

---

10 Pogrom perpetrators (Russian).
11 Cherikover, *Antisemitizm*, 49.
12 YIVO Archive, file 208, 18509–12; see also Miljakova, *Kniga Pogromov*, 408.
13 Jeff Goodwin, James M. Jasper, and Francesca Polletta, eds., *Passionate Politics: Emotions and Social Movements* (Chicago: University of Chicago Press, 2009).

In other words, the period of augmented violent narrative that preceded physical conflict served to heighten such emotions as fear, disgust, and hate, which further separated attackers-to-be and their prospective victims, in order to bring them together in a powerful clash.[14]

Within the highly ritualized environment of the pogrom, the period of the victims anticipating violence, and "pogrom talk" by the offenders that initiated the public dehumanization of future victims, became an integral part of pogrom script. During this period, the crowd of the soon-to-be pogrom perpetrators fed the impulse that later propelled the pogrom itself. The transition from threats to acts of violence occurred through the ritual of anti-Jewish rumors, accusations, and slogans that were disseminated and repeated over and over. Smith writes that "[t]hose threats were not mere markers of identity or cultural codes in the precise sense of the term. Rather they were speech acts uttered in the context of violent ritual."[15] The shouted speech and the circulating rumors altered the physical state of the offenders and the victims, causing agitation and thrill among the offenders, and fear and apprehension among the Jews. This emotional arousal caused by outcries like "Beat the Jews" or "Jews are traitors" augmented the separation between Jews and non-Jews and promoted rapid consolidation of the aggressive crowd, united by the common enemy.

What was considered by contemporary Jewish leaders and scholars to be pogrom agitation by certain ringleaders was, as most scholars agree,[16] rarely masterminded, but represented mostly grassroots processes of talk and gossip in public spaces that exacerbated antisemitic sentiment and emphasized popular accusations against Jews. The most popular accusation laid against Jews that permeates the history of the pogroms in Ukraine during the Civil War was the already mentioned Judeo-Bolshevik canard, based, among other loose arguments in favor of it, on the common belief that majority of the Bolsheviks were Jewish, and therefore acted in the Jewish interest. The alleged Jewish alliance with Bolsheviks was evidenced in popular opinion by the fact that Bolsheviks denounced pogroms and persecuted pogrom instigators in furtherance of the principles of internationalism. It is important to mention that the Bolsheviks often branded Jews "capitalists" and punished them by expropriation of property and forced labor.

---

14 Sara Ahmed, "Collective Feelings: Or, the Impressions Left by Others," *Theory, Culture & Society* 21, no. 2 (2004): 25–42.

15 Smith, *The Continuities of German History*, 132.

16 Christopher Gilley, "Beyond Petliura," 45–61.

Labeling Jews as Bolsheviks while the Red Army was fighting on the territory of Ukraine justified both the persecution of Jews by various authorities and the anti-Jewish violence by belligerents of all sorts, and ignited pogrom activity. In the aftermath of the infamous Proskurov pogrom in February 1919 that took lives of almost two thousand Jews, ataman Semesenko, who justified the massacre as a punitive expedition against Bolsheviks, explained the mass killing of the peaceful Jewish population thus: "I can't take the blame [for the murder of the innocent Jewish population] when even the Jewish elderly, women and children are all Bolsheviks."[17]

There is no information on what exactly triggered the pogrom in Kanev on November 6, but the Jewish community and the local population all over Ukraine could as a rule accurately foretell a pogrom on market day or a religious holiday, when the combination of Jewish vulnerability, antisemitic sentiment, and the joint enthusiasm of the non-Jewish crowd became particularly potent. Pogroms on market days and on religious holidays happened in many towns all over Ukraine in 1917–18, among them Borodyantsy, Zhabokrych, Zhivotov, Kamenka, Kupel, Lyakhovtsy, Rakitino, Skvira (Skvyra), and many others. Most of requests to the Jewish Secretary/Ministry for armed protection came from the Jewish communities ahead of scheduled market days. The letter from the Transcarpathian town of Lyakhovtsy on the farthest western border of Ukraine that was received on January 10, 1918 appealed for urgent protection: the market was scheduled for January 15, and the local hoodlums and the partially disarmed soldiers of the army regiment that was stationed in town acted as if a pogrom was a foregone conclusion.[18]

Another factor that commonly precipitated pogroms was the presence of armed troops in the area, whether it was divisions of the Russian army moving to and from the fronts of the First World War, regiments of the new Ukrainian army that was being hastily formed by the Ukrainian government, or any other armed forces. Idle and often undersupplied soldiers were the major perpetrators of the pogroms in 1917–18. Jewish properties and businesses were an obvious, easy, and highly visible lucrative target. Soldiers also sought to retaliate against Jews, branded as traitors responsible for the losses at war, and through pogrom violence vent their frustration with the revolutionary chaos and war that engulfed Ukraine. Even the mere presence of armed men created a tense atmosphere of impending disturbance and contributed to the buildup

---

17 YIVO Archive, file 659, 56263.
18 Ibid., file 18, 1128.

of energy that propelled anti-Jewish violence, which usually started with spo-radic extortion and plunder. The towns of Western Ukraine, particularly in or near Galicia, hosted the most armed detachments not currently engaged at the front. At the end of November 1917, two regiments were quartered in the Miropol (Miropil) shtetl[19] close to the front line; the soldiers first simply stopped paying for the goods in Jewish shops, but shortly afterward the iso-lated incidents accumulated into a pogrom. In Rashkov,[20] the Cossack regi-ment that passed through the town at the end of December 1917 shot two Jews to scare the rest of Jewish population and looted Jewish property, joined by the local peasants.

The local *militsia* (police) and law enforcement were very poorly orga-nized. More often than not, the units dispatched to stop the violence themselves joined in the pogroms with enthusiasm. It became a ubiquitous phenomenon due to weak control on the part of the Ukrainian government. A representative example is the pogrom in Gogolev, a small village adjacent to the larger com-munity of Brovary, less than thirty miles to the east of Kiev, where in March 1918 a cavalry detachment of 120 soldiers entered the town, looted Jewish property, and publicly tortured and humiliated Jews.[21] During the day, soldiers thrashed the Jews with the whips, and two Jewish men were murdered in front of their families; and at night soldiers would raid Jewish houses, demanding money and vodka.

The pogroms of 1917–18 were a starting point of genocidal violence rather than the true precursor of the pogrom waves of 1919. The death toll of the pogroms was low, and there were no rapes reported, although some reports hint at instances of gender violence. About a year of pogroms during 1917–18 was followed by a break in continuity in the anti-Jewish violence. Indeed, from the establishment of the German protectorate headed nominally by Hetman Skoropadsky until the Directory took over late in 1918, the outbreaks of civil unrest were suppressed by the military power. According to Tcherikower, who analyzed several pogroms that took place during that time, Ukrainian peasants, forced to provide for German and Austrian armies, rioted against economic policies rather than against Jews, but attacked urban centers, where Jews con-stituted the majority.[22] The situation changed dramatically when the Alliance troops retreated, and the Ukrainian National Army advanced towards Kiev.

---

19 Ibid., file 19, 1164–64a.
20 Ibid., file 19, 1203–14.
21 Ibid., file 18, 1001–13.
22 Cherikover, *Antisemitizm*, 178–79.

"PETLIURA'S POGROMS"[23]

In February 1919 many Ukrainian army detachments moved through the busy railway junction of Mironovka (Mironivka) about sixty five miles south of Kiev, on the line that connected the port towns of Southern Dnieper with the Western Ukrainian provinces. The village of Rossava (Rosava) lay to the north of the station. In the beginning of 1919, it had a population of five thousand, of which one thousand was Jewish. Two hundred and ten Jewish families were engaged in crafts and trade that served the local peasant community and the station. It is not clear if there had been any pogroms there in 1917–18, although neighboring shtetls and towns, Kanev among them, suffered from violent outbreaks. However, since the Directory came to power in Kiev and the German protectorate was over, the pogroms became a regular occurrence in Rossava, as every passing detachment and regiment of the Ukrainian army engaged in plunder and beatings of the Jews. The Jewish community lost track of how many regiments and under whose command passed through the station from February through July, but the scenario of the events, once the next group of armed men disembarked from the train, initially followed the same pattern. At first, the soldiers arrived from the station to pick up some items in Jewish shops without paying, then, under the guise of searching for Bolsheviks, they rummaged through Jewish homes and beat Jews. By February 1919, this became normal behavior, and the Jewish community came to regard it as such. Then, the Ukrainian regiments retreated and the Red Army detachments arrived. The Bolsheviks didn't rob Jews; but shortly after the Reds retreated, the Ukrainian army moved in once again. The public beatings of Jews and the plundering became more ferocious and unrestrained, while all the Jews were branded as traitors and Bolsheviks. Several other regiments moved through Rossava one after another, and almost every time a pogrom erupted. The desperate Jewish community sent its emissaries to the neighboring town of Boguslav (Bohuslav) in search of any power that was in control to seek protection, but to no avail. The pogroms in Rossava continued and the pogrom brutality soared, breaking the understood forms and norms, and creating a vicious cycle of violence.

Inspector of the Committee for Relief to Victims of Pogroms (EVOBSCHESTCOM) I. S. Braude, who later interviewed Rossava's remaining Jews,[24] reported that the brutal treatment at the hands of a regiment of

---

23 This is the way the pogroms of the first half of 1919 were commonly described by contemporaries and early researchers.

24 YIVO Archive, file 183, 15832–960.

Petliura's army that encamped at the station in late spring escalated very quickly and lasted for several weeks. Torture of Jews became exceedingly violent and humiliating, and was carried out in public. Soldiers would beat Jews and lash them with whips and rods, while making them run around the square naked. Braude recorded among others one gruesome episode, when pogrom perpetrators intently watched a Jewish man and his father-in-law eat dirt for over ten minutes, while his wife was made to witness this humiliation. Then, soldiers proceeded to rape the woman on the spot in front of her husband and father.[25] This horrifying episode is exemplary and illustrative of what was inflicted on Jews all over Ukraine, and of what the pogroms had turned into. The "carnival of violence" that was staged and played out, "in a deeply sinister sense of the word 'play,'" as William Hagen pointed in his landmark study of the Lvov pogrom,[26] transformed the pogrom into a communal act. Ritualized scripts as performed by the pogrom perpetrators carried a specific message and meaning that ultimately degraded and dehumanized the victims, paving the road to genocidal violence.

CARNIVAL OF VIOLENCE: RITUALS OF DEHUMANIZATION

This dramatically staged performance of violence focused on symbolic acts that stripped victims of their dignity and social standing. Flogging with rods was widely practiced as a penalty in the Russian army and civil courts. Performing this punishment instantly positioned Jewish men as inferiors to their assailants. This metaphor of military subordination was stretched even further, as the Jews were forced to run around the square used as the *plats*, or military training ground. Rossava Jews were forced to engage in soldier routines under the command of pogrom perpetrators, who thus asserted their power over their "subordinates."

In January 1919 at the railway station of Romodan, near shtetl Lubny in the Poltava province, to the east of Kiev, the UNA soldiers forced Jewish men to undress and run naked in the snow; in order to exacerbate the gruesome entertainment, the victims were also ordered to sing, while the soldiers shot at them randomly.[27] To the west of Kiev in the shtetl Peschanka, in the Podolie province, an armed gang of unknown allegiance in blue uniforms entered the town and started the pogrom: Jewish men were forced to dance naked in the

---

25 Ibid., file 183, 15848.
26 Hagen, "The Moral Economy of Ethnic Violence," 203.
27 YIVO Archive, file 182, 15823–31.

square, while soldiers shot at them.[28] There are many more similar incidences of pogrom perpetrators forcing their victims to engage in an activity that was either inappropriate for them, like military exercise, or out of place, like dancing. This gruesome "circus" activity entertained the offenders, but also humiliated and degraded the victims even further, as pogrom perpetrators ordered Jewish men to undress and perform naked. Forced nakedness that was observed by the pogrom perpetrators as well as the Jewish and non-Jewish population amounts to acute torture and humiliation. While the sexual aspect of violence will be addressed later in greater detail in the context of the mass rape of Jewish women, it should be noted that forced male nakedness has always been (and continues to be) a powerful tool of torture and punishment.[29] Publicly stripped of their clothing, their Jewishness emphasized by the exposing of their circumcised genitalia, men were robbed of their dignity and reduced to an unclothed, uncivilized, animal-like state. This carnivalesque, visceral ritual was played out to hurt victims' emotions before inflicting physical harm on them.

The sinister circus of torture described above, when the Rossava Jews were forced to eat soil, aimed to destroy all aspects of a victim's social standing and exclude him or her from the world of the living. The soil or dirt is clearly an "un-food," the opposite of human nourishment, and at the same time it symbolizes death: filling the mouth with soil invokes the imagery of burial. Subjecting two generations of the same family, a father-in-law and his son-in-law, to the same torture aimed to destroy the hierarchy of the traditional family, and attempted to ruin the respect of children for their parents, and of youth for seniors in general, symbolically undermining the basis of traditional society.

The humiliation was augmented through females witnessing the torture, which not only further undermined the family and social structure, but targeted the gender structure, by undermining masculinity and the dignity of men in front of the women. Rape of women in front of their kin endeavored to achieve a similar result. And while mass rape of Jewish women will be discussed in greater detail in the following chapter, it is crucial to place it within the context of the pogrom script as it developed. In fact, Braude, who recorded the

---

28   Ibid., file 177, 15377–84.
29   Philip G. Zimbardo, *Lucifer Effect* (Indianapolis: Wiley Online Library, 2007), 141, 402. See also Andrés Zarankin and Melisa Salerno, "The Engineering of Genocide: An Archaeology of Dictatorship in Argentina," in *Archaeologies of Internment* (New York: Springer, 2011), 207–27; Kathy Phillips, "Mass Nakedness in the Imaginary of the Nazis," *War, Literature & the Arts: An International Journal of the Humanities* 27 (June 2015): 1–19.

atrocious episode, stopped short of narrating the rape. He writes that soldiers "attempted" to rape the wife in front of her husband, although most probably the soldiers succeeded in their attempt. However, he writes, "for obvious reasons" (the formula most commonly employed), cases of rape are not discussed openly, although a lot of Jewish women were raped during the pogrom, and only "the sadly lowered eyes of the Jewish women betrayed the horrible secret."[30]

The reports of the pogroms in Rossava that continued on and off in the first half of 1919, as the troops passed through the busy station, contained many more gruesome examples of the humiliating torture exercised by the perpetrators: the soldiers ordered Jews to make footcloths for them out of tefillin (prayer shawls), an elderly matriarch was beaten into bloody pulp in front of her family, perpetrators murdered children in front of their parents, and parents in front of their children, etc. There were no limits to the brutality and the perverse creativity of the violent rituals, all of which aimed to demonstratively undermine the position of Jews in society, to destroy social and communal structures and hierarchies, and to exclude Jews from the world of humans.

The Rossava pogrom, emblematic of the ongoing violence, claimed a lot of Jewish lives, and the bodies of sadistically beaten and murdered Jews, scattered alongside the road, lay there while the Jews were forbidden to bury their dead for a while. By contrast, in Peschanka, the Jews were forced to bury their dead on Sabbath, which is prohibited in Judaism, while bandits randomly shot at them. The bandits engaged in this macabre entertainment while stationed in the town—in between fights with Bolsheviks. After one of the retreats and counteroffensives, the fighters claimed that the Jews fired at them from their windows in support of Bolsheviks, and proceeded to murder most of the Jewish population in retaliation.[31] The narrator of an account of these events, a Jewish doctor named Flek, who was forcibly conscripted into the UNA to treat the wounded, was horrified to hear that soldiers of his regiment told the story of this pogrom with great satisfaction.

It is evident that the violent discourse of the pogroms and death threats readily resulted in the murderous spree. The death toll of the pogroms in the first half of 1919 surged tremendously compared to the casualties of 1917–18. The number of Jews murdered during "Petliura's pogroms" could be estimated in tens of thousands without exaggeration. The death toll of each individual pogrom differs, depending on multiple factors: what regiment or gang engaged

---

30 YIVO Archive, file 183, 15848.
31 Miljakova, *Kniga Pogromov*, 273–74.

in violence, how much time the offenders stayed in town, if the offenders were retreating at the moment or attacking, etc. The transition from the "traditional" violence to the slaughter of the Jews required transitional social rituals to ease the transformation. The exceedingly violent circus of torture, rape, and humiliation not only transformed the Jews into unworthy victims, stripped of humanity, but also relieved pogrom perpetrators from moral restraints. The nature of those inhibitions and restraints and how they were broken made the pogroms gyrate out of control into intimate genocide, defined by the complicated relations of the various groups of offenders with the Jews. The concept of "intimate" genocide juxtaposes the close personal involvement of the assailant and the victim to the previously common understanding of genocide as a killing machine.[32] Deep personal involvement with the victims is very characteristic of the later genocides of the twentieth century,[33] as well as of pogroms during the Holocaust.

The deadliest pogrom of the period that was masterminded and carried out as a military operation, while breaking the pattern, sheds light on how deeply the victims and the perpetrators were involved. Proskurov, in the Podolia region of western Ukraine,[34] was one of the five largest towns in the area and home to a flourishing Jewish community. The well-documented pogrom[35] occurred on February 15, 1919, when Ukrainian army troops under the command of ataman Semesenko entered the Jewish neighborhood and methodically massacred the Jews with bayonets. Up to sixteen hundred Jews were killed in one day. Ataman Semesenko later defended and justified the slaughter as a punitive expedition against an enemy—the Bolsheviks. There was in fact an attempt at a Bolshevik uprising before the pogrom, but it was minor and unsuccessful. The retaliation against the Jews of Proskurov, who were summarily branded Bolsheviks, was beyond disproportionate. The Proskurov pogrom's atrocities astonished and frightened even Petliura's government.[36]

The Proskurov massacre was presented by Semesenko almost as a holy crusade against Judeo-Bolshevism, and the legitimacy of such punishment

---

32 Kopstein and Wittenberg, "Intimate Violence: Anti-Jewish Pogroms."
33 Madeline Hron, "Intimate Enemy: Images and Voices of the Rwandan Genocide," *African Studies Quarterly* 10, no. 2–3 (2008).
34 Proskurov was renamed in 1954 as Khmelnitskyi, in official commemoration of the union between Russia and Ukraine. Bogdan Khmelnitsky, who led the rebellion against the Polish king in 1654, was also responsible for a series of deadly anti-Jewish pogroms in the area.
35 YIVO Archive, files 180–81; also see Cherikover, *Di Ukrainer Pogramen.*
36 Semesenko was temporarily imprisoned, and, according to some sources, executed.

was validated by complete and intentional disengagement from any personal engagement with the victims. No plunder, torture, or rape, which would turn the punishment into a pogrom, were allowed. This distinction between "pure" massacre and "dirty" pogrom, taken to the extreme, demonstrated the opposite: the personal aspect of the pogrom was recognized by the assailants. The soldiers who participated in the pogrom truly believed that sparing Jews of emotional and material involvement justified their actions.[37]

In Balta, a large town to the south of Proskurov, the pogrom also started in early February 1919, and lasted on and off through the spring of 1919. The death toll by March was approximately around one hundred, but many people were wounded, over 120 women were raped, and many houses burned down. In the midst of the ongoing violence, a group of Ukrainian soldiers and officers came to the magistrate and requested an officially signed document stating that during the pogrom they exclusively murdered Jews as Bolsheviks, but didn't participate in pillage.[38] Tcherikower, who described this episode in his notes, adds that in the neighboring town of Ananiev in late February 1919 Ukrainian soldiers, who murdered forty-four Jews during the pogrom, did not allow the dead to be buried until the rabbi wrote and signed a document that declared all the murdered Jews Bolsheviks. Only after the document was procured were the soldiers allowed to bury "Judeo-Bolsheviks."[39]

"DENIKIN'S POGROMS"[40]

The pogroms of the second half of 1919, perpetrated by Denikin (White Army) regiments, although generally similar to the pogroms committed by Petliura's soldiers and various gangs, were not as numerous, but were more violent, brutal, and murderous than the pogroms of the previous six months. The White Army was much smaller than the Ukrainian National Army, but was very well trained and organized. Denikin's army consisted primarily of Russian army officers of all ranks and Cossack regiments. Unlike the Ukrainian army or the assorted gangs, Denikin's army had a very clear goal and direction: the Whites fought against the Reds and advanced toward Moscow. Ukraine, its people, and its politics were of no concern to the officers and Cossacks, who treated it as a resource base.

---

37 YIVO Archive, file 659, 56260–64.
38 Ibid., file 659, 56269–70.
39 Ibid.
40 The common way by which pogrom contemporaries and early researchers defined the pogroms of the second half of 1919 perpetrated by White Army regiments.

The majority of White officers shared antisemitic views, and also branded Jews as Bolsheviks and blamed them for their loss of influence, property, and the fall of the Russian Empire in general. The Cossacks, who fought Bolsheviks to protect their militarized communities and privileges, traditionally shared the antisemitic sentiment. The opportunity to enrich themselves through the looting of Jewish property was another incentive for Cossacks to join the Volunteer Army.

The first detachments of Whites arrived at Rossava in August 1919 during the advance toward Kiev. The pogrom broke out immediately after the Cossacks entered the town. The Jewish community that had already suffered continuous pogroms by Petliura's soldiers could not believe that the Whites had started the pogrom, and for some time believed them to be impostors, not the real Cossacks.[41] In the eyes of the Jews, the Volunteer Army represented the authority of the tsar and the government of the Russian Empire, so why would they commit atrocities like the gangs and the Ukrainian army did? Disillusioned by the Ukrainian Revolution and abused by the Ukrainian army and various gangs, the Jews of Ukraine hoped for the restoration of the "real power," which had in the past offered protection and some order along with discrimination.

During the previous waves of pogroms, the vertical relationship between Russian Jewry and the Tsarist government known as the "royal alliance" was broken, because the Jews could not entrust their protection to the authorities, who were "increasingly unable, or unwilling, to tame popular antisemitism," as Elissa Bemporad has convincingly proven[42] in her latest research. The Jews had previously experienced the Tsarist government not preventing pogroms and siding with the perpetrators more than with their victims, but it was Tsarist troops that usually interfered in the end to stop pogroms. And while the Jews did not expect a lot of protection from the Russian tsars, they had had significant practice through the ages in dealing with them. While it is doubtful that the Jews greeted White Army troops as liberators, they probably viewed them as the lesser evil.

The false expectations of the Jews determined their actions during the pogrom: almost always when the Whites were expected, the Jews formed a delegation to greet the incoming troops and present them with a gift of money in hopes that the Jewish community would be spared a pogrom. White officers

---

41 YIVO Archive, file 209, 18769.
42 Quote from the unpublished manuscript of the book by Bemporad, *Legacy of Blood*, with author's permission.

did accept the money or even demanded more, but never did they prevent the pogrom or stop it. In Borispol (Boryspil), a town immediately to the southeast of Kiev, the Jews organized a delegation once they heard that the Whites were approaching. They collected some money and the traditional offering of bread and salt and went out of town to greet the command. At the same time as the officers of the avant-garde mocked and humiliated the delegation and refused to parley, the pogrom had already started.[43] Groups of officers and soldiers brutally raped Jewish women, while others knocked on Jewish doors demanding money and girls, and killed Jews in the streets. When the self-appointed commandant Colonel Karpov finally received a delegation of Jewish representatives weeks later in November 1919, Jews begged him to stop the pogroms. The commandant replied, "You have been suffering for only two weeks, but you have been torturing us already for over a year. Get out!"[44] The colonel implied that all the Jews were Bolsheviks by definition, and thus retaliation in a form of a pogrom was due.

There are numerous examples of how Jews attempted to employ the traditional, archaic scenario to deal with the Whites. In the tiny agricultural colony of Kalnibolot in southern Ukraine, the richest and well-respected Jews of the community also greeted the Denikin troops at the end of August 1919 with the traditional bread and salt. White officers in response hit members of the delegation over the heads with their sabers.[45] In Kagarlyk (Kaharlyk), another shtetl immediately north of Rossava, a crowd of Jews similarly awaited the White regiment to greet them with bread and salt. The greeting ceremony turned into a plundering and looting spree. Three Jewish men were killed on that day, August 16, 1919; one of them was murdered as he tried to protect his wife from rape. The pogrom continued for several weeks, becoming "chronic," and did not stop until most of the Jewish population left town, according to the report of the Kagarlyk refugees.[46] The traditional script did not prevent or stop pogroms, but nevertheless it was been repeated over and over, since no alternative existed and Jews themselves were not accustomed to any other behavior. The White officers also acknowledged the traditional scenario and awaited the arrival of Jewish emissaries with the "tribute."

Pogroms perpetrated by Whites were all very much alike, following very pronounced scripts and unfolding according to a more or less uniform scenario.

43 YIVO Archive, file 206, 18288–300.
44 Ibid., file 206, 18294 reverse.
45 Ibid., file 208, 18500–504.
46 Ibid., file, 208, 18488–96.

Rossava Jews had barely recovered from Petliura's army pogroms in February and March, when Denikin's army avant-garde entered the town on August 13, 1919. The Cossacks of General Shkuro's squadron immediately went looking for Jewish homes and shops, and started the pillage, particularly looking for jewelry and money. Plunder and looting became, as a rule, the major activities of the first day of the pogrom, when the Jewish population had not yet had a chance to hide or re-hide their possessions, while *pogromschiki* rushed to get the best spoils. Cossacks divided into groups and spread all over the Jewish quarter ransacking homes. They broke into the only remaining shop that served the needs of the impoverished Jews of Rossava, and robbed it bare in a matter of minutes. Cossacks meticulously searched for any valuables, even inside pillows and mattresses, forcing Jews with threats and beatings to reveal any caches they had made. The loot was loaded onto a carriage and hauled to the railway station. In the evening, the local population joined the Cossacks, following in their footsteps, and took whatever they could remove from the barren Jewish flats. The shtetl looked dead and deserted, as Jews tried to hide from the raging Cossacks, but the quiet was disrupted in the middle of the night as Cossacks detonated the strongbox in the office of the savings bank. Jews, driven out of their hideouts by the explosion, tried to return, but the pogrom was ferociously rekindled, as Cossacks finished the plunder and began the "entertainment."

The carnival of violence, complete with scenes of torture, rape, and murder, played out on the second day of the pogrom as "celebratory street theater."[47] Pogrom perpetrators purposefully drove Jews into the streets and hunted down their victims. The streets of the Jewish quarter in Rossava turned into a public performance arena, where acts of torture took place in front of an audience of pogrom perpetrators, the local population, and frightened Jews. The ritualized violence reiterated the previous pogroms, but often in a more grotesque and horrifying form. The elderly couple Yudko Gurshevoy, aged seventy-five, and his wife Brukha, mad with fear, were stripped naked and forced to run through the streets as hunted animals, cheered by the Cossacks.[48] *Pogromschiki* bayoneted their victims, careful not to kill them, but to leave the wounded to suffer and bleed to death in agony that lasted sometimes for several days. Elderly parents were left to die, while their families were not allowed to help them. Children were mortally wounded in front of their parents. *Pogromschiki* made sure that all the apothecaries were wrecked, and there were no medical assistance; the only

---

47 Hagen, "The Moral Economy of Ethnic Violence," 217.
48 YIVO Archive, file 209, 18770.

remaining non-Jewish medical practitioner was strictly prohibited to provide any help to the Jews on pain of death. The Vinokur family was murdered in front of their four little children. While the husband died immediately, his wife Masya slowly bled to death over the next day on the threshold of her home. Armed Cossacks rode through the streets whooping and shouting, forcing Jews to flee in panic. The Jews were not allowed to attend to the wounded or care for the dead, and bodies remained lying in the streets, preserving the macabre scene for greater effect. The local population refused refuge to surviving Jews, who desperately tried to hide at the riverbank in sedges. The howls and wails of the raped women became the constant accompaniment of the pogrom. The mass rape of Jewish women continued on the second and the third day.[49]

On the third day the Cossacks hunted the Jews who hid by the riverbank and in the ravines, shooting up the underbrush. The local population meanwhile ransacked Jewish homes for any movable objects, including furniture. After the Cossacks succeeded in shooting and bayoneting the Jews they had discovered, the regiment withdrew. Rossava was left by the Whites in the hands of the local gang leader and former member of Petliura's army Demian Lazarenko, who together with his friends continued to rob and abuse Jews through the night. In the morning on the fourth day of the pogrom, some Jews attempted to sneak back to their houses to collect and bury the dead. Apparently, the Cossacks, who had not left but were camped at the station, galloped back into town and massacred whomever they could find. After that, the pogrom became an ongoing affair, as Cossacks continued their daily raids while the local gang terrorized the shtetl. On August 27, two weeks after the Volunteer Army regiments entered Rossava, the remaining thousand Jews, starving and almost naked, among them many wounded, raped, and beaten, left Rossava and walked toward the nearby shtetl of Boguslav seeking refuge.[50]

The pogrom that devastated the Rossava shtetl is emblematic of the pogroms by the hands of the Whites. On the one hand, the pogrom employs the same components as Petliura's: plunder, murder, and demonstrative punishment of the Jews. On the other, the Denikin army pogroms strike us as more violent, more structured, and ultimately more deadly. Peter Kenez analyzed and reconstructed the typical pogrom by the Volunteer Army, and attributed its "success in murdering as many Jews as all other armies put together" to three

---

49 See more on the Rossava pogrom and mass rape in Chapter 3.
50 YIVO Archive, file 209, 18776.

factors: the pogroms were well organized, carried out as a military operation, and strongly ideologically motivated.[51]

The concept of an organized pogrom appears to be problematic in the context of the latest scholarship of pogrom violence and current research. There is no data that proves that pogroms were in fact masterminded or premeditated; rather, the pogroms were considered by Whites, as well as Ukrainians before them, to be the normal—and thus the proper—way to punish Jews, to visit on them due wrath and indignation. Genocidal violence against Jews that was strongly backed by the convictions of the White movement and traditionally supported by the Cossacks was never curbed, and unfolded through pogrom scripts that did not require any organization or planning, unlike a military operation.

Detailed analysis of numerous pogroms suggests that the "efficiency" of the pogroms of the second half of 1919 stemmed primarily from the fact that Denikin's army had better structure and training, and overall was more homogeneous than any of Petliura's troops or bands. Petliura's pogroms were pogroms of local thugs, of poorly trained peasants, very often former neighbors. The Denikin army pogroms were carried out by highly trained soldiers and officers, who had no regard for Jews, for the local population, or for Ukraine in general.

During the Civil War, the pogroms engulfed Ukraine and created a "pogrom universe" defined by genocidal violence. Inside this microcosm, framed by the free reign of violence, the brutal mass rape, and the torture and humiliation, all inhibitions became obsolete. The phenomenon of the pogrom in Ukraine in these years developed its own internal mechanics, an endless cycle of violence that spun out of control. Ritualized pogrom scripts appealed to visceral impulses and emotions and, when performed over and over, required escalation of violence to maintain the excitement and awe of the exhibition of gruesome public punishment. The previously committed violence caused even more violence.

Shtetl Kazatin (Koziatyn), home to approximately three thousand Jews, was an important railway junction to the west of Kiev. Through 1919, the Jews of Kazatin suffered from pogroms perpetrated by various regiments and platoons of different armies that traveled through this railway hub, as the shtetl changed hands constantly. In September 1919, the passing Denikin army regiment publicly hanged three Jews and left the bodies on the gallows for three

---

51 Kenez, "Pogroms and White Ideology," 302.

days. "But for the Jews such execution already was a trifle, of course,"[52] told one Goldfainag, the teacher of the Jewish secondary school in Kazatin. He proceeded to say that all ended well and that the Jews there were lucky, because that regiment stayed for only three days. This evidence demonstrates that the concept of normality was totally betrayed and ruined by endless cycles of pogroms, because the public execution of *only* three Jews became considered a lucky escape. Ever growing violence continuously adjusted the moral scale of both assailants and their victims. Indeed, the dam of inhibitions broke and destroyed the Jewish Ukrainian community as it was.

Not murder or plunder but publicly performed acts of violence became central to the intimate genocide that unraveled on the territory of Ukraine[53] during the Civil War. Pogrom perpetrators clearly distinguished between robbing and murdering Jews, and punishing Jews. Mass rape of Jewish women became the most characteristic trait of the pogroms in 1919. The scope and brutality of gendered violence during pogroms was unprecedented, and the mass rape of Jewish women became in many ways focus of genocidal violence during Civil War.

---

52 YIVO Archive, file 208, 18497.
53 And Belarus. See the Introduction to the current publication.

CHAPTER 3

The Perfect Weapon: Mass Rape as Public Spectacle

The pogrom that broke out in Skvira, a large town at a railroad junction southwest of Kiev and home to the Chernobyl Hasidic court, in December 1919, was the eighth since October 1917. For two weeks, the Denikin army troops had terrorized the Jews of Skvira: at least sixty people had been killed, over three hundred were wounded, and a "huge" number of women were raped, with almost twenty of them subsequently requiring medical help.[1] The Jewish women of Skvira had been repeatedly raped by various pogrom perpetrators throughout 1919, but the rapes were seldom voluntarily reported, because of the humiliation and shame associated with them. However, as the pogroms intensified, and mass rape of Jewish women overwhelmed Jewish communities, people started to narrate their experiences. As one Roitbok, a victim of the fifth pogrom in Skvira in August 1919 by the Zolotonoshsky unit of Petliura's army, described his dreadful experience minute by minute,[2] he painstakingly focused on some seemingly insignificant details but apparently left some obvious gaps in his witness account.

A group of twenty-four Jews had congregated in one house waiting for the pogrom that was about to break out; however, they had been caught off guard, and had not managed to escape to a hideout across the street. The "bandits," as Roitbok called the assailants, had dragged all the Jews out and divided the men and women in two groups, but had kept them in the same space. Petliura's soldiers intended to rape the Jewish women, and wanted it to hurt the most, so they had arranged the scene in a way that would augment the upcoming

---

1   YIVO Archive, file 209, 18792–94.
2   Miljakova, *Kniga Pogromov*, 227–28.

violence. The violent rites of the pogrom had unfolded according to social gender codes, and pogrom perpetrators deliberately and strategically utilized them. After separating men and women, the *pogromschiki* had tortured and tormented their victims in an effort to extort as much money and jewelry as they could, and had robbed the apartments. Once the initial loot had been acquired, the bandits proceeded to a macabre entertainment: torture and rape. One girl had been selected and raped in turns by a group of soldiers on the spot, in front of the gathered Jews. The other three attackers had beaten the witness's cousin until she fell on the floor, where one of the men proceeded to punch her chest and abdomen. The victim managed to run out of the house. She had been crying on the porch, apparently unable to move because of the shock and pain, when another group of *pogromschiki* came by, dragged her inside the house, raped her in turns, and shot her dead afterward. Her sister had been separated from her mother, dragged by the soldiers into the next room, and raped. Her aunt had been murdered by the youngest bandit, who had been left behind to guard her but got bored with his task. One of the bandits began to abuse Roitbok's eleven-year-old sister. He then told Roitbok to kiss the girl goodbye and shot her on the spot. After that, he dragged the crying Roitbok to the apothecary across the street, where they forced him to produce some money to pay for the bullets and the wear and tear on the whip that the bandit had used to beat him. After the bandit left, Roitbok, shaken and exhausted by the pogrom experience, sat on the chair in the deserted apothecary and fell asleep for two hours, as if his whole being could not cope with the trauma.

Most of the female members of the Roitbok household were subjected to brutal rape, carried out in front of witnesses and by the group of pogrom perpetrators. This single narrative of one episode of one of the pogroms is illustrative of the mass rape of Jewish women, as the rape scenario was repeated over and over throughout 1919 with striking similarity. Even this particularly violent episode should be considered within the larger perspective, as it was one of many that happened in the course of the fifth pogrom, which means that Jews of Skvira had already been victims of pogrom violence, or at least had witnessed it, four times, and would yet suffer similar experiences thrice in the course of a few months.[3]

---

3   The first pogrom at the end of 1917 by local peasants and the third pogrom in March 1919 by Red Army troops produced no casualties, but looting, beating, and abuse did take place. The second pogrom by Petliura's retreating platoons in February 1919 and the third by Tyutyunik and Zheleznyak gangs in June 1919 brought devastation and left behind casualties. Roitbok and his family had been already exposed to the pogrom violence before, and survivors had yet to live through another Petliura's pogrom in September, a pogrom by the Makhno gang that terrorized Skvira through October and November 1919, and a pogrom by Denikin's army in December.

The pogrom script, as it evolved during the Ukrainian Civil War, focused on intentionally horrific violence against Jews with the intent of not only killing the Jews but also of destroying Jewish life first and foremost. The objective of the genocidal violence was to destroy the very basis of Jewish existence, to demolish all sacred values of Jewish life, and to inflict maximum suffering onto Jews through both violence and the exposure of violence. The Jews were destined to become witnesses to their own disgrace.

In the context of a violent conflict like wars or riots, there is a type of violence other than murderous that does not aim to achieve death of an enemy as its primary target, but aims to destroy the very core of the human being—the able self—while keeping the body alive. Slavery, torture, and rape rob the victim of the ability to control his or her actions and his or her body, and aim to inflict suffering that is continuous. Often, slavery, torture, and rape are interwoven, and employed at once, and the distinction between the three can become blurred. Theoretically, torture and slavery are not gender-based, and can have practical goals, such as extraction of labor or of information, although that is not a requirement. Rape, regardless of a victim's identity, is always a gender crime, which does not and cannot have purposeful goals, but can inflict maximum suffering on the victims, the gazing crowd, and the larger community.

The mass rape of Jewish women became a prominent feature of the violent pogroms all over Ukraine. Tcherikower in his notes seems to have exhausted his vocabulary trying to give a name to the massive occurrences of rape during the Civil War pogroms that he refers to as an "epidemic."[4] Though rape had been a feature of anti-Jewish violence throughout Jewish history, and in the history of pogrom violence in particular, it was not a significant part of the pogroms in 1917–18. In 1919, however, the number of rapes of Jewish women surged tremendously. Mass rape of Jewish women affected, according to very conservative estimates, no less than half of Jewish women in the places where pogroms occurred. It is very difficult to assemble the exact rape statistics because rape generally was seldom reported, as it was unanimously understood as shameful for the victim, but at the same time recognized by the Jewish population of Ukraine as an integral part of the traditional pogrom script. As a result, nobody, neither pogrom survivors nor persons who assessed pogroms and interpreted the data, wanted to discuss rape publicly, but they shared the understanding that rape had taken place in the course of pogroms. However, as pogroms unfolded, more and more reports would account for the mass rape

---

4   YIVO Archive, file 659, 56269.

of Jewish women. Very cautious at first for "obvious reasons,"[5] the reports of the growing number of rapes became more explicit and precise as mass rape of Jewish women ruptured Jewish communities beyond repair.

Mass rape should be regarded within the context of genocidal violence, and specifically of how this brand of violence strategically targeted the interiority of every victim, every witness, and every victimized community. The concept of genocidal rape has been developed by a number of feminist scholars, particularly Claudia Card,[6] and is increasingly recognized by the international community. The purpose of genocidal rape, according to these thinkers, is to assert the power and superiority of the perpetrators, destroy publicly the dignity of women, and, in doing so, victimize the whole community through humiliation. The shame and disgrace of rape endures long after the execution of the crime, and is transmitted from generation to generation. The traumatic experience dramatically impacts the victimized community. Mass rape thus aims to promote the social death of the community which, along with its physical destruction, is the ultimate objective of genocide.

Integral to the strategic goals of gender violence utilized by most of the belligerent armies involved was the creation of a public spectacle of mass rape, which augmented the humiliation and impacted more observers. Almost without exception, rape was perpetrated collectively and in the presence of witnesses. The public rape performance fit into what we have termed an evolving pogrom script. The street theater aspect played out through carnivalesque rituals in a way immediately recognized by Jewish communities from their historical and more recent experiences. In 1919, however, the level of anti-Jewish violence spun out of proportion and manifested itself in both an unprecedented death toll, excess of humiliating torture, and brutal, visceral rape. The mass rape had evolved within this archaic scenario, and often became its culmination.

THE PUBLIC SPECTACLE OF RAPE

Spectacle makes mass rape genocidal. During the pogrom in Rossava that has been discussed at length, the public rape of a Jewish girl emerged as the central performance in the theater of violence, a focal point of the pogrom,

---

5   This is a quote from the EKOPO Report of the pogrom in Vasilkov, but similar quotes are present in most reports about rapes. YIVO Archive, file 165, 1400–29.

6   Card, "Rape as a Weapon of War"; Card, "Genocide and Social Death"; Claudia Card, *The Atrocity Paradigm: A Theory of Evil* (Oxford: Oxford University Press, 2002).

and its culmination.[7] Here, Cossacks brutally raped every other Jewish woman and girl in the town on the first evening, leaving them naked on the streets to bleed to death. The *pogromschiki* did not differentiate by age or physical condition: they raped a seventy-year-old woman before her husband's eyes, the twelve-year-old daughter of a local distiller, and a new mother who had just given birth. According to eyewitnesses, the parents were hacked to pieces as they tried to cover the naked bodies of their daughters. The mass rape continued into the second day of the pogrom. On the third day of the pogrom, the White officers summoned Rossava's entire population to the central square. Roza Kozlova, who had been raped by a group of Cossacks on the previous day, arrived at the gathering with her parents. It is clear that the previous rape had happened in public, since the anonymous witness, and probably everyone else, knew about it. The Cossacks shot Roza's father on the spot. After that, her mother "was picked up on the sabers," forcing her daughter to observe the killing of her parents, while the whole scene was exposed to the public. Then the Cossacks dragged Roza to the shed in the square, gang raped her again, and after that pushed her outside into the crowd. Apparently this horrible display of rape was the essential communication from the Cossacks and their command to the crowd of peasants, and to the Jews, regardless of what the official reason for the summoning was. This dramatized rape performance unfolded at the peak point of the pogrom, after the looting, general torture and beatings, and mass rape of Jewish women had already taken place in public spaces. The spectacle of Kozlova's rape was an intentional and significant statement of power and ultimate domination, the culmination of the grand performance of the pogrom.

A common pattern emerges in the theater of pogrom violence: every rape and every act of violence is executed as a spectacle, which together coalesces into one big performance that often culminates in a grand finale. A meticulously staged spectacle concluded the November pogrom in the small shtetl of Bobrovitsy, located to the east of Kiev and a long distance away from Rossava. The pogrom unfolded according to the same common script: the Cossacks first announced a "tribute" to be paid by the Jewish community, then went around the houses, tortured the Jews, and collected the loot; and the Jewish women were raped at homes in front of their families or in the streets by groups of Cossacks, who also specifically targeted unmarried teenage girls to be brutally raped in public. After the pogrom was over, the Jewish population of Bobrovitsy assembled at the cemetery to bury the pogrom victims. At the exact time when

---

7   YIVO Archive, file 209, 18770–71.

all the Jews gathered at the cemetery, a large group of Cossacks rode back into the shtetl, forced their way into the cemetery, and raped the fifteen-year-old *shammes*'s (a sexton in a synagogue) daughter right there in front of every-one present.[8] In Bobrovitsy, the spectacle of rape was orchestrated to achieve maximum dramatic effect to punish and disgrace Jews: it brutally deprived the Jewish community of the appropriate mourning for their dead, symbolically vandalized the sacred space, and humiliated Jews further by public destruction of female dignity and honor.

The street theater of pogrom violence, ritualized and exposed, appealed to the most bestial and primal emotions of perpetrators, victims, and bystanders. For *pogromschiki*, this macabre circus became a source of satisfaction and enter-tainment, which derived primarily not from physical gratification, or sadistic pleasure, but from the mortification and suffering of the punished victims. The rapists acted as a group with a collective purpose, and the rape of Jewish women in Rossava or Bobrovitsy, and all the other shtetls and towns, had been per-formed as a public statement.

Claudia Card argued that "one set of fundamental functions of rape, civilian or martial, is to display, communicate, and produce or maintain dom-inance."[9] The spectacle of rape delivers the message of dominance to the vul-nerable community, and transforms an individual act of sexual violence into a calculated assault on the community in general. In other words, public expo-sure and ritualized performance of rape is a strategy aimed to remove the act of rape from a private domain, to strip it of the emotional and intimate aspect of sexuality, to absolve a perpetrator from responsibility, and to validate rape as an act of punishment in the public domain.

No discussion of public punishment is possible without referencing the classic work by Michel Foucault, *Discipline and Punish*.[10] Foucault described the practice of public torture and execution, and its demise in modern history. The purpose of public scaffolding in premodern history was to establish and emphasize absolute monarchial power over subjects. The public execution that appeared "to exceed . . . in savagery the crime itself"[11] appealed to the most bestial feelings of the crowd, and established a potent image of absolute power as the body of the condemned was subjected to elaborate torture. As society, challenged by modernity, changed its values and objectives, Foucault argues,

---

8   Ibid., file 206, 18233–40.
9   Card, "Rape as a Weapon of War," 7.
10   Foucault, *Discipline and Punish*.
11   Ibid., 9.

the spectacle of public scaffolding has been substituted with the public trial that focuses on the prosecution of justice, while the actual punishment is carried out away from the public view and is based on discipline—an inverted version of spectacle, when the condemned are subjected to constant scrutiny.

Foucault described how the public spectacle of violence disappeared in the nineteenth century. In the twentieth century, it made a comeback as a strategic weapon of war and genocide. Bergoffen has analyzed the politics of gender in modern warfare through the public rape of women to further genocidal objectives:

> The public rape strategy exploits the ways that the rape spectacles create images of horror that inflame feelings of shame and disgust either by staging a Sadean challenge to the incest taboo, manipulating fantasy of masculine sovereignty or disrupting (if not destroying) the gender identities of men and women.[12]

Bergoffen argues that in peacetime rape reinforces gender identities indigent to the patriarchal society: rape serves as a punishment for the woman who placed herself in harm's way by leaving the protection of her family.[13] Wartime and genocidal rape aim to destroy publicly the traditional gender identities of the community, feminizing men and instrumentalizing women. The spectacle of rape targets not just women whose bodies are violated and degraded, but "their men" as well, who are degraded and humiliated in the eyes of the enemy, of the onlookers, of their peers, of their tortured women, and in their own eyes.

Roitbok's narrative[14] of his experience of the Skvira pogrom illustrates how he, in his designated role of observer, was involved in gender violence. He and other Jewish men were forced to watch the rape of women they knew and were related to. The shame and humiliation of the spectacle were acutely experienced by Roitbok, and he omitted all the descriptions of the actual act of rape, while going into a lot of minor details about other actions of the pogrom perpetrators. The logic of the narrative suggests that Roitbok[15] intentionally did not mention all the instances of gender violence inflicted on his close relatives and possibly on his little sister. Roitbok is closely involved in the unraveling

---

12 Bergoffen, *Contesting the Politics of Genocidal Rape*, 50.
13 In reality, Bergoffen remarks, domestic rape defies this narrative, because in this case rape is perpetrated by men charged with protection of women. Ibid., 51.
14 Miljakova, *Kniga Pogromov*, 227–28.
15 For the reasons to be discussed at length in the following chapters.

visceral performance—the bandits address him when they are deciding what to do with his little sister and suggest that he "kiss her goodbye"[16] after she was murdered. The crying Roitbok was humiliated further by the suggestion that he pay for the tear and wear of the whip he was beaten with. Roitbok was physically exhausted by his role of observer and fell asleep after he was left alone, which appears to be a sign of an adaptive response to his extremely traumatic experience.

Gender and sexual politics establish how the spectacle of rape impacts the most visceral and bestial human emotions, and causes the most damage to human interiority. The pogroms in Ukraine were not carried out as an ethnic cleansing campaign or a religious war, or rather were never described as such, and lacked the single ideological set of violence narrative. The pogrom genocide was narrated and rationalized in strictly political terms and utilized the infamous Judeo-Bolshevik canard, which by no means reflected the real motivations of the groups of perpetrators. Considering that pogroms were perpetrated by a number of armed forces, who fought for absolutely different reasons and goals, the messages that they communicated through anti-Jewish violence were poles apart. To some groups of pogrom perpetrators, the rape spectacle proved to be more instrumental than to others. Specifically, the White Army did utilize Foucauldian public punishment on several different levels, as a genocidal strategy and simultaneously in the form of a narrative of monarchial power, reenacted by both assailants and their victims.

The reenactment of the monarchial narrative as Foucault's "spectacle of the scaffold" perfectly served the White Army's faux representation of the Tsarist regime. For the White Army, with its unclear goals and objectives, anti-Jewish violence became a technique to define themselves and their enemy. The reenactment of monarchial ceremonies, as discussed in the previous chapter, was reinforced by the public display of cruel punishment. The original mechanism of public punishment, as described by Foucault, focused not on the original crime that caused the retribution, but on the monarchial rite to exact this punishment. Only a certain kind of power exerts itself directly on bodies and is exalted and strengthened by its visible manifestations.[17] Such power, or a simulacrum of power in the case of White Army vis-à-vis the Jewish community, best asserts itself through militarized order, treats real or imaginary breach of rules or laws as a betrayal that requires vengeance, and retaliates

---

16 Miljakova, *Kniga Pogromov*, 228.
17 Foucault, *Discipline and Punish*, 57.

against disobedience as if against an act of hostility. The crusade unleashed by the White Army against the Jews was grounded in popular prejudice, which was at the same time deeply rooted in ages of animosity. The White Army represented not a real authority that could enforce its laws, but an imaginary one that fed off demonstration of force against its enemies, and, in Foucault's own words, "in the absence of continual supervision, sought a renewal of its effect in the spectacle of its individual manifestations; of a power that was recharged in the ritual display of its reality as 'super-power.'"[18]

The publicized violence strengthened the White Army's image as a monarchial absolute power and ensured and furthered genocidal objectives. Foucault did not and could not discuss rape as a form of public punishment as exercised by monarchial power. However, it was in a form of publicly exposed rape that "spectacle of the scaffold" made a comeback during the pogroms and became the focal point, the culmination of the spectacle of violence practiced by all pogrom perpetrators. Genocidal rape, as was discussed earlier,[19] emerges as an extremely versatile form of weapon, which inflicts maximum damage on the victimized community. This heinous strategy works best when communicated through ugly spectacle, fitting perfectly into pogrom script, which is also based on publicly executed violent rites. The rituals of mass rape are almost identical in most pogroms; however, the secondary details specific to each pogrom demonstrate how the meaning of rape was emphasized.

The shtetl of Borzna, located northwest of Kiev, was of no specific significance, as it was rather far away from the two closest railway stations, but nevertheless lay directly on the line between Kiev and Moscow. The Jewish population of Borzna numbered approximately three hundred and fifty families. From the end of August to the beginning of September 1919, White Army regiments forced the Bolshevik troops out of Borzna, but the Reds managed to recapture the town. Borzna changed hands up to nine times, although the evidence is conflicting;[20] some anti-Jewish violence took place every time regardless of which troops took over. Finally on September 15 (old style) the White cavalry regiment known to the local Jewish population as the Blue Cuirassiers or the Hussars of Death came into town. The pogrom broke out immediately: "they came in at four o'clock in the afternoon, but already in half an hour the piercing female screams were heard from everywhere,"[21] recalled Rivka Raskovskaia,

---

18 Ibid.
19 See Introduction.
20 YIVO Archive, file 206, 18272–87.
21 Miljakova, *Kniga Pogromov*, 286.

sister of the leader of the Borzna Jewish community. Raskovskaia's evidence is very restrained compared to other accounts of Borzna pogrom, but she also singled out mass rape as the most defining aspect of pogrom violence. Almost all Borzna pogrom narratives focus on the horrible and exceedingly brutal rape of Jewish women, and particularly young girls. The death toll of the Borzna pogrom was relatively low, compared to many other shtetls—twenty-four Jews died, and many were tortured by partial hanging, pulling out of beards, etc. Murders, torture, and beatings of Jewish men are mentioned as a background to the spectacle of rape: large groups of Cossacks undressed young Jewish girls in front of their families and other people, flogged them, and then brutally raped them. Raskovskaia mentions one thirteen-year-old Jewish girl raped in her house in front of the girl's father and grandfather; other reports name one more victim, Yoffe, a fourteen-year-old girl; and although only one case of rape was registered officially for "obvious reasons," all respondents talk about the epidemic of syphilis, and a lot of pregnancies that resulted from the pogrom.[22]

The pogrom perpetrators in Borzna deliberately built up tension and fear by gradually approaching the culmination of the performance: undressing, then flogging, and after that—the greatest punishment—rape. In this case, the "punishment" aspect of rape was stressed through the public flogging—a basic form of punishment that would be understood as such by a spectator of any age and social status. Forced undressing aimed to cause more shame for the victims and their families, and to stress the subservient position of the Jews. The elaborate and malevolent choreography of the Borzna pogrom illustrates how rape culminates in a public spectacle as a focal point of the pogrom. But the Foucauldian "art of torture" would be pointless if there were no one to observe it. The spectacle of rape required an audience, and in Borzna, like in other pogrom-stricken towns, the audience was carefully selected.

With the established function of the public mass rape of Jewish women as a strategic weapon, the role of the spectator becomes a crucial one. The humiliating aspect of the torture is validated only when witnessed and comprehended as such. Without witnesses, the sadistic act remains an individual performance of assault and torture, but once the event gains spectators the rape becomes an act of public punishment, an act of war, which requires no vindication or justification. Foucault wrote: "In the ceremonies of the public execution, the main character was the people, whose real and immediate presence was required for the performance."[23]

---

22 YIVO Archive, file 206, 18272–87.
23 Foucault, *Discipline and Punish*, 57.

The main function of the audience is to observe, to look. The practice of looking or observing, unlike simply seeing, is one of the basic ways to interpret the world, like writing or speaking, Sturken and Cartwright argue in "Practices of Looking."[24] Looking is irreversible, as an image once seen cannot be wiped out from consciousness without a trace. The practice of looking involves the relationship of power: images communicate a message and cause a spectrum of emotions from pleasure to horror; through looking people can influence and be influenced. The complicated process of looking that establishes the relationship between the image and the observer is described in psychoanalysis as the gaze. The Lacanian concept of the gaze,[25] usually applied to film and fine arts, fundamentally describes the pleasure and desire experienced by the spectator in a particular set of social circumstances. Feminist scholarship argued early on that visual culture is traditionally structured around the "male gaze" that disempowers woman by making them objects of voyeurism.[26] Sturken and Cartwright proceed to argue that the concept of gaze is not restricted to subjectivity and the spectator, and, according to Foucault's theory, there are institutional gazes that establish the relationship of power between individuals within its realm. The images can exert power and act as its instruments.[27] All the meanings and functions of gaze were simultaneously employed in the context of mass rape of Jewish women during pogroms, inflicting maximum suffering on the maximum number of people.

The audience of pogrom rape consisted of three groups of people: large groups of pogrom perpetrators, the local non-Jewish population, and the Jews. The local non-Jewish population identified with the perpetrators during the UNA pogroms, and was not necessarily present during Denikin's pogroms. Whenever the non-Jewish crowd was present to witness the spectacle of rape, it provided yet another gaze to intensify the suffering of the victims. Whether mass rape took place in front of a large crowd, like in Rossava,[28] where all the population was forced to assemble in the central square, or inside the houses, like in Skvira as described by Roitbok,[29] the assailants endeavored to perform

---

24 Marita Sturken and Lisa Cartwright, *Practices of Looking* (Oxford: Oxford University Press, 2003), 9–12.

25 Jacques Lacan, *The Split between the Eye and the Gaze*, in *The Four Fundamental Concepts of Psycho-Analysis*, vol. 11 (New York: W.W. Norton & Company, 1981), 71.

26 Laura Mulvey, "Visual Pleasure and Narrative Cinema," in *Visual and Other Pleasures* (New York: Springer, 1989), 14–26.

27 Sturken and Cartwright, *Practices of Looking*, 101–5.

28 YIVO Archive, file 209, 18771.

29 Miljakova, *Kniga Pogromov*, 227–28.

the rape in front of the family members of the victims. The composite audience provided the gaze, which, to Sturken and Cartwright "is the process in which the object functions to make the subject look, making the subjects appear to himself or herself as lacking."[30] The transitional function of the gaze turned the Jewish audience into victims and perpetrators at the same time: by actively witnessing the spectacle, the Jewish audience added to the suffering of the women being raped, and inflicted further suffering onto themselves by both watching the execution of their own and by recognizing themselves as doing so.

The pogrom perpetrators recognized the power of the gaze and sought to intensify it by involving close relations of the victim: parents, children, and other family members were very often forced to witness the rape of their daughters, sisters, and mothers. During the pogrom in Cherkassy, the father of two teenage girls being raped in front of his eyes began pulling out his own hair and crying, and the Cossacks murdered him.[31] For the father the pain of association with the perpetrators on top of the pain of witnessing his own daughters' suffering was unbearable, so he tortured himself to punish himself further, and to compensate for the horrible spectacle that devastated him. The Cossacks did murder the girls' father in the end; however, it is probable that it was done to harm his daughters more than the father himself, for whom the death could be a redemption. As violence of the pogroms in general and rape in particular intensified, the murder of the Jews provided less gratification for the perpetrators than the elaborate spectacle of their suffering.

The sexual component of the gaze, described in psychoanalysis, was most definitely present in the spectacle of rape. Jewish women were undressed and raped in front of Jewish men's eyes, forced Jewish men to join in the gaze, which "carries the negative connotation of the powerful, if not sadistic, position within the game."[32] By forcing Jewish men to desire women who were being raped, perpetrators made Jewish men, however briefly and unconsciously, rapists of their own women, inflicting on them further shame and suffering. One particularly horrific episode illustrates this: during a pogrom in Smela, a husband was forced to be the thirteenth to rape his own wife, and the Cossacks made sure that he "was not faking it."[33] Rapists were seeking to humiliate their

30 Ibid., 122.
31 Ibid., 356.
32 Sturken and Cartwright, *Practices of Looking*, 124.
33 Joseph B. Schechtman, Naum Iul'evich Gergel', and I. M. Cherikover, *Pogromy Dobrovol'cheskoi Armii na Ukraine: K Istorii Antisemitizma v 1919–1920 gg.* (Ostjüdisches Historisches Archiv, 1932), 120.

victim and her husband, and to ruin them emotionally as well as physically, as this forced act of rape would inevitably impact, if not completely ruin, this particular Jewish family.

There is no evidence about rape during pogroms provided by rape perpetrators and their leaders, so the scholars have to evaluate circumstantial evidence to establish how the rape strategy fitted into the agenda of rape perpetrators. The following case study is focused on a single well-planned raid, which was glorified by the White Army as a victory, and was committed by one of the most famous of its commanders, known not for their viciousness, but for their honor and dignity. The story of the pogroms committed outside the former Pale of Settlement during this infamous episode illustrates that mass rape was evidently and casually recognized as an integral part of the pogrom script, and that mass rape was understood, at least by the high command of the White Army, as a just and adequate punishment of the Jews.

General Mamantov[34] was a well-known charismatic leader of the Cossack army who commanded the Don Cossack Host before and after the Revolution. Unlike the infamous general Shkuro, who elicited dread even among his comrades-in-arms with his ruthless and vicious violence, General Mamantov was widely regarded as a wise and thoughtful leader, mild-mannered, kind, an exemplary officer, and a very refined, well-educated, ascetic person, who shunned strong drink and detested cigarette smoke.[35] From the end of August until the middle of September 1919, General Mamantov led his very best battalions on a cavalry raid in the rear guard of the Red Army in Central Russia. The official goal of the raid was to distract the Bolshevik command from a counteroffensive, and to instigate a peasant uprising against the Soviets; however, it turned out that there was another motive for the raid, probably no less important. In less than a month, Mamantov's Cossacks broke through the Red Army front line, conquered several Russian towns, violently yet meticulously perpetrated pogroms, and ravaged small Jewish communities in those cities. The White Army command did not approve of the raid, although among Cossack armies it was treated as a glorious victory, especially when the enormous convoy laden with loot crossed back into Ukraine, and Mamantov sent a victorious greeting over the White Army radio channels.[36] The peasants in the territories raided by Mamantov's troops did not rise

34 Also spelled as Mamontov.

35 A. N. Grishchenko and A. V. Lazarev, "Konstantin Konstantinovich Mamantov," *Voprosy Istorii*, no. 1 (2012).

36 Petr N. Vrangel', *Zapiski: (Nojabr' 1916 g.–Nojabr' 1920 g.)* (Kosmos, 1991).

against the Bolsheviks, and the Jewish communities in towns such as Kozlov and Yelets were utterly devastated.

The pogrom in Yelets lasted six days, although the Jews of Kozlov were told that the Cossacks were entitled to at least twenty-four to forty-eight hours of plunder,[37] and were carried out with frightening precision, as described by the Bolshevik officials who were sent to investigate, but obviously had no previous experience with pogroms and could not fully comprehend and describe the disaster.[38] The Cossacks were not interested in finding and punishing the "real" Bolsheviks at all; they went into the town in large groups, entered Jewish homes, assembled Jewish families in their apartments, raped Jewish women in front of their families, looted anything that could be found, and then took the surviving Jews outside of town, where they were undressed, tortured, the Jewish women were raped again and again, and then the surviving victims were killed. Everything happened very fast, with military precision, but followed the same script as all the pogroms perpetrated by the White Army.

The military raid into the Russian interior turned into a punitive expedition against Jews, and all the atrocities were committed with the full knowledge and approval of the command. When General Mamantov was approached by the representatives of the local Russian intelligentsia, who were astounded and shocked by the rape, torture, and murders, he said that Jews in fact should be shot not in small groups but in the hundreds.[39] This general, known for his impeccable personality, who was rumored to have forced his Cossacks to destroy all the alcohol in one of the towns to preserve morale,[40] considered the rape, torture, and murder of Jews to be right and just.[41] Mamantov undoubtedly knew about rape and torture and approved of it, as the discipline in his regiments was always perfect.

Mamantov, like most officers in the White Army, was a very well-educated man, born and raised as a member of the privileged class, who was exposed to modernity and enjoyed its benefits for most of his life; and still he considered barbaric punishment by public rape an adequate means of retaliation.

---

37 Miljakova, *Kniga Pogromov*, 784.
38 YIVO Archive, file 206, 18463–64.
39 Miljakova, *Kniga Pogromov*, 785.
40 Grishchenko and Lazarev, "Konstantin Konstantinovich Mamantov."
41 Similarly, twenty-five years later the Russian high command, including Stalin himself, considered wartime rape to be a reasonable response to the German invasion. See also Giles MacDonogh, *After the Reich: The Brutal History of the Allied Occupation* (New York: Basic Books, 2009).

Rape statistics of the pogroms during the Civil War suggest that not only the visceral cruelty of mass rape was intentional, but also that it was understood by at least some pogrom perpetrators and their leaders as the way to maximize suffering among the victims, also exposed to education and secularism, who would be able to comprehend the ugly barbarity of their punishment. The gaze as a practice, according to Foucault and Sturken and Cartwright, belongs to modernity. The complex relationship between the spectator and the spectacle, and between the observer and the observed, gains crucial importance in the modern image-permeated society,[42] and, according to Foucault, would serve as its major regulatory force. The return of public punishment during pogroms in many respects relied on the modernized gaze of the audience. The return of violent spectacle in a form of genocidal rape was directed at the inhomogeneous Jewish community of Ukraine that had been partially exposed to secularism and modernity. Likewise, the perpetrators of the genocidal rape constituted an inhomogeneous multitude of groups of people, who sought to achieve different goals and communicate different messages through the mass rape of Jewish women.

---

42 A. Freidberg, *The Mobilized and Virtual Gaze in Modernity*, with introductions by N. Mirzoeff (London: Routledge, 1998).

CHAPTER 4

Inventing Vengeance: Who and Why Punished the Jews

In the shtetl of Rakitino,[1] the second pogrom broke out on August 14, 1919, after the leaders of local peasants, who perpetrated the previous pogrom in February, invited the Cossacks, posted at the railway station, to help with the pogrom. A group of Cossacks had joined enthusiastically, and the pogrom started immediately and lasted for over two weeks. A young Jewish girl named Povolotskaia was stripped naked in the central street and raped by a group of Cossacks right there despite her desperate pleas. Three sisters from the Reikhman family were brutally raped in front of their parents' eyes. Khava Ochakovskaia, fifty, was killed while she tried to protect her three daughters, aged twelve to nineteen, who were taken consecutively to the railway station and repeatedly raped there by groups of Cossack soldiers.[2] In total, about a hundred Jewish women aged from twelve to sixty were raped by groups of eight to ten Cossacks.

Cossacks, stationed at the railway terminal outside the shtetl, had come deliberately to rape, extort, and torture. The rapists always acted in a group, usually of eight to ten men, who raped one victim after another. There is evidence of groups of other sizes as well, but this particular number appears more often than any other. In the large town of Cherkassy, where the pogrom had been perpetrated by different armed forces—the insurgent soldiers under

---

1   Tcherikower, following the report of the Committee to Aid Pogrom Survivors of the Russian Division of the Red Cross, gives the name of the shtetl as "Rakitino"; however, it appears that the established name is Rakitno, or Rokytno. This shtetl was located in the vicinity of the regional center and railway junction Belaya Tserkov, south of Kiev, in close proximity to Rossava, Boguslav, Skvira, and other places already discussed.

2   YIVO Archive, file 209, 18762–64.

the command of ataman Grigoriev—the Red Cross inspector Tsifranovich reported that the male Jewish population aged sixteen and over had been killed almost completely, with their bodies mutilated so horribly that it had been almost impossible to recognize them, since their arms and legs were cut off. The report goes on: "The rapes were of a horrible character. The victim was tortured by eight–ten people consecutively, and they gathered the Jews to make them watch the barbaric atrocity (The rapes were not registered)."[3]

Group participation of *pogromschiki* in the mass rape of Jewish women was an essential factor, which had a very specific primary function—to communicate a message. The first and the most straightforward message of rape is the message of domination, of absolute power and superiority. Violent pogrom rituals[4] communicate the very same message by symbolically restoring the "correct" hierarchy of the society, but the act of rape, and particularly mass rape, has a much more powerful impact. Rape is a violent crime that "derives from a system of dominance and subjugation"[5] and maintains this system on a larger scale. Claudia Card takes this concept further with regard to wartime rape: "If there is one set of functions of rape, civilian or martial, it is to display, communicate and produce or maintain dominance."[6] The message of wartime rape has two major targets: the victim and the audience receiving the message.

Women who suffered rape clearly were the primary victims of the pogrom rapes: their bodies were forcefully penetrated, violated, tortured, and mutilated; and they had their integrity ruined publicly, may have been impregnated against their will, and may have been infected with sexually transmitted diseases. All Jews of pogrom communities who observed rape directly, or were otherwise exposed to rape, became victims of rape as well. The Jewish community became the primary audience of rape, but there was another audience: the group of rapists who perpetrated the rape together. Each single act of group rape communicated two quite different messages at the same time: one directed at the victims, and another directed internally.

According to philosopher Louise du Toit, gang rape often conforms to the model of rape as a performance, a theater that requires an audience, but at the same time "cements the truth of rapist's world," promoting bonding and camaraderie.[7] This is particularly true for the two waves of rape that swamped the

3　Ibid., file 191, 16558 on reverse.
4　Hagen, "The Moral Economy of Ethnic Violence."
5　Allen, *Rape Warfare*, 39.
6　Card, "Rape as a Weapon of War," 7.
7　Du Toit, *A Philosophical Investigation of Rape*, 93.

shtetls in Ukraine in 1919. The mass rapes during the first and second halves of 1919 followed generally the same scenario, but communicated a distinctly different internal message to various groups of assailants. The perpetrators of the mass rape of Jewish women in the first half of 1919 were soldiers of the Ukrainian National Army, various gangs, and even Bolshevik troops, who ultimately belonged to a group of people that can be defined by one word— "locals." The White Army and the Cossacks, who perpetrated mass rape in the second half of 1919, were by and large not natives of Ukraine and their objectives were radically different. In the context of mass gender violence, rape communication as a driving force of violence and part of the identity structure of pogrom perpetrators will be revisited later in the book. Red Army rape perpetrators fell either into the same category as soldiers of the UNA or military gangs, who indeed switched their allegiances with ease, or they were Cossacks, who had previously served in the White Army. The lack of unique identity vis-à-vis anti-Jewish violence among Red Army soldiers was also sustained by the politics of internationalism conducted by the Red Army command, which led to politics of pogrom prevention and persecution of the offenders, so no specific Bolshevik *pogromschiki* profile could be formed or singled out.

UKRAINIAN ARMY SOLDIERS AND BANDITS

On July 10, 1919, Braude, the representative of the Aid Department of the Russian Red Cross, reported on the situation in the pogrom-stricken shtetls in the region to the south of Kiev around the important railway junction in the town of Uman. Various gangs and Petliura's army regiments perpetrated pogroms in Uman and shtetls like Lodyzhenka, Golovanievsk, Dubovo, etc. Braude, who visited the region during the short break of relative calm provided by the advance of the Red Army, assessed the situation thus: "Around the towns and shtetls [there are] bandit packs, insurgents, groups, mobs, or simply peasants with pitchforks and scythes, with various slogans, with all sorts of demands, or without all these 'gauze curtains';[8]—all of them beat, torture,[9] mutilate Jews. There are many dozens of chieftains. Almost all of them have nicknames borrowed from the folk tales or pulp fiction."[10] This is, in fact, a very precise evaluation of the chaos that engulfed Ukraine in 1919, and Braude's

---

8   Here meaning "pretense."
9   Here the term means anything from humiliation to, most probably, rape.
10 Miljakova, *Kniga Pogromov*, 204–5.

description is valid for the whole of Ukraine in 1919. Most of the other inspectors and witnesses tried to comprehend the rampant anti-Jewish violence through political analysis on the micro-level, and inevitably became drawn into arguments about whether Jews were or were not Bolsheviks, missing the larger picture altogether. Braude, however, recognized that political slogans served to camouflage the real objective of harming the Jews, and that perpetrators of the pogroms in the first half of 1919 were a chaotic mixture of all sorts of armed men, a patchwork of various regiments and platoons with no coherent plans or goals. Braude was also very keen to notice that despite the chaotic appearance these people shared some common characteristics: for one, they were in desperate search of a name, or rather identity. Moshe Rekis survived Grigoriev's pogroms in the Cherkassy-Smela-Elisavetgrad area in May 1919, and provided a detailed account of his experience. Rekis indeed searched for political rationalization, but, in sync with Braude, he defined Petliura's soldiers as "demoralized . . . Ukrainian village 'Cossack[s]'" and "prostitutes of the Civil War,"[11] recognizing their false identity and vague allegiance.

Petliura's army, just like the various military gangs (*bandas*), was composed of locals. "Local" is the key adjective in this case: they were native to the land, and long-term neighbors of the Jews they were now attacking. This circumstance implies a certain pattern to the relationship of the Jews and *pogromschiki* in the first half of 1919. On one hand, Jews generally did not recognize the Ukrainian National Army (UNA), unanimously referred to as Petliura's army, and the *bandas* as legitimate representatives of power. In the eyes of the Jewish communities the new Ukrainian army and the military gangs, although they constituted a real threat and, indeed, a mortal danger, did not represent valid authority that consequently would have enjoyed real respect and trust (in a positive rather than negative sense). In other words, Jews did not know what to expect from the new power and, what is more, did not believe the new power to be viable or capable of imposing any solid, long-term order. On the other hand, the people who joined the UNA, the gangs, or even the Bolshevik army, had been uprooted and were no longer peasants connected to their land, although a lot of Ukrainian soldiers were of peasant ancestry. By the beginning of 1919, the bulk of the Ukrainian army and gangs consisted of former soldiers, or people without a particular profession or landholdings, who shared at the moment of a pogrom a common characteristic—they were constantly on the go.

---

11 YIVO Archive, file 183, 15936.

This group of people was perceived by Jews as thugs. In the eyes of their victims, Petliura's pogroms were pogroms of criminal elements. These were people whom Jews might have known personally, or were similar to people they knew. As a result, Jews feared the Ukrainian *pogromschiki*, but did not respect them. The fact that the majority of pogrom perpetrators were either neighbors of their victims, or recognized as similar to the same, adds yet another dimension to the common portrait of the *pogromschiki* of the first half of 1919 that set the first wave of pogroms apart from the second. The UNA soldiers as well as various bandits and the new Bolshevik recruits were all native to Ukraine. The land they were roaming was their own, not a foreign land they did not care for. This influenced the course of the pogroms as well as made a tremendous difference in the way both the *pogromschiki* and local non-Jewish neighbors approached Jewish property during the pogroms: as much as the *pogromschiki* did not care about Jewish lives, they did care about their property and the local settlements in general.

The self-identity of Petliura's army appears to be problematic. The UNA soldiers were not Cossacks although they called themselves by that name most of the time and insisted that others do so. The real Cossacks lived in closed, militarized communities that maintained themselves in the Russian Empire mainly in the regions of Don, Kuban, and Caucasus. Cossacks provided excellent military service to the Russian tsars—they formed elite regiments and, unlike regular soldiers, were very loyal to the tsars, who relied on the Cossacks to suppress uprisings and revolts. The Cossacks were active on the front lines during wars as well, and their fighting prowess justified for the Tsarist government the existence of the anachronism of a privileged military estate in the twentieth century. The real Don and Kuban Cossacks, and some from other regions, did take part in the Civil War in Ukraine and perpetrated pogroms. However, they joined the Volunteer Army of General Denikin, not that of Petliura.

The real Cossacks would certainly not have called themselves "Ukrainians." Their identity lay elsewhere, and it was a very strong identity, so powerful that for the rest of the world, and for Ukrainians themselves, it became a symbol of Ukrainian identity and has remained an emblem of Ukrainian national and cultural identity until today. The image of the Cossack was extremely charismatic and appealing, not least because it included the concept of liberty—*kazatskaya volnitsa*, which Ukraine and Ukrainians had lost. After ages of Ukrainian existence as part of the Russian Empire under the official name "Lesser Russia" (*Malorossiya*), the image of the strong, independent, and militant Cossack appealed both to the Ukrainians and to the outside world as a more attractive and desirable vision of Ukrainians in their own free country. In the wake of social revolution, the young Ukrainian state was searching for symbols of national identity to organize and unite a people that had lived without an independent statehood for centuries. In 1917 the civic militia had adopted the name Free Cossacks. By 1918 and even more so in early 1919, the new Ukrainian troops began calling themselves Cossacks and making use of other specific Cossack terms and names. This provided the military with the appropriate terms in the Ukrainian language that otherwise they would have had to borrow from other languages, and it also boosted the national self-consciousness and patriotic feelings of the army. Insurgents, as the UNA soldiers were most commonly called, utilized the rank of "ataman" for a leader of any military detachment or gang, and named some detachments *kurens*, after Cossack tradition. The most infamous was *Kuren Smerti* (The Clan of Death), under the command of Ataman Palienko, one of the generals close to Petliura, which perpetrated the pogrom in Berdichev in January of 1919[12] and in many Jewish settlements after that.

These self-proclaimed Cossacks were not a homogenous group of people, but former peasants, former soldiers, and all sorts of workers and professionals who had chosen to pledge their allegiance to the Ukrainian army, subordinate to the Directory and Petliura personally, or to one of the numerous military units (*bandas*), which roved the countryside. These self-labeled Cossacks, often referred to in the pogrom narratives as "insurgents" or "bandits," did not usually share strong allegiances or convictions, and swiftly changed their acquired identity. In fact, the people who fought in the Red Army hardly differed from the "New Cossacks," except the Red Army accepted Jewish recruits in the name of internationalism. During the Civil War, soldiers changed sides freely, as did some of the atamans, like the infamous Grigoriev.

Grigoriev started his short career as an officer in the Tsarist army, than served independent Ukraine, after that pledged his allegiance to Hetman Skoropadsky, subsequently joined the Red Army, but soon betrayed the union, and finally assembled his own huge army and fought the Reds in the Cherkassy region, where his army perpetrated vicious pogroms. After Grigoriev had been defeated by the Bolsheviks, the majority of his army, numbering up to fifteen thousand soldiers, rejoined the Bolsheviks, while Grigoriev himself escaped to the headquarters of another infamous ataman—Makhno. Later in the summer of 1919, Grigoriev was murdered on Makhno's orders, as they failed to find

---

12   Ibid., file 161, 13772.

common cause. Changing sides became a commonly employed tactic by various Petliura regiments and armed gangs, who would join the Red Army instead of fighting it. A witness of the pogroms in shtetl Volodarka near Skvira concludes his story: "Former pogrom perpetrators signed up with the Red Army—and thus protected themselves from the upcoming punishment."[13]

Rekis believed that Ukrainian soldiers, bandits, and peasants, who changed sides so readily, were the reason why the Red Army had not rescued Ukrainian Jews from the pogroms. Rekis observed that whenever Grigoriev's soldiers felt threatened and defected to Bolshevik side, they were received "in a celebratory and pompous manner."[14] Detachments of the Red Army perpetrated a number of pogroms throughout the Civil War in Ukraine; however, the Bolsheviks did follow through on the denunciation of anti-Jewish violence, punishing at least some pogrom perpetrators and instigators.

In 1919 there were few choices available to men in Ukraine, which was overwhelmed by chaos, war, and poverty. The first was to join the Bolsheviks, whose ideas in general appealed to the impoverished uprooted population, but lacked any immediate reward, and restrained anti-Jewish violence by accepting Jews and prosecuting pogrom instigators. Another option available to Ukrainian men was to join the Ukrainian National Army that, in theory, was fighting a patriotic war and provided a rather vague form of Cossack identity in return. The third choice was to join one of the militant gangs or *bandas* that were loosely associated with Petliura's army or cause but generally were gangs of armed men fighting under the command of a chieftain. Peasant unrest in the country, which was devastated by wars and revolutions, and the large amount of weaponry and particularly firearms accumulated by the local population amid the anarchy in the countryside created a window of opportunity for various individuals to organize militarized gangs of their own and become "atamans" themselves. The atamans would often be active in their native villages and regions, and terrorize and rob the Jewish population, with whom they were previously neighbors.

This extremely diverse group of uprooted men with vague goals and perspectives was in dire need of a common locus. The mass rape of Jewish women provided much needed bonding and camaraderie, and also served to establish an identity, or rather to simulate an identity, across age gaps and different

---

13 Miljakova, *Kniga Pogromov*, 206.
14 YIVO Archive, file 183, 15935 reverse.

backgrounds. The *pogromschiki* of the first wave of the Petliura's pogroms adopted a simulacrum of Cossack identity to fill a void, but truly established it through the mass rape of Jewish women. By brutally raping Jewish women in public, the new Ukrainian Cossacks defined themselves as a powerful authority, united by common action, and proved their dominance and importance to the Jewish population, who had previously dismissed their former neighbors as thugs and bandits.

The reinforcement of the acquired joint identity during the pogrom often unfolded as an ostentatious theatrical performance, complete with stage props and costumes. Makhno and his anarchist army spent only twelve days in shtetl Kazatin at the end of summer 1919; during this time Makhno's soldiers killed and tortured many Jews, and brutally raped at least forty Jewish women. Amid the chaos and devastation of the pogrom, Makhno also ordered the Jewish population to provide raspberry jam and silk lining for his coat.[15] Clearly, by demanding luxury items and fancy food from the robbed and impoverished Jews, who often were left even without their underwear and deprived of the last scraps of flour to bake bread, the atamans sought to establish their superior rank and privileges. In the same context, the rape of Jewish women was often played out as an imitation of symbolic service and entertainment: in shtetl Gornostaipol, atamans Laznyuk and Struk perpetrated pogroms from January through May 1919. The latter ordered the Jews to prepare him and his gang a feast to be served by thirty Jewish girls, all of whom were raped. Performance of rape as service and entertainment, provided by serfs to their masters, aimed to redefine the relationship between Jews and their neighbors in terms of dominance and hierarchy. Besides Makhno and Struk, many atamans utilized the very same combination of luxury and carnivalesque rape and torture: for example, atamans Angel and Kozyr-Zyrka were particularly known for such sadistic practices. Kozyr-Zyrka was described as wearing rich silk garments and demanding young Jewish girls for his pleasure as well as for the pleasure of his comrades, while torturing Jewish men for entertainment.[16]

Braude, who inspected many shtetls after the pogroms, interviewed the "lucky refugees" who had escaped from shtetl Ladyzhenka during the last pogrom in July 1919. An unnamed gang had entered Ladyzhenka and orchestrated the pogrom show: in the synagogue they gathered thirty remaining Jews, mostly the elderly, the sick, and the women, who had survived previous

---

15 Ibid., file 170, 14598–601.
16 Ibid., file 177, 15294–327.

pogroms. The Jews, locked in the synagogue, had been stripped nearly naked and denied medical help and food. Often soldiers would drag the Jews into the square one after another and force them to dance or crawl naked, or perform other humiliating acts for the entertainment of soldiers and peasants. Later, Braude interviewed two Jewish girls who had been among those locked in synagogue. Both had been repeatedly raped, their faces horribly mutilated—one of the girls had her nose cut off—and both had contracted venereal diseases, which Braude called "dirty disease."[17] That was the end of the Jewish community in Ladyzhenka, which at the beginning of 1919 had 1,400 members,[18] and by July 1919 those few who had survived the ordeal of the last pogrom left the town. Braude makes another observation that proves how effective the tactic of mass rape and torture was: he writes that the "success" of the pogroms against the backdrop of constant violence encouraged further bandit activity. "A village boy scratches his head and comes to a decision [to organize a gang], then simply yawns, tempts eight to ten shepherd boys, with sweets almost,[19] they grab some clubs—and here comes the gang. And the Jews, their faces contorted with obsequiousness and grief, kiss their dusty pants and pay them the tribute (this is a fact proved by the witness protocol)."[20] This remarkable evidence both reveals the despair of the narrator and uncovers the mechanics of the relationship among the pogrom perpetrators. Braude disclaims that gang members or soldiers formed any long-term relationships or strong bonds, and describes the connection between them as something insubstantial, circumstantial, and temporary. The joint performance of anti-Jewish violence, and particularly the participation in gang rape of Jewish women, became the unifying force that held the members of a gang or regiment together.

Gang rape is particularly important in the context of genocidal rape, as a "prevalent form of military sexual assault" that "is valued for building soldier's morale," writes Bergoffen, who concludes that "comrades in arms are now comrades in rape."[21] Gang rape bonds its perpetrators on many levels, and not only a positive identity is forged as a result. The gang members and soldiers of Petliura's army, as well as those Red Army regiments that perpetrated pogroms, built their positive identity by mass rape of Jewish women, and also used rape to secure their internal bonds. Every rapist is symbolically connected to his

---

17 Miljakova, *Kniga Pogromov*, 204–6.
18 YIVO Archive, file 174, 14991–5000.
19 Meaning, some uneducated teenagers.
20 Miljakova, *Kniga Pogromov*, 204.
21 Bergoffen, *Contesting the Politics of Genocidal Rape*, 42.

group through participating in the initialization ritual of joint rape, when every participant observes and is being observed by his comrades. At the same time, group rape unleashed further rape and torture on a larger scale, as joint participation in rape loosened the moral boundaries of the assailants and diffused personal responsibility.

A number of accounts illustrate with great precision how gang rape unravels during a pogrom. For instance, in May 1919 the Grigoriev gang perpetrated a pogrom in Elisavetgrad, a large town south of Cherkassy between Uman and Kremenchug. The soldiers broke into smaller groups and went from courtyard to courtyard, meticulously searching for Jewish families. Fanny Gitel, aged twelve, witnessed as all the Jewish families in their courtyard were brutally robbed, raped, tortured, and killed.[22] In the nearby courtyard another (not named) Jewish family was standing silent as ordered while the soldiers robbed and looted their apartment. Then the soldiers started to threaten Jewish men and women, and were obviously priming themselves for further action. The situation was very tense, as the Jews stood in fear of horrible torture and violence, and pogrom perpetrators, temporarily united by joint action, paused in anticipation of anything that would trigger and unleash their wrath. One of the girls could not stay silent and broke out in cries of fear. The bandits immediately grabbed her and took her to the next room, where they raped and tortured her in turns, making her father stand next to her and watch. The moment of the start of the gang rape is crucial to the group of assailants that are not well connected or confident in their actions. Such groups often lack the impulse and energy to propel their actions, but every step of the rape powers every following step, spinning the rape frenzy out of control and freeing the actors from any moral inhibitions. The grabbing and dragging of the victim served as the prelude to the theater of rape, or, if the action unfolded in the public space, rapists often stripped their victims naked in the street.

In Elisavetgrad, where the pogrom became exceedingly vicious in May 1919, more and more sadistic rituals were added to the mass rape, as the pogrom violence gained momentum and the energy of the assailants drove the level of violence to previously unwitnessed extremes. Sixteen-year-old Donya

---

22 Fanny's non-Jewish neighbors jointly robbed them and plundered their apartment, but the very same neighbors favored Fanny and her family and hid them in the cellar. Grigoriev soldiers murdered all other Jews in the courtyard. Fanny's neighbors, who were so kind to the girl's family, kept the bodies of the murdered Jews and produced them to the *pogromschiki* as a proof that all "their" Jews have been murdered already and thus saved Fanny's life. YIVO Archive, file 168, 14346–97.

Kogan was raped by the gang of Grigoriev's soldiers in front of her brother, and then she was terribly mutilated. Denying her a quick death, the rapists instead threw her into a cellar, where she died slowly of blood loss.[23] All over town Jewish women were brutally gang raped, their breasts cut off, and their abdomens ripped open.

Horrific scenes, like the ones that occurred during the pogroms in Elisavetgrad, became a fact of life by the summer of 1919. The retreating Ukrainian army and numerous atamans raped the Jewish female population to promote and demonstrate their superiority to their former neighbors, and to build strong bonds and camaraderie inside their groups. Amid the chaos and terror, the advance of the White Army in August 1919 promised some relief for Jewish communities, who hoped for the restoration of law and order. All those hopes were shattered, as the new wave of pogroms proved to be more brutal than ever, and mass rape of Jewish women surged even further.

THE WHITE OFFICERS

The Whites, like the Ukrainian soldiers and bandits, gang raped Jewish women publicly, and did so with exceeding brutality and visceral hatred. Even contemporary observers recognized that the Cossacks and officers had raped their victims in the manner that would inflict the most suffering, both physical and emotional. Schechtman, who published a volume on the pogroms of the Volunteer Army as part of Tcherikower's series in 1932, wrote that "this trait of *purposeful humiliation* characterizes the rape by the Volunteer Army."[24] Like the soldiers of the Ukrainian army and the bandits, the Whites used the same anti-Jewish rhetoric, branding the Jews as Bolsheviks responsible for the fall of the Russian Empire, and also sought to penalize Jews as well, but did so in retaliation, and with a greater degree of emotional involvement.

Smela (Smila), a large town immediately to the west of Cherkassy and north of Elisavetgrad, had been home to a thriving Jewish community since the seventeenth century; before the Civil War, seven and a half thousand Jews constituted half of Smela's population. In May 1919 Grigoriev's soldiers turned the pogrom in Smela into a bloodbath, raped an indeterminate but very large number of Jewish women, and left the town in a state of total devastation. In August 1919 Denikin's army perpetrated a violent pogrom as they advanced to

---

23 YIVO Archive, file 168, 14346–97.
24 Schechtman, Gergel', and Cherikover, *Pogromy Dobrovol'cheskoi.*

Moscow and repeated it during their retreat in November–December 1919. Rekis, a survivor of the May pogrom, collected evidence about Volunteer Army pogroms in the same area and interviewed survivors. A story narrated by Rabbi Men of Smela is emblematic of the Volunteer Army pogroms.[25] According to Rabbi Men, on August 5, 1919, the Bolsheviks left Smela and the city expected Denikin's vanguard to arrive soon thereafter. A special interim guard committee prepared to greet the new power and inquire about their "wishes and demands,"[26] because the anticipation of Denikin's army's arrival had aroused expectations among both the Jews and the non-Jewish population. When the Cossack "Wolf Division" under the command of General Shkuro appeared in Smela on the night of August 7, the Cossacks were enraged to see Jews in the city guard, and immediately started a pogrom. Rabbi Men and the delegation of the most educated and wealthy Jews went out to parley with Major General Markevich, the head of Shkuro's headquarters. After the delegation waited for a very long time, the general granted them an audience, but received Jewish representatives with a lot of resentment and refused to stop the pogrom. General Markevich explained his decision thus: "How can I forget that a Jewish Commissar in Rostov[27] killed my mother and my sister? My soldiers are embittered against Communists, and all the Communists are Jewish. We can't allow a Jewish kingdom in Russia."[28] When Rabbi Men argued that young Jewish girls had nothing to do with politics, the general replied: "The first four or five days my boys need to unwind. There is nothing to be done about that, my Cossacks are good fighters but also good looters. If you just killed Trotsky all that would end."[29]

At last, General Markevich promised to send sentries to the Jewish hospital, where thirty-five Jewish girls were hiding. The pogrom, however, did not stop, but simply became less violent when the Wolf Division finally left the town. The Whites left behind a guard unit of local people who were familiar to the Jewish community, as they had originally belonged to the Grigoriev *banda* that committed the horrible pogroms in May. The command of the guard consisted of three local landlords who busied themselves with extorting money from the local Jewish population, while the members of the guard would periodically raid Jewish homes. In November 1919, Colonel Romanov

---

25 YIVO Archive, file 209, 18795–812 on reverse.
26 Miljakova, *Kniga Pogromov*, 333–34.
27 Russian town.
28 Miljakova, *Kniga Pogromov*, 334.
29 Ibid.

of Denikin's army led the elite Preobrazhensky regiment into Smela. Romanov was surprised that a Jewish delegation did not greet him. He sent emissaries the following morning to Rabbi Men's house to inquire about the absence of greeting from a Jewish delegation headed by the rabbi. The Jews had managed to collect twenty-five thousand rubles as a welcoming bribe and hurried to greet the colonel. Romanov accepted the bribe and announced that Jews had always sabotaged the White Army and that his regiment would take revenge with a ferocious pogrom. After this opening threat, Romanov requested more donations of linens, sugar, and oil from the Jewish community and said that he would restrain his soldiers. The "slow" pogrom did not stop, but after the Preobrazhensky regiment left and the Drozdovsky cavalry regiment entered Smela, the pogrom resumed with a new force, and the officers participated in it even more actively than the soldiers. Again the pattern repeated itself: Rabbi Men, representing the Jews, and the Russian Orthodox town representative went to Colonel Prihodko, the commander of the Drozdovsky regiment, and offered him a bribe of hundred and twenty thousand rubles to stop the pogrom, and offered to have the whole population of Smela go outside to greet him, if he liked, if only he would do something to stop the pogrom, but to no avail. Drozdov's regiment left the city on December 17. When leaving, the commanders of the regiment warned the Jews that the officers and soldiers had been good to them, and that the next coming regiments would "show their true face"—and it would be horrible for the Jews. And indeed this is what happened. The Chechen regiments (i.e., of Cossacks from the Caucasus, the same as the Wolf regiment of General Shkuro), which were known to be the most ruthless and merciless to Jews, entered the city and began murdering the Jews (twenty-seven killed in the first hours) and raping Jewish women and girls on a massive scale. The dead bodies of the Jews were mutilated and left lying in the streets. The number of wounded was enormous, and more victims proceeded to die because of wounds, typhoid, venereal diseases, and trauma. A significant body of evidence depicting all aspects of anti-Jewish violence was collected after the Smela pogroms.

Vengeance and retribution—those were the two driving forces behind the pogroms, clearly articulated by various White Army officers. The Volunteer Army adopted as a way of justifying the anti-Jewish violence a very similar anti-Bolshevik/anti-Jewish line of reasoning, but its origin was different from that of the Ukrainian army, because the Volunteer Army operated on an entirely different basis. Former Tsarist generals and officers were mostly foreign to Ukraine, its society, and culture. Professionally trained officers, many of noble lineage, had rarely come in contact with Jews, or even the common civilian population, in the course of their lives. The officers spoke Russian, but it was a refined Russian, and very different from the language of the majority of the Ukrainian population. Denikin and his command declared the restoration of the Russian Empire as it had existed before the Revolutions of 1917 to be their primary goal. In this framework, an independent Ukraine did not exist, and was just one of the provinces of the empire; there was nothing to establish, no contacts or ties to maintain. Thus, the Volunteer Army leadership and the population of the south of the former Russian Empire remained hostile and alien to each other, and, at the same time, the relationship between the Cossacks and the White movement was far from ideal: the Cossacks and the Whites were at best fellow travelers and never truly shared the same goals and ideology. The White Army's encounter with Jews on the territory of Ukraine lasted for only about half a year, from midsummer 1919 until the beginning of 1920, and happened twice in this short period: during the advance of the White Army and during its retreat. The territories occupied by the Whites were heavily settled with Jews, and many Jewish settlements had already suffered from the pogroms in previous periods.

Peter Kenez argued that antisemitism became an obsession for the Volunteer Army.[30] The absolute majority of the officers, church leaders, political figures, and Denikin personally were vigorous and fervent antisemites; and only the necessity to cooperate with foreign powers made Denikin issue an official denunciation of the pogroms. The Special Department of Propaganda of the White Army produced a wide range of materials, including a falsified "documentary," all aimed to prove the old canard that all Jews were Bolsheviks and thus enemies of Russia.[31] General Denikin, whose memoirs were heavily edited later in France to camouflage his antisemitic views in the aftermath of Petliura's assassination and the trial of his killer, had denounced the White Army participation in pogroms and adduced a series of self-contradictory arguments to marginalize the issue of pogroms, and blame them, among other reasons, on "animal instincts" of some army men. However, he leaves the following remark: "If the troops only had some reasons to suspect that the higher authority would look on the pogroms with approval, the destiny of the Jews of South Russia would have been much more tragic."[32] In light of the horrible atrocities

---

30 Kenez, "Pogroms and White Ideology," 301.
31 YIVO Archive, file 211, 19202.
32 Anton Ivanovich Denikine, *Ocherki Russkoj Smuty*, vol. 3 (Moscow: Ajris, 2006), 536.

committed by the Volunteer Army, this statement sounds cruelly derisive, betraying a lack of conviction of the White Army command toward the denunciation of the pogroms.

In the absence of any positive ideology, antisemitism became the only ideology, almost an idée fixe for the White movement.[33] Officers of the Russian army grew disillusioned by the Russian monarchy after the inglorious defeats in the Russo-Japanese War, the losses in the First World War, the growing civil unrest, and the deteriorating economy. On the other hand, the Bolshevik Revolution had robbed Russian officers, a lot of whom were of noble descent, of their possessions, homes, futures, and their civilization. A lot of Russian soldiers joined the Red Army, and the officers were left to fight Bolshevism with the army that had more command hierarchy than fighting power. The two key problems of the White Army were the lack of soldiers and the lack of positive goals. The White Army maintained decorum and proclaimed the restoration of the Russian Empire as its objective, but there were no viable plans or long-term goals. There was a void inside the White ideology that led to the development of a negative concept of life—the retaliation for everything that was lost. The punishment of Jews, equated with the Bolsheviks, became the single clear and, more important, feasible objective of the Volunteer Army. This philosophy led to the degradation of the officers of the White Army, and of the army in general, rapidly losing their very thin veneer of humanity and civilization. The rage and despair of the stateless Volunteer Army, on a scene already overwhelmed with violence against an unprotected minority that was perceived as the enemy, turned the formerly polished, educated, and civilized officers into sadists who found amusement in gruesome torture.

These mutations were shocking and frightening, especially for those victims who witnessed both sides of a person and who saw the moment of transformation. Dr. Sara Margolin, who lived in Cherkassy, a large town near Smela, described her interaction with two officers during the pogrom.[34] The two officers who entered her house made at first a very good impression—one had a very intelligent face, and Margolin compared him to Russian writer Chernyshevsky; the other one had a "shaved face" like an actor. The officers ordered her to bring them tea, and then engaged in a conversation with the Russian girls, who rented rooms at Margolin's, and with the lady of the house. Margolin, a highly educated woman herself, admitted that the conversation was very lively and that one of the

33 Kenez, "Pogroms and White Ideology," 308–11.
34 YIVO Archive, file 209, 18795–812; Miljakova, *Kniga Pogromov*, 330–33.

officers discussed the situation in Soviet Russia and how he was fighting against the Commissars (who were all Jews) and the "fat Jewish profiteers," but declared Margolin's property to be under his personal protection.[35] The two officers, courteous in the beginning, grew more impatient as the tea did not immediately appear. Tea was served with bread rusks, the only provision Margolin had. One of the officers drank his cup and gave an order to the Cossack soldiers who accompanied him. The house of Dr. Margolin was full of sick people—both relatives and strangers—because she was a doctor and treated people at home. On the officer's order, several soldiers took her sick brother-in-law out of bed and made him dance a Russian dance, spurring him on by hitting him with whips. Cossacks and the officers began pillaging the rooms, grabbing anything of value that they could carry, taking things from people sick with typhoid, and beating whoever was in the house. In one of the rooms, they found several girls, and two of them were brutally raped by a large group of Cossacks. Officers actually encouraged more soldiers to come in and participate in the pogrom and rape. Margolin described a sudden transformation of two people whom she at first even considered to have looked intelligent into totally different beings. "We saw only the faces of savages around us, livid, sweaty from the tea they had just drunk, blazing with hatred towards us. This is the first time in my life I had to observe such hatred towards people, such loathing and cruelty towards Jews, as is difficult to imagine even towards the filthiest animals."[36]

Transformation of the well-bred and cultured individual into a wild beast similarly astonished another witness from Smela, a local anonymous homeowner, who hosted White officers in his home and reported his experience with bitter sarcasm: "Those three [officers] who stayed permanently, who lived permanently, and permanently loved, loved not just me but my tea, my sugar, my breakfast, my dinner, my supper; they loved my clean linens and everything that was left after the first arrival of Denikin's soldiers, let their memory be damned."[37] The narrator described the officer as "young, handsome, tall, with an intelligent and sophisticated face,"[38] who raised his heavy fist on him as a way of greeting. The stark contradiction between the appearance of the officer and projected expectations of his behavior stupefied the homeowner, who returned to this frightening transformation several times in the course of his short narrative: "Frequently we conducted long conversations, and often

---

35 Miljakova, *Kniga Pogromov*, 331.
36 Ibid., 331–32.
37 YIVO Archive, file 209, 18795–812.
38 Ibid.

discussed various subjects, and particularly those that interested us the most. The assaults and robberies. They were afraid that maybe this would stop soon and they would not be able to ship home everything they looted; I was afraid that, conversely, it would last longer and I would not live long enough to witness their demise. All my tenants were of the intelligentsia. They were people of blue blood, thin fingers, and exquisite, pristine faces."[39]

The language of the two very different witnesses is very similar in the way they juxtapose the savage actions of the officers with their assumed image of well-bred, cultured, and refined men. The notion of intelligentsia in the Russian Empire and later in the Soviet Union is a way of describing people who share cultural and educational identity that nevertheless cannot be simply defined by level of education, origin, or profession. This elaborate identity was readily recognized by the majority of the population of the country and implied certain expectations for their conduct. Jewish witnesses had naturally assumed that the officers, noble, refined, and educated as they were, would fit in with the intelligentsia identity and behave accordingly. As the Jews did not previously anticipate that their neighbors turned atamans would wield real power in the first half of 1919, so they did not expect vulgar and cruel brutality from the White officers in the second half of 1919. But neither had Jews expected a favorable treatment from the White officers, as suggested by their previous encounters, the latest of which happened during the First World War.

White officers perpetrated pogroms against Jews in retaliation and vengeance, but also in frustration and despair. Unlike Petliura's soldiers and various gang members, who vied to establish their identity, Volunteer Army officers conformed to a powerful preexisting identity, and sought to reinforce it through genocidal violence, specifically through genocidal rape. The paradox of the White–Jewish encounters during the Civil War was that both sides possessed a strong image and concept of their antagonist, but those assumptions were dramatically incorrect. For Whites the Jews, zealously branded as Bolsheviks, became an embodiment of the ultimate enemy, responsible for all misfortunes and losses. From the Jewish perspective, the Volunteer Army carried the halo of the monarchial authority of the Russian Empire that evoked a long history of oppression, but also of order and firm power.

The Russian monarchy victimized and oppressed Jews but, with the memory of previous "royal alliance" still fresh in their minds, the Ukrainian Jewry expected the Volunteer Army to restore the Tsarist regime and establish

39 Ibid.

order and peace. Jews did not expect any favors from Denikin's command; they just wanted the pogroms to stop. Ukrainian Jewry, as was discussed in the previous chapter, employed known scripts and tactics in dealing with the White Army as representatives of Russian tsars. Rabbi Men and his fellow community leaders did not know any other way to negotiate with the officers except to greet them in the most servile manner and offer bribes and gifts, while the officers had nobody to represent but themselves, and had no constructive plan to act on. The second paradox of the White–Jewish encounter was that despite this false identity, Denikin's army continued to act as emissaries of the Russian Empire and employed imperial tactics in dealing with Jews—because they had no alternative and had never been exposed to alternate modes of communication with the Jewish community.

The Volunteer Army officers expressed retribution for their misfortunes and the loss of their "civilization" through the public punishment of Jews. The progression of the brutal retaliation compromised the cultural identities of the officers, who devolved into wild, vicious savages in front of their victims. The Jews were frightened and astonished by this transformation of the officers; however, the actions of the Cossacks did not fail Jewish expectations.

THE COSSACKS

The Volunteer Army lacked not only positive goals but soldiers as well. Most soldiers of the Russian army joined either the Red Army or the Ukrainian National Army, and the White movement commanders sought alliance with Cossacks. As a result, according to Kenez, "the great majority of the fighting men were Cossacks, who fought for their own purposes."[40] Cossacks lived in organized military communities, or hosts, that had enjoyed a variety of privileges under Tsarist rule, such as independent government and administration. Leaders of the Volunteer Army, after long and complicated negotiations, managed to strike an alliance with Cossacks, who agreed to join the Volunteer Army in Ukraine and became its major fighting force. The Cossack support of the Volunteer Army was always conditional, and the Cossacks tried to maintain their independence under the Whites.

Cossacks became the major perpetrators of genocidal violence, and they carried it out vigorously. The roots of Cossacks' traditionally violent antisemitism remain obscured since Cossacks historically did not encounter Jews. Peter

---

40 Kenez, "Pogroms and White Ideology," 297.

Kenez agrees with Richard Pipes that the "Jewish question" was not essential for the Cossacks.[41] Looting was an important incentive for the Cossacks to participate in pogroms, and Pipes believes that it was the only one, but that does not explain the deliberate massacres, mass rapes, and torture of Jews, which still has to be thoroughly researched.[42]

Indeed, the immediate and very powerful motivation for the Cossacks to join with the White Army were the pogroms themselves. Cossacks looked forward to the pogroms as a source of enrichment. Kenez calls looting and plundering a "driving force" behind the Cossacks' participation in the campaign, and on occasion women came from the Cossack home communities to participate in the distribution of the acquired wealth and take it home in carts. Cossacks sometimes sent their loot home by the railcar, as reported by the Jewish witness Iliya Dvorkin in the town of Kremenchug, a port town on the Dnieper River downstream from Cherkassy.[43] In July 1919 in Rovnopol, a Jewish agricultural colony in southern Ukraine in close proximity to Cossack lands, the Cossacks drove out all the cattle and horses and took all the hens and chickens; they took even the last four pounds of flour in a paper wrap from a widow with four children, and took all the paper, books, and quills from the local teacher. The Cossacks told the local Jews, who were trying to hide their daughters in the fields to protect them from rape, that they were taking the horses, because "you don't need the horses to harvest the crops since we are going to slaughter all of you anyway."[44] Plundering and looting were not consistently discouraged by the Volunteer Army command, which could not organize a regular supply of food and ammunition and could not support the fighting men. Aside from the practical reasons for allowing if not legitimizing the plunder of Jewish (and on rare occasion, non-Jewish) homes, the officers lacked the power over the Cossacks to stop them. Like Petliura, who rode the wave of anti-Jewish violence, unable, if not unwilling, to stop the pogroms, the Volunteer Army command (that had a rationale to favor the pogroms) would not have been able to stop them, even if they tried.

Cossacks, like White officers, had a similar motive to fight against the Bolsheviks, because they had lost their special privileges as a result of the Revolution, and the Bolshevik policies against Cossacks were very

---

41 Richard Pipes, *Russia under the Bolshevik Regime* (New York: Vintage, 2011), 105.
42 Ulrich Herbeck, "National Antisemitism in Russia during the 'Years of Crisis,' 1914–1922," *Studies in Ethnicity and Nationalism* 7, no. 3 (2007): 181.
43 YIVO Archive, file 208, 18559–89.
44 Ibid., file 209, 18756–60.

straightforward: they announced their intention to dissolve the Cossack armies and abolish Cossack privileges and land ownership, and suppressed as counter-revolutionary any attempts to preserve the original units. Cossacks, known as excellent horsemen and soldiers, had served Russian tsars directly, maintained their status for ages, and resented Bolshevik attempts to reduce their freedoms. Cossack military communities were located for many centuries on the territory then known as the "wild field"—the steppes that stretched from the Northern Caucasus and South Urals through southern Russian and southern Ukrainian lands to the lower reaches of the Dnieper. After the October Revolution, Cossack leadership faced a deep crisis as some commanders had allied themselves with Bolsheviks, while others declared independence. As the result of intense negotiations, three Cossack armies from the Terek Host in Caucasus, from the Don River Host, and from the Kuban Host had allied themselves with the Volunteer Army. The Cossacks definitely shared the conviction that all Jews were Bolsheviks, but the Cossacks were not as unanimous and fervent foes of Bolshevism as the Whites were.

Cossacks did not experience identity crises the way Ukrainian nationalists or Whites did. The remarkably strong self-identity of the Cossacks was a stable characteristic of these military groups. The popular image of a Cossack proved extremely attractive to their "non-Cossack" Ukrainian neighbors and very recognizable to others on the territory of the former Russian Empire and beyond its borders, and remains ever present in contemporary culture across the world. Cossacks presented the image of freedom, and what is more important, the freedom of a common person—a rare commodity in the Russian Empire. The image of Cossacks as masters of the land, and ruthless but jovial fighters, is rooted deeply in Russian and Ukrainian folklore, songs, and literary works of famous writers, such as Gogol, Tolstoy, and Sholokhov.[45] However, the popular image does not reflect all of the complexity of the Cossack identity, and significantly simplifies the picture. Although technically all the structures of Cossack life had been destroyed under the Soviets, the Cossacks maintained their identity in the Kuban, Don, Terek, and some other hosts throughout the Soviet years. On some occasions, Cossacks started riots and fomented disturbances even during the postwar Soviet period. During the Second World War, the Cossacks fought both on the side of the Soviet Union and on the side of the Third Reich under the command of some of the Cossack generals like the

---

45 E. M. Beletskaia, *Kazachestvo v Narodnom Tvorchestve i v Russkoi Literature XIX veka: Monografiia* (Tver': Zolotaia bukva, 2004); Leila Gadzhieva, "Mir Kazachestva v Izobrazhenii N. V. Gogolya, L. N. Tolstogo, M. A. Sholokhova" (Moscow: Moscow State University of Humanities, 2007).

infamous Krasnov and Shkuro, perpetrators of the most horrible pogroms, who emigrated to Europe after the Bolshevik victory. Some of the White officers joined Hitler as well. After the collapse of the Soviet Union, Cossack communities reorganized themselves and regained some of their privileges.

Bolsheviks wanted to win the Cossacks over from the very beginning of the Civil War, but it was not until the end of 1919, when the First Cavalry Army under the command of Semyon Budyonny prevailed over the Cossack regiments of the White Army that Cossacks began to change sides. Initially only a marginal number of poor Cossacks joined Budyonny, but as the Civil War went on, more Cossacks changed sides, but did not change their basic convictions. The Red Army command after 1919 had to deal with the growing controversy: on the one hand, the ongoing war on the Polish front and the continued resistance of the White Army and the bandits forced the Bolsheviks to recruit vigorously among enemy soldiers, while on the other, the number of pogroms perpetrated by the Red Army surged in 1920, when more and more former Ukrainian soldiers and bandits joined in, and increased even further as Cossacks began to defect to the Bolshevik side. The Cossacks who perpetrated pogroms all over Ukraine after 1919, as described by Babel,[46] most probably had perpetrated a number of pogroms while being a part of the Volunteer Army, and did not alter their practices. In May 1920, for example, a Red Army detachment terrorized Korsun—a significant shtetl in the Cherkassy region—for an entire week, and the Red Army pogrom followed the same script, complete with the public mass rape of Jewish women, just as they previously suffered at the hands of the Ukrainian army and the White Army.[47] However, the Bolsheviks proceeded to enforce an anti-pogrom policy, and did investigate and prosecute at least some pogrom instigators and perpetrators, as was done by the Revolutionary Military Council (*Revvoensovet*) of the First Cavalry Army after the pogroms in Priluki (Pryluky) and Vakhnovka, where the council decided to disband and reorganize some of the detachments that had perpetrated the pogroms.[48]

Cossack identity was not based on their ethnicity but on their community. The Cossacks were not an ethnically homogeneous group of people, and they did not identify with either Russians or Ukrainians. Different Cossack hosts maintained different uniforms and a particular appearance, which clearly

---

46   Isaac Babel, Carol J. Avins, and Harry Taylor Willetts, *1920 Diary* (New Haven, CT: Yale University Press, 2002).

47   Miljakova, *Kniga Pogromov*, 358–62.

48   Ibid., 424–26.

distinguished the Cossacks from the "insurgents and bandits" who tried to imitate them. Because of their distinctive appearance and dress, it was easier for witnesses to identify Terek Cossacks, infamous among the Ukrainian Jews for especially brutal pogroms. Ukrainian Jews called them "Chechens," because the latter were known as treacherous and merciless foes, reflecting the popular image of Chechen fighters, and because Terek Cossacks looked very much like members of other Caucasus nations. The Terek Cossacks, the White Army, and other Cossacks borrowed much of the traditional costume of Caucasus militants since Russia had been almost constantly engaged in a war in the Caucasus in the nineteenth century. Especially outstanding was the distinct Circassian coat—a long outer garment fitted at the waist with special small pockets to hold bullets. The Cossacks also borrowed the *papakha*—a tall fur hat—from their Circassian neighbors. Many White officers began to wear this hat too. The distinct appearance and garments made the Terek Cossacks and also their neighbors the Kuban Cossacks highly recognizable and universally dreaded by the Jewish population, and especially so the Wolf Division under the command of General Shkuro that perpetrated the most vicious pogroms. Shkuro's career had advanced rapidly during the First World War, when he suggested organizing a special regiment of the most ruthless Cossacks, originally from the Kuban Host, to raid the enemy rear and disrupt communications and logistics, attacking the enemy from the back wherever possible. In less than four years, Shkuro had been promoted from the lowest rank to general, and his Wolf Division recruited the most wild and bloodthirsty Cossacks from different hosts. Shkuro reinforced this image by designing a special emblem, a wolf's head on a black background, and by attaching a wolf's tail onto his soldiers' high fur hats. It was this alternating image of a Cossack as a ferocious fighter and a sadistic torturer that had become lodged deeply in Jewish popular culture.

In East European popular culture, the terms "Cossack" and "pogrom" are forever connected, as well as Cossacks being associated with the rape of Jewish women, and it is reasonable to assume, based on the pogrom evidence, that Cossacks also harbored a traditionally negative image of Jews as greedy and cunning enemies of Christian people. Jews and Cossacks had a very definite negative image of one another, even though most Cossack hosts had no prior systematic contact with the Jews: Terek and Kuban Cossacks that perpetrated the most horrible atrocities against Jews had no interaction with Jews at all. Until the First World War, when Cossacks serving in the Russian army participated in the expulsion of Jews from the front line, there was just one negative but extremely notable encounter between Jews and Cossacks. In 1648, Cossacks from the Zaporozhsky Host, led by Hetman Khmelnitsky, massacred

Ukrainian Jewry.[49] Since then the Jewish community feared the Cossack as a violent enemy. Antisemitism was not crucial to Cossack identity as a bonding tool, but Cossacks proved nevertheless to be ardent antisemites who sadistically tortured Jews during pogroms, and in particular raped Jewish women in groups "for the show."[50]

The most disturbing conclusion that results from the study of pogrom evidence is that for Cossacks, and for the officers as well, violent mass rape and torture of the Jews became a source of satisfaction and entertainment, which had nothing to do with sexual intercourse as such, but everything with the public celebration of power that is free of restrictions. Rabbi Men of Smela quoted a White general who referred to the popular concept also expressed by many others that Cossacks for several days (from three to five) were entitled to plunder and ravage a captured town. This was the observed rite whenever Cossacks entered small shtetls or larger towns, like nearby Korsun[51] (a large railway junction) and Yablonevo[52] (a small place of no industrial significance). Several days of "deserved" pogrom included not only looting, but actions described by Russian word *gulyat'*, meaning to carouse, to have fun, to enjoy oneself, to entertain oneself wildly. Pogroms, and particularly rape and torture, became the Cossacks' visceral entertainment, a way of emotional release. Officers and Cossacks were not shy about the fact that they enjoyed pogroms, and articulated it openly. For example, a student of a girl gymnasium, A. Teitelbaum, quotes the White officer who participated in the pogrom of their apartment in Kiev, abused them, and bragged about his pogrom experience: "I am an intelligent person [he belonged to the intelligentsia], but when I see Jewish blood I feel moral satisfaction. It's nothing to kill a person [by shooting]; the true pleasure is to stab them."[53]

The continuous cycle of violent pogroms in shtetls demonstrates how the offenders became carried away in their search of the satisfaction of violent punishment of the Jews. Before August 1919, the Jewish community of Korsun was considered "lucky," because Jews there got away with just bribes and other forms of extortion. Korsun even had a rather successful and well-armed self-defense unit. During the August advance of the White Army, the Cossacks paused

---

49 Shaul Stampfer, "What Actually Happened to the Jews of Ukraine in 1648?," *Jewish History* 17, no. 2 (2003).
50 According to the witness, that is how Cossacks raped young girls. YIVO Archive, file 209, 18747–48.
51 Ibid., file 207, 18536–58.
52 Ibid., file 210, 19058.
53 Miljakova, *Kniga Pogromov*, 310.

to "have fun" for three days, which included "hundreds"[54] of rapes and about twenty murders. The publicly exposed rapes were particularly humiliating: among the raped were two seventy-year-old women, one dying young girl in agony, and apparently a few new mothers. Another witness confirms the estimates and adds that "Chechens" were the worst—they murdered "in a wink."[55] The local population joined in with the plundering enthusiastically, following in the Cossacks' footsteps, and removed even roofs from some houses. The Jewish community of Korsun could barely recover before the White Army retreated in December 1919, and the endless platoons and regiments passed through the shtetl that was dangerously close to the railway station. The Cossacks' and officers' entertainment became even worse. One woman lost her teenage son, and her sixteen-year-old daughter was brutally raped, became pregnant, and had to have an illegal abortion.[56] The daughter of the wealthy merchant Pokras, while she was lying in bed in fever with pneumonia, was viciously raped by several groups several times and strangled to death. Assailants continued to torture and rape her dead body. Fifteen-year-old Sigalov had to watch her parents slashed with sabers, and then she was raped many times in front of her dying parents, and only after that her parents were murdered, while she was left to suffer.[57] About two hundred Jewish women were locked in the local brewery on the riverbank and raped continuously. Some young women escaped by jumping into the river.

The Korsun pogroms, typical of the White Army pogroms, clearly demonstrate that officers and Cossacks were emotionally involved in the humiliation of and violence against Jews. Gang rape of Jewish women became a demonstrative sadistic show in which assailants participated as both perpetrators and the audience. Mass rape of Jewish women combined with elaborate torture provoked in the pogrom perpetrators an ever-growing hunger for greater punishment, because the one that Jews had survived was never enough. *Pogromschiki* constantly searched for ways to escalate the humiliation and disgrace they inflicted, aiming to surpass previous acts of violence. There were no more moral inhibitions, no restraints, no limitations: terrible acts of violence gyrated out of proportion, provoked by acts of violence already committed, and created a self-propelling vicious cycle. This vortex of violence enveloped the Jewish community of Ukraine and damaged its life often beyond repair.

54   YIVO Archive, file 207, 18538.
55   Ibid., file 207, 18539.
56   Ibid., file 207, 18545.
57   Ibid., file 207, 18547–49.

CHAPTER 5

Describing the Indescribable: Narratives of Gendered Violence

The period of Denikin's army rule in Smela began and ended with a pogrom. In truth, it is very hard to determine exactly when the first pogrom ended and the second began. Four months of unhinged Volunteer regiments doing as they pleased in the shtetl was one endless pogrom. The Jewish population had not a single minute of peace and quiet. Many military regiments had passed through Smela—the Preobrazhensky regiment, as well as the Izmailovsky, the Semenovsky, the Pavlovsky,[1] and many others.

The greeting of the "guests," the volunteer [regiment], at the end of August was commemorated with the true pogrom in the modern style with all the [appropriate] trappings and particulars. The heroic pogrom undertaking was performed by the Special Plastun (scouting) Division under the command of general Khazov. The Second Kuban Partisan Platoon has particularly excelled in the endeavour. First of all, the drunken Cossacks burned down the Jewish cooperative [shop] in the middle of the shtetl. Starting from there the fire spread onto nearby buildings and destroyed them to the ground. While the fire raged, the Cossacks happily sang a song that became very popular around the pogrom pale: "We beat the Jews, we beat the Commune."[2]

At the same time, as some [of the Cossacks] enjoyed the fire, other groups of volunteers [soldiers] have spread around the town and have

---

1 Formerly elite regiments of the Russian Tsarist army.
2 Meaning the Communists; beating of Jews equated to beating (defeating) of Communists and Communist (Bolshevik) regime.

begun to act with vim and vigor: robbed apartments, killed, cut, etc. [Pogrom perpetrators] directed their special efforts to chasing Jewish girls and women, whom they dishonored[3] right there on the street in front of everybody. Hysterical screams and sobs of the ill-fated victims stabbed at the soul. Two of my brothers-in-law, V. and A. Z-s, had witnessed how the whole group of about twenty drunken Cossacks in the cellar gruesomely violated one young Jewish girl. The rape was accompanied by vicious torture. Every rapist invented a new, more horrible way to ravish their victims. The poor girl, I was told, committed suicide after this eventuality.

Among the raped there are a lot of elderly women. For example, I personally know Ms. M., who is an old woman aged 60. People are embarrassed to tell [about the rape] and very often hide such facts. Doctors, however, say that a lot of women, especially young girls, sought their help after the pogrom. It is a terrible misfortune as many of them contracted venereal diseases. . . .[4]

This account of the pogrom in town of Smela, located to the southeast of Kiev in the Cherkassy region, was provided by I. Galperin,[5] in November 1920. Smela and the nearby town of Cherkassy, as well as the surrounding smaller shtetls like Rotmistrovka, Aleksandrovka, Medvedovka, etc., suffered devastating pogroms in May 1919 by ataman Grigoriev's army and in August and December 1919 by White Army troops during their advance and retreat.

Galperin, in accord with other witnesses, estimates that at least four hundred women were raped during the first White Army pogrom in August,[6] and about a thousand during the second pogrom in December.[7] It is also important to remember that hundreds of Jewish women were raped in Smela in May during the Grigoriev pogrom.[8] Considering that before the pogroms the Jewish population of Smela had been approximately seven and a half thousand,

---

3   Meaning—raped.
4   YIVO Archive, file 209, 18800–18803.
5   The precise identity of the witness is unknown, although the Galperin family was very prominent and well established in Jewish community of Cherkassy (www.jewishgen.org). The narrative was collected by the prominent Yiddish publicist and activist Abram Yuditsky, who at the time worked as a representative of the Pogrom Victims Aid Department of the Russian Red Cross.
6   Also, twenty-two Jews were killed and about 300 wounded.
7   YIVO Archive, file 209, 18800–18803.
8   Ibid., file 185, 16045–77.

and constituted about half of town's population, approximately half of Jewish women in Smela were raped in 1919.

At the same time, it is obvious that no definitive data on the rapes exists or could have been collected "for obvious reasons," as most pogrom reports confirm. In the comprehensive catalog of short pogrom summaries assembled by Tcherikower, the number of rape victims in most communities is described as "a lot," "many," "undefined," and "all," while the numbers for the killed and wounded are given in numerical values.[9] The first-person narratives of rape are practically nonexistent, and the number of short responses of women to direct inquiries into rape is negligible. Everyone knew that large numbers of women had been raped, and in some small shtetls all Jewish women had been raped without exception; and, moreover, members of Jewish community knew most of the victims and their ordeal all too well, but no woman would admit it. The majority of witnesses also were reluctant to identify victims of rape. Galperin even disguised the names of his brothers-in-law and did not give any hints about the identity of the girl whose atrocious rape his relatives witnessed, although all rapes were publicly exposed, and everyone definitely knew who the poor victim was.

Galperin, who survived at least three major pogroms in Smela, described it as "true pogrom in the modern style with all the [appropriate] trappings and particulars,"[10] unmistakably recognizing the pogrom script, its archaic origin, and its new features. Among the honed-to-perfection violent tactics of the pogrom perpetrators, Galperin identifies the rape of Jewish women as the most heinous of them all, and recognizes the long-term impact of rape both physical, in pregnancies and venereal diseases, and emotional, in the traumatic and disgraceful experience that sometimes led to suicide.

Galperin's evidence, which is much more comprehensive, is exemplary of how an educated Jewish man sought to relate the tragic events of the recent past and to make sense of them; and how he failed to at least do the latter. Galperin demonstrates acute awareness of and sensitivity to both the traumatic pogrom experience and its inner dynamics and implications, and yet he struggles to express himself. The first striking feature of Galperin's evidence is that almost every paragraph is written in a different style, as if the narrator had been searching for the right tone and voice, but could not find one. The second paragraph of this remarkable evidence is full of bitter sarcasm, while the passage about

---

9   Ibid., files 271–74, 25498–6286.
10 Ibid., file 209, 18800–18803.

rape that follows reads as a lament. This narrative, like many others, demonstrates that pogrom survivors wanted to tell the story, but did not know how to describe the indescribable. This short passage, like a magnifying glass, highlights the major issues of how the Jewish community of Ukraine was affected by mass rape during pogroms and responded to it.

Pogroms were a gendered phenomenon, and response to mass rape falls along gender lines. Women, who had been physically violated and survived, suffered terrible wounds, contracted venereal diseases, and became pregnant, on the one hand, and suffered devastating emotional trauma, on the other. Jewish men, who were involved in spectacle of rape as observers, were deeply traumatized by the experience. Thereafter Jewish women and men experienced and narrated rape differently. In the course of this chapter, I will evaluate the immediate, physical impact of rape on the Jewish community, and how Jewish women and men expressed traumatic experience in their narratives.

Gender violence is probably the most subversive form of violence, because it targets the very core constructs of the human being and society, such as gender and sexuality. Mass rape was already discussed as a genocidal strategy, and what moved its perpetrators was discussed in the previous chapter; the current discussion concerns yet another aspect of gender violence during pogroms—in what ways it impacted the lives of the Ukrainian Jews, their interiority, and how they responded to it.

"Rape is a gendered and symbolic crime," argues Bergoffen, and it "depends on accepted gender codes."[11] According to the fundamental gender paradigm, the female body, which can be tamed and forced into submission by rape, is weak and fragile, and requires protection. The relationship of dominance in exchange for protection puts a social value on the untainted female body. The established gender identities position a man in charge of protecting "his" women: wife and the unmarried members of the household. Female chastity thus acquires value and meaning that is woven into the very fabric of patriarchal society. Man, as the designated guardian of the female "honor" in his household, is defined by it as well. If his daughter's chastity is ruined, it negatively impacts her marriage prospects, dishonors her family, and damages her father's position in society. The same principle can be extrapolated onto the community in general: female dignity is integral to the dignity of the whole community.

The application of patriarchal gender norms, as they are discussed in the context of gender violence, to the Jewish community is highly problematic and

---

11 Bergoffen, *Contesting the Politics of Genocidal Rape*, 24.

yet necessary. First of all, the definition of Jewish community is different from what is commonly understood by "community" in, for example, European history. Jewish community in imperial Russia, then the largest Jewish diaspora in the world, emerged as a result of unique encounters with the Russian government,[12] and even the briefest discussion of these encounters would not fit the framework of the current project. The distinctive challenges of the Jewish community in the Russian Empire, which the Ukrainian Jewish community was part of, included, but were not limited to, assimilation, modernization, and secularization, against the backdrop of increasingly anti-Jewish government politics. Some of those processes correspond to similar challenges encountered by other Jewish communities in Europe and America, while some are specific to Russian Jews. It is clear that the Ukrainian Jewish community that suffered pogroms during the Civil War cannot be straightforwardly identified as patriarchal or homogeneous. There is extensive scholarship that discusses the gender structure of the Jewish community in Russia, describes gender roles within the community, and how they evolved in the late nineteenth to the beginning of the twentieth century.[13]

Notwithstanding, for the sake of this research it is possible to discuss impact of gender violence vis-à-vis traditional gender codes that define social and moral implications of rape. Gender violence scholarship unanimously suggests that however extensively altered the gender structure of the victimized community is by the processes of modernity, the rape targets very fundamental gender norms that are still common for a variety of victimized communities in the twentieth century.[14] Inexorably tied to basic gender norms, the rape acts by forcing shame on the victims and violating their dignity and honor. Wartime rape, as has been already discussed, is not an act that substitutes for consensual sexual intercourse, as many still believe,[15] but rather a violent crime that targets the dignity of a human being, whose sexual self is the most vulnerable aspect of its personal and social identity.

---

12 Benjamin Nathans, *Beyond the Pale: The Jewish Encounter with Late Imperial Russia*, vol. 45 (Berkeley: University of California Press, 2004).

13 ChaeRan Y. Freeze, *Jewish Marriage and Divorce in Imperial Russia* (Hanover: University Press of New England for Brandeis University Press, 2002); Paula E. Hyman, *Gender and Assimilation in Modern Jewish History: The Roles and Representation of Women* (Seattle: University of Washington Press, 1995); and Aviva Cantor, *Jewish Women/Jewish Men: The Legacy of Patriarchy in Jewish Life* (Harper: San Francisco, 1995).

14 Bergoffen, *Contesting the Politics of Genocidal Rape*; Brownmiller, *Against Our Will.*

15 Katharine K. Baker, "Sex, Rape, and Shame," *DePaul J. Health Care L.* 8 (2004).

International humanitarian law today defines wartime rape as a violation of women's dignity and honor,[16] as dignity and honor are considered to be basic human rights in the modern world. The concept of dignity, however, preexisted the notion of a "human right" by many ages. The notion of dignity originated in connection with the social status of a person,[17] and, although the concept of dignity is interpreted in philosophy in many different ways, for the purpose of this current research I will focus on the social aspect of the term. Dignity and honor are ethical and moral indicatives that define the human being within the *socium*: they convey respect and acceptance, and ensure one's status among people who share similar moral codes. The loss of dignity reduces the person to a lower position in the community, strips the individual of respect and esteem in the eyes of other people, and potentially excludes this person from the community altogether. Publicized rape strips victims of their dignity and intentionally degrades them. The instrument that destroys dignity and honor is shame.

Personal and social identity is sustained and validated through the emotional reactions of the community, which shares a joint code of emotions. The concept of emotional communities, developed by Rosenwein,[18] suggests that human coexistence inevitably results in a commonly shared set of emotional responses. The members of real and imaginary emotional communities experience and express the same emotions in response to their experiences. The variety of emotions, on the other hand, is formed as a result of cultural politics[19] rooted in joint history and collective codes, particularly the gender code.

Shame as an emotion of an individual emerges when another is present to witness and judge.[20] Shame is based on the set of moral norms shared by society. Emotional community and gender codes are at the very center of it, as they dictate the family structure and define sexual taboos. Shame is a social emotion, because it "necessarily depends on other people's thoughts, feelings

---

16 Theodor Meron, "Rape as a Crime under International Humanitarian Law," *The American Journal of International Law* 87, no. 3 (1993): 424–28; Yougindra Khushalani, *The Dignity and Honour of Women as Basic and Fundamental Human Rights* (Leiden: Martinus Nijhoff Publishers, 1982).

17 Michael Rosen, *Dignity: Its History and Meaning* (Cambridge, MA: Harvard University Press, 2012), 11.

18 Barbara H. Rosenwein, "Worrying about Emotions in History," *The American Historical Review* 107, no. 3 (2002): 821–45; Barbara H. Rosenwein, "Problems and Methods in the History of Emotions," *Passions in context* 1, no. 1 (2010): 1–32.

19 Sara Ahmed, *Cultural Politics of Emotion* (Edinburgh: Edinburgh University Press, 2014).

20 Claire Pajaczkowska and Ivan Ward, *Shame and Sexuality: Psychoanalysis and Visual Culture* (London: Routledge, 2014), 1.

or actions, as experienced, recalled, anticipated or imagined at first hand, or instantiated in more generalized consideration of social norms or conventions."[21] Considered from the perspective of social emotion, rape is one of the most "shameful" of crimes in a society where the value of female chastity is integrated into individual and communal identities. The shame and humiliation of rape become powerful regulators in patriarchal society, where rape serves as a form of punishment, laying foundations for the phenomenon known today as "victim blaming."[22]

Rape destroys female dignity, subjecting the victim to shame and dishonor in the eyes of the community. Wartime rapes "were calculated to expose and exploit the women's unique vulnerability—the fragility of their honor,"[23] so women sought to conceal rape in order to avoid the shame that would inevitably tarnish their reputation. Genocidal rape strategy does not just make rape into a spectacle to degrade women of the victimized community, but also utilizes it to degrade and emasculate the men of the community, who are unable to protect "their" women. The status of a humiliated and undignified victim extrapolates onto the whole community, or, as Claudia Card argues: "martial rape domesticates not only the women survivors who were its immediate victims but also the men socially connected to them, and men who were socially connected to those who did not survive."[24]

THE EXPERIENCE OF RAPE

Iosif Kramarovsky, aged fifteen, son of the medical orderly who worked in the Smela Jewish hospital, described the last pogrom by the White Army regiments in December 1919: " A lot of Jews, and especially young girls, were hiding in the almshouse next door [to the Jewish Hospital]. . . . Volunteer gangs took a lot of girls from the almshouse, and their [the girl's] screams of horror caused panic among the peasant women who passed by in the street. Many peasant women who had been carrying their pots from the market and walked along this street became so scared of the heartbreaking screams of poor girls that they threw

---

21 Shlomo Hareli and Brian Parkinson, "What's Social about Social Emotions?," *Journal for the Theory of Social Behaviour* 38, no. 2 (2008): 134.

22 This was briefly discussed in the previous chapter. For further discussion, see Bergoffen, *Contesting the Politics of Genocidal Rape*, 50–51.

23 Ibid., 27.

24 Card, "Rape as a Weapon of War," 7.

their pots on the ground and ran away."[25] According to Rabbi Men, during the first White Army pogrom in August 1919, the almshouse was used as a hiding place for Jewish girls, but the White general was extremely reluctant to offer any protection for the girls hiding there.[26] Another witness, Eidelshtein,[27] described the outrageous mass rape in greater detail: "In order to describe the inconceivable torture to which victims succumbed, I can tell you about one raped girl, who had been bitten by her tormentors from head to toe. I saw her. Because of the bites, the body of the poor thing began to swell. And she was not the only one."[28] Another witness, Dubinsky, who escaped the first pogrom in his native shtetl of Rotmistrovka and moved to Smela, where he survived the first White Army pogrom in August, emphatically argues that most of the Jewish girls in Smela had been already sexually assaulted at that time. Dubinsky remarks that hardly any of the girls could really escape rape.[29]

The pogroms in Smela were not extraordinary, and rape practices were similar everywhere where pogroms happened, as was the aftermath. Outbreaks of sexually transmitted diseases always followed the mass rape, along with unwanted pregnancies and rape-related wounds. Rape-related data was rarely reported during the first wave of pogroms in 1919, but occasional reports suggest that this lack of evidence was due to collective attempts to conceal rape. Tcherikower in his notes provides an account of a pogrom in the town of Balta, where in February–April 1919 mass rape became "an epidemic," with at least one hundred and twenty women violated, most of whom contracted venereal diseases.[30] By the time the second wave of pogroms hit the Jewish communities in Ukraine, the epidemiological situation spiraled out of control. Jewish hospitals, short on supplies and medical staff, could not provide urgent care for all pogrom victims who were suffering from various wounds, while typhus claimed victims in large numbers everywhere. Emissaries of various aid organizations who collected information about the pogroms at the end of 1919 and

---

25 Miljakova, *Kniga Pogromov*, 338.
26 Ibid., 334–35.
27 This narrative is part of the evidence collected in the Smela-Cherkassy region by M. Rekis. The copy of Eidelshtein's evidence from Tcherikower's archive in YIVO indicates that he described the last pogrom by Denikin's army in Smela; however, the copy of the same evidence from the Russian State Archive indicates that the evidence refers to the Cherkassy pogrom. Since the events in both towns are very similar, I decided to use the evidence without geo-location. Ibid., 339.
28 YIVO Archive, file 209, 18796.
29 Ibid., file 209, 18797.
30 Ibid., file 659, 56269.

afterward were able to obtain more information about the number of women raped, and witnesses voluntarily described the most outrageous cases, like the one quoted above concerning the badly bitten victim. Although many statistics about rape, pregnancies, traumas, and diseases were still withheld in an attempt to protect the victims' dignity, more and more pogrom survivors and inspectors recognized the vital importance of this information.

The Editorial Board envoy in the region of Cherkassy and Smela, where indescribably vicious yet emblematic pogroms took place throughout 1919, collected some unique and invaluable data about gender violence. Rekis, whose fervent efforts to collect evidence on mass rape will be discussed further at greater length, questioned local doctors and midwives about the care they had provided for the rape survivors. Considering the general pattern of gender violence during pogroms as it is revealed everywhere else, it is legitimate to regard his collected narrative to be representative of all gender violence during pogroms. Rekis and his respondents clearly understood and indicated that the number of rapes and rape victims was much higher than that known to the medical professionals who treated their patients officially. The overwhelming shaming stigma of rape prevented a lot of women from seeking the necessary medical assistance. In Cherkassy, Rekis collected the oral testimonies of Dr. Goldman (gynecologist, chief doctor of the Jewish city hospital), Dr. Shendarevsky (epidemiologist, chief regional epidemiologist), Dr. Shendarevskaia (a female physician, possibly wife of Dr. Shendarevsky), nurse-midwife Ruvinsky, and nurse-midwife Lipkova. In Smela, Rekis questioned Dr. Gandlevsky (a doctor in the city hospital in Smela), Dr. S. Polyak (another female physician), and Dr. Zlochevsky.[31] Doctors recognized the extreme cruelty of the rapists who targeted both extremely young girls who had barely reached puberty and elderly women. Dr. Shendarevskaia of Cherkassy reported seeing rape victims as young as ten years old; Dr. Polyak related that Dr. Radzevich in Smela had treated girls as young as twelve. The rape of underage Jewish girls as young as ten was also reported by various witnesses in Borovitsy, Volchansk, Golta, Dymer, Ekaterinoslav, Kodlubitskaia, Pavoloch, Priluki, Korsun, Smela, Cherkassy, Krivoe Ozero, Popelnya, Severinovka, Stepantsy, Fastov (Fastiv), and many other places. Most of the accounts of the interviewed doctors agree that most rape victims were Jewish women from thirteen to fourteen to fifty years old, although in some cases women as old as seventy had been raped. Most of the

---

31 Ibid., file 209, 18795–812 reverse, and file 210, 19013–39. See also Miljakova, *Kniga Pogromov*, 342–43, 353–56.

victims who sought medical assistance after the rape were young unmarried women. The severely limited data does not allow for affirmative conclusions, but married women might have considered themselves more experienced in the gynecological area, and thus better able to resolve the consequences of the rape themselves, while young women, especially orphans, required outside help.

One of the tragic consequences of mass rape was numerous unwanted pregnancies. Dr. Polyak in Smela sent twenty of her fifty patients to have abortions.[32] Dr. Goldman in Cherkassy avoids discussing abortions but claims that rape was so traumatic for many victims that they stopped menstruating, so it was sometimes difficult to establish pregnancy; Dr. Goldman did, though, undertake "measures to prevent unwanted impregnation."[33] Dr. Shendarevsky claims that about fifty percent of the raped women were pregnant. He as well as other doctors admitted to many abortions underwent by Jewish women, but never directly said that he had performed them. "There are a lot of abortions. Doctors abet this. Unfortunately, many sought help too late, while others, because they were ashamed, did this at home (using different methods), or sought assistance from quacks or old wives, etc. These sometimes ended in fatal outcomes."[34] The doctor carefully avoids the term "abortion," but, like Dr. Goldman, he recognizes this measure as necessary to deal with rape consequences. Doctors and midwives from Smela—Polyak, Zlochevsky, and Dobrovolsky—did not shy away from the term, but were a bit vague; they simply "referred [their patients] for abortion."[35] The abortions were not legal in Russia, although at the end of the nineteenth and the beginning of the twentieth century, abortion became a more common practice in Russia, and there was a move to decriminalize this procedure.[36] Jewish law did not approve of abortion either, but it was a measure to deal with unwanted pregnancy that had been known to Jewish women as well.[37] It is unclear who performed the abortions, and it would seem that most doctors and midwives did so, although there was a certain discrepancy in what medical practitioners considered to be an abortion. Nurse-midwife Ruvinskaia said that she didn't perform a lot of abortions, "because [Ruvinskaia] usually managed

32 Miljakova, *Kniga Pogromov*, 343.
33 Ibid., 354.
34 Ibid., 355.
35 YIVO Archive, file 209, 18804–10.
36 Laura Engelstein, *The Keys to Happiness: Sex and the Search for Modernity in Fin-De-Siecle Russia* (Ithaca, NY: Cornell University Press, 1992), 349–51.
37 ChaeRan Y. Freeze, "Lilith's Midwives: Jewish Newborn Child Murder in Nineteenth-Century Vilna," *Jewish Social Studies* 16, no. 2 (2010): 9–10.

to expel the fetus in time (in the very beginning)."[38] Abortion was considered by most to be almost as shameful and as painful as rape itself, and many Jewish women preferred to terminate a pregnancy in secret, risking to carry out the procedure themselves, or with the help of incompetent self-trained midwives, to whom Dr. Shendarevsky referred as "quacks and old wives." Some women could not recognize their condition, especially the younger girls, and sought help when it was too late to terminate their pregnancy. Dr. Shendarevsky regretted the "fatal outcomes," and as an example singled out two raped girls—Shalif, nineteen, and Panorova, eighteen—who chose homemade abortions and died as a result. To emphasize the loss, the doctor claimed that both of the deceased were well-known beauties. Dr. Shendarevsky also talked about the rape of disabled Jewish women, deaf or mentally retarded, who could not recognize their condition; apparently such women carried their children to term, although the doctor did not elaborate further.[39] There is absolutely no information of any kind that may shed light on the fate of the children that were born as a result of pogrom rape.

Venereal diseases became another highly disturbing consequence of mass rape, and because the pogrom perpetrators had gang raped a lot of Jewish women over and over during the Civil War, venereal diseases became endemic. The most common sexually transmitted diseases that were contracted by the raped Jewish women, and subsequently their husbands and families (since some sexually transmitted diseases are not transmitted exclusively by sexual intercourse), were gonorrhea and syphilis.[40] Doctors had treatments for gonorrhea at the time, and in some cases for syphilis; however, the medical supplies were insufficient, and many victims concealed their condition or mistook their symptoms for those of typhoid. Both Dr. Shendarevsky and Dr. Shendarevskaia closely questioned their patients, whom they treated for typhoid rash, if they were "touched" by Cossacks; that was often the case, and victims were then treated for venereal diseases as well.[41]

As pogroms and rapes continued, Jewish women apparently developed a sort of routine to deal with contagious venereal diseases. The evidence collected in the town of Kremenchug, a large city in the lower reaches of the Dnieper River, with a flourishing Jewish community that totaled approximately thirty-five thousand prior to the Revolution, is as unique as the materials that

---

38 Miljakova, *Kniga Pogromov*, 356.
39 Ibid., 355.
40 YIVO Archive, file 209, 18795–812 reverse, and file 210, 19013–39. See also Miljakova, *Kniga Pogromov*, 342–43, 353–56.
41 Miljakova, *Kniga Pogromov*, 355.

originated in Cherkassy. The history of the Kremenchug pogroms is very similar to Cherkassy and Smela since Kremenchug lies along the same route to Kiev. In May 1919, Kremenchug experienced the Grigoriev pogrom,[42] and in July and August, the White Army pogroms.[43] There are a number of responses to the inquiries obtained from pogrom survivors in Kremenchug, and among these responses are some of the only first-person narratives of rape—recorded very tersely, in a very formal way, and yet invaluable for this research. Jewish men and women, when questioned after the pogroms were over, demonstrated hands-on knowledge of the basic medical procedures that they followed after rape.

Leiba Surgin told the inspector that about fifteen to twenty Cossacks had entered their apartment, took his wife to the next room, and raped her there, while he was crying in the next room. Surgin also said that after the incident his wife "lay down" for two days and then began medical treatment and douching, but thankfully did not contract any sexually transmitted disease.[44] Douching appears to be commonly practiced as a prevention method against venereal diseases; it did not always work. Leiba Toporsky, twenty-two years old, was injured during the war, leading to his disability, and was staying at home with his wife, who was twenty-one, and their five-month-old baby. Cossacks kept coming all day and all night, and once there was nothing left to rob, two of the Cossacks raped his wife. Toporsky's wife had had a miscarriage a week earlier. The very next morning after the rape, she ran to the clinic to have the douching and was advised to come back in a week's time. Three weeks later, she and her husband were diagnosed with gonorrhea.[45] On rare occasions, a previously contracted venereal disease saved girls from another rape. The data is so limited that it is impossible to argue whether it became a regular tactic. There is a story by a Jewish man Gurvich, who was sixty-eight, who hosted two Nurkin sisters both in their teens, refugees from Likhovka. When the Cossacks wanted to rape both of them, they claimed that they had contracted gonorrhea when they were raped by the Grigoriev soldiers, thus saving themselves from another rape.[46]

Many rape victims were badly wounded during rape, and many more died as a result of their wounds. Rapists often tortured their victims in horrible ways, sometimes cutting off their breasts and hands. Many victims had wounds to the

42   YIVO Archive, file 173, 14815–958.
43   Ibid., file 208, 18559–89.
44   Ibid., file 208, 18572.
45   Ibid., file 208, 18572.
46   Ibid., file 208, 18573.

head inflicted by sabers. In Stepantsy, a small shtetl northwest of Cherkassy on the road to Kiev, White Army regiments and Makhno's (anarchist guerilla) regiments perpetrated pogroms in August 1919. An unknown Jewish man wrote a letter to his apparent relative in Kiev and related that none of his family members had any clothing anymore: his daughters and wife had nothing but underwear, and he did not own even a pair of pants. His older daughter, who most probably had been raped, was discharged from the hospital with unhealed wounds to her chest and arm, because there were no bandages available. A lot of women died after they had been raped, because Cossacks and other *pogromschiki* cut their arms and breasts off. The correspondent concludes his letter with the description of further atrocities of the White Army's appointed commandant and his aides, who sadistically raped girls and killed some of them by stabbing them continuously with a fork.[47] Sadistic torture became a part of the violent cycle of genocidal rape. However, the rape-related wounds have been never reported separately, so most of the evidence is hearsay. Doctors who treated rape survivors in Cherkassy and Smela provided details only for the particularly gruesome and tragic cases. Dr. Shadarevsky reported that a ten-year-old refugee from shtetl Moshe was raped by a group of assailants and as a result died from extensive hemorrhage.[48] Nurse Ruvinskaia described one seventeen-year-old victim, a worker at a confectionary plant, who was raped by a group of Cossacks both vaginally and orally. They exchanged derogatory remarks and "silenced" their victim. As a result, the victim's mouth was very badly wounded, and the experience left her to suffer from constant convulsive vomiting for a long time. The mere thought of the horrible experience triggered the vomiting and made her sick.[49] Most rapes during pogroms were perpetrated by gangs of assailants who, among other goals, pursued bonding and camaraderie through joint perpetration of gender violence. In this context, the masculinity and dominance of the perpetrators could not be compromised by any "perversions," so there was no rape of Jewish men, and most rapes appeared to be vaginal. The fact that the detailed description of the ordeal of the seventeen-year-old victim presented this particular rape as extraordinary testifies to the latter.

This last narrative of rape and the subsequent post-traumatic suffering of the victim leads to a discussion of the psychological trauma of rape and its impact on the Jewish community then and in perspective. In many ways,

---

47 Ibid., file 209, 18816–21 reverse.
48 Miljakova, *Kniga Pogromov*, 355.
49 Ibid., 356.

trauma and its lingering effects is the objective of genocidal rape, which continues to harm the victimized community for generations to come. Acute shame and damaged dignity effectively silenced the traumatized Jewish community. The silence of the victims is deeply meaningful and becomes, in Ilana Szobel's words, a "powerful silence."[50] In order to study the traumatic experience of these women, it is essential to analyze the pogrom narrative, which falls along gender lines.

THE RAPE NARRATIVE: WOMEN

One of the most immediate responses of the Jewish community to the pogroms was the effort to collect and preserve evidence of the inhumane atrocities. The Editorial Board, created by Elias Tcherikower, sought to assemble a body of evidence that would represent the pogroms from multiple perspectives and include thousands of witness accounts of pogroms. This collection is unique and also the first of its kind, which also implies that respondents of the pogrom inquiries had no set scripts to follow, and they created their narratives anew. Just as the violence in the pogroms emerged as a gendered phenomenon, so the narrative about the pogrom fell along very clearly defined gender characteristics that are essential to properly interpreting it.

The pogroms by the Ukrainian National Army in the first half of 1919 resulted in fewer firsthand narratives of the survivors. The silencing effect of the shame and the shock of the first wave of violent pogroms left the Jewish community almost mute on the subject of rape. During the White Army pogroms in the second half of 1919, the surge of violence and the sheer enormity of mass rape broke the dam of silence and generated more firsthand and secondhand accounts of rape and torture. These stories are not merely evidence of traumatic experience, but rather are a part of it.

There are no established ways to tell the story of rape. This is because rape is shameful for the victim, and there is no possibility of escaping the shameful connotation. It was a commonly shared understanding at the time that a woman who had been raped was spoiled and, the fact that she had been abused and her behavior had been honorable notwithstanding, she was stigmatized, lowered in social stature, and became almost unacceptable as marriage

---

50 Ilana Szobel, *A Poetics of Trauma: The Work of Dahlia Ravikovitch* (Lebanon, NH: University Press of New England, 2013), 102.

material. The only socially acceptable way to deal with the stigma of rape was to silence it, to deny it and pretend it never happened, and more often than not the camouflaging of rape became a communal effort, which created a strange phenomenon when everyone kept secret that everyone knew. This is evident from almost any pogrom narrative. Because of the stigmatization of rape, there were no preexisting rape stories a narrator could relate to in order to communicate her own experience. Not only was it hard to admit the fact of rape, but also there were no acceptable narrative patterns or clichés that might have enabled rape victims to share their personal experiences.

Ann Burgess, a renowned specialist in psychiatric care who coined the term "rape trauma syndrome" in 1974, argued that until recently rape thrived on "prudery, misunderstanding and silence."[51] But even the anecdotal evidence of the rape narrative available to her strongly suggested common patterns of response to the trauma of rape, which included "the sense of personal outrage over intimate violation; a lack of clarity concerning how to characterize the event even to oneself, and even how to characterize oneself following the event."[52] The rape narrative is deeply rooted in trauma, which determines survivors' tactics in relaying their stories. Traumatic experience, according to Ruth Leys, an expert on the psychology of trauma, complicates the relationship between victim and memory and narration.[53] The victim usually is haunted by the traumatic experience, so one of the coping mechanisms, which was almost the only one available to pogrom rape victims, is to shutter it in. Dori Laub, a Holocaust survivor, professor of psychiatry, and cofounder of the Holocaust Survivors Film Project, wrote that the imperative to tell the story is "inhibited by impossibility of telling, and, therefore, silence about the truth commonly prevails."[54] So, in fact, the female narrative of genocidal rape is the narrative of silence, and the tactics women choose to translate their experience into words derive from it. Narrative analysis of the evidence provided by victims of genocidal rape in other places, such as Bosnia and Herzegovina, are similar to the pogrom rape stories, with one crucial exception: victims from Bosnia

---

51 Ann Wolbert Burgess, "Rape Trauma Syndrome," *Behavioral Sciences & the Law* 1, no. 3 (1983): 99.

52 Ibid.

53 Ruth Leys, *Trauma: A Genealogy* (Chicago: University of Chicago Press, 2010), 227–29.

54 Shoshana Felman and Dori Laub, *Testimony: Crises of Witnessing in Literature, Psychoanalysis, and History* (Oxford: Taylor & Francis, 1992), 79.

and Herzegovina were patiently questioned by specialists,[55] and the current research aims to similarly "question" the existing body of evidence.

Ida Shwartz, a twenty-eight-year-old widow who survived the pogrom in Kremenchug in August 1919, responded to the pogrom inquiry and said the following: "My Christian neighbor told me that Cossacks are coming, but I couldn't leave because my child was sick with measles. I begged the Cossacks and kissed their hands, but they have raped me anyway, while my father was locked in the next room. When leaving the Cossacks robbed me of 20 thousand rubles."[56] Ida's narrative is really singular only because she presumably had no choice but to admit the fact that she had been raped, but otherwise her story has all the essential characteristics common to the women's narratives. Evidence provided by female pogrom survivors about rape often is more restrained than male evidence, betrays less personal emotion, and contains very few adjectives. Most of the descriptions in the women's narratives are very cliché, modeled on the literary, journalistic, and bureaucratic rhetoric of the late Russian Empire— exaggerated and pompous. There are narratives the style and tone of which do not fit into the general description, but overall the reader is tasked to decipher the female narrative in order to be able to read into it and comprehend it. Considering how many Jewish women were raped, how few admit to it, and how many sought to conceal their experience "for obvious reasons," it is logical to assume that rape survivors disguised their experience in the evidence they provided. The current research delineates several distinct narrative scripts that enabled victims to communicate their stories without admitting to anything.

Substitution is a powerful tool used by female respondents to exclude or omit the tragic experience but tell the story anyway. The only details that distinguish the otherwise often blunt narratives that lack a lot of important details and emotions are the ones regarding material loss. Besides the obvious fact that women very often responded to the questioning anticipating some compensation or support in return, the meticulous description of how much money and in what currency was taken away, how many pairs of shoes removed, and what color curtains were destroyed is in fact a way to mute the painful experience but preserve its value, substituting physical and moral loss with its material equivalent. Emblematic of this form of narrative is an appeal dictated by Basya Gershtein (probably illiterate) to the Berdichev City Council on February, 10, 1919, after

---

55 Inger Skjelsbaek, "Victim and Survivor: Narrated Social Identities of Women Who Experienced Rape during the War in Bosnia-Herzegovina," *Feminism & Psychology* 16, no. 4 (2006): 373–403.

56 YIVO Archive, file 208, 18570.

an extremely violent pogrom by the Ukrainian National Army, in which she lists her losses, such as "... two curtains—80 rubles, 4 bed sheets—320 rubles, eight women's undershirts—800 rubles, one silver cigarette case—120 rubles, two nickel-plated tea kettles—100 rubles...." In the last line of her appeal, Gershtein adds that she is alone with two children, and her husband does not make any money, because he was so badly beaten during the pogrom that he has been in hospital these past four weeks.[57] While it is very hard to establish for sure what really happened during the pogrom with this survivor, some evidence is more telling than other. Khaia-Sura Rabinovich from shtetl Dubovo near the large town of Uman described her experience thus: "from my daughter's ears they pulled out beautiful earrings, and from my fingers they pulled off the rings";[58] however, the narrator, who survived the third pogrom in four months, failed to mention rape at all, although most probably she and her daughter had been raped like almost all the Jewish women of the shtetl, as the other evidence from Dubovo suggests.[59]

"MY DEAR CHILDREN"

There are no memoirs of women that describe their pogrom experience. Notwithstanding this, there is one absolutely unique narrative which exists in several copies, not all of them identical. During the Civil War, Feiga Meril Shamis survived a number of pogroms in shtetls in Western Ukraine, where she lived at the time: Verbe, Dubno, Shumsk, and Kremenets; her husband died at the beginning of the war from a chronic illness, and she lost to pogroms at least two of her children. After escaping to Warsaw in 1920, Shamis sent two of her younger children, Rose and Manes, aged eight and ten, to South Africa with a group of two hundred Jewish orphans who lost their parents in pogroms, sponsored by Isaac Ochberg.[60] Shamis, who moved to Palestine with one of her daughters, met her son, now Manes Favish, who had been adopted by a South African Jewish family, in 1941, when Manes served in Egypt during Second World War with the South African army. This very short but no doubt emotional meeting resulted in Feiga's attempt to explain her life to some of her surviving children in a form of a memoir letter. Two families of Feiga's descendants

---

57 Ibid., file 163, 16852.
58 Ibid., file 167, 14295 reverse.
59 Ibid., file 167, 14289–317.
60 Susan L. Tananbaum, "From Local to International: Cape Town's Jewish Orphanage," *Jewish Historical Studies* 46 (2014).

shared with me their copies of the memoirs, which were written in Yiddish, but were translated by local volunteers into English. One of the copies, addressed to Manes Favish, was published privately,[61] and another, addressed to Feiga's daughter Tilly Froman, was typed up and never published.[62] This long introduction is necessary to explain the origin of this distinctive narrative, which deserves designated research.[63] Feiga's dramatic story, among other things, illustrates all of the tactics of the pogrom narrative employed by Jewish women who survived pogroms. The detailed life story similarly, yet not identically, provides the necessary context that allows me to discern the narrative techniques with confidence.

Feiga Shamis describes in great detail her struggle to survive during the pogroms, focusing on minuscule details of financial negotiations and the tremendous efforts that included bribing of the officials, producing moonshine brandy, trading in wet sugar and used army sacks, hiding every single possession in the neighbor's cellar, and negotiating rents, transportation, and documents.[64] Feiga's ordeal strikes the unprepared reader not only with its tragedy but also with the glaring lack of certain details. Feiga Shamis does not mention the names of all of her children, and the two copies of the memoir provide conflicting insights into their fate. We know that there were twelve children, and the youngest daughter Yentele was born after the Civil War had begun; however, Feiga mentions only in passing that she lost two children during the pogroms, and again the data in the different copies does not match exactly. Considering the urgent yearning with which she addresses her children, whom she misses bitterly, the little inscriptions on the photographs, and indeed the fact that she wrote this memoir, which obviously pains her to write, it is impossible to deny Feiga deep true feelings. Notwithstanding, Feiga's narrative is missing any emotional references to her loved ones and their lives, and her story depicts a hostile world full of strangers whose worth is measured by their benevolence, which sometimes means simply lack of violence, and their wealth, which means survival. The idea of wealth permeates the story and becomes the only object of pronounced envy and desire.

Feiga Shamis's story demonstrates how a painful emotional experience, like the death of a child during a pogrom, is substituted with a different set of

61 Feiga Mirel Shamis, *Shalom Shalom My Dear Children* (Johannesburg, 1998).
62 Feyge Mirel Shammas, *The Memoir* (n/a).
63 I am proud to be part of the team that made the first documentary on pogroms, http://www.mydearchildrendoc.com/.
64 Shamis, *Shalom Shalom My Dear Children*, 13, 23–30.

values. The issue of rape does not surface even once in Feiga's story, although the circumstances strongly suggest it: the young widow traveled a lot through war-stricken territory, hosted soldiers and officers of various armies and gangs, was involved actively in trade, and her lodgings were ambushed on many occasions.[65] Feiga's story is not unusual, as many Jewish women during the Civil War had to travel, to become breadwinners, to take care of the children, and to suffer all sorts of violence. For example, Slava Shubb, who traveled by train from Kremenchug to Kiev to buy medicines for the Jewish hospital, had spent all the money she had with her to ransom out nine Jewish women from Kanev who had been taken off the train, raped, and could have been murdered. In her emotionless report, Shubb describes how she, with several other non-Jewish passengers (she traveled with the documents of her Russian friend), went to watch the Cossacks kill (and rape) Jewish women. Cossacks actually invited passengers to become an audience for the spectacle, and many agreed. Shubb wrote a petition to the Odessa Jewish community, describing her ordeal, in order to be compensated for her expenses.[66]

Feiga Shamis, like Shubb or many other women who told their stories, had a purpose, although her purpose was not of a material nature. Shamis recorded her story in search of redemption; she tried to justify her choices for her children. Feiga's dynamic drama unfolded against the backdrop of a narrative that could be described as a lamentation with elements of a fairytale. On every page she cursed her terrible bad luck and the numerous *tsores* (troubles) she had to deal with; however, she had been rescued from every tight corner and dreadful situation that she chose to describe, not just due to her efforts, but also because figures of authority had been charmed by her, and wanted to help her, or even marry her and take her to Moscow (an offer she claims to have declined).[67] Feiga's narrative is full of miracles, but those miracles are not joyful. This is a fairytale in which a happy ending is substituted with no ending, the ending when the most terrible thing did not happen. Notwithstanding this, in reality the horrible thing could have happened, and more likely than not, it did.

TELLING ANOTHER STORY

Many rape survivors managed to communicate their tragic personal experience of rape through altering the story by omission. This kind of narrative would

---

65 Ibid.; Shammas, *The Memoir*.
66 Miljakova, *Kniga Pogromov*, 327.
67 Shammas, *The Memoir*, 20–27.

unfold gradually, chronologically accounting for the pogrom events, leading to the inevitable. For example, twelve-year-old Rosa Rosenvasser from shtetl Vasilkov tells how the *pogromschiki* came in and looted their home, tortured and assaulted her father and wanted to kill him, how he was trembling from fear, so she was screaming and crying and pleading, and rushed in and covered her father in a warm shawl. It is important to notice that the protagonist of the story, a suffering female character, takes an active part in the unfolding events. So the officer grabs her by her hair, drags her to another room, and ... lets her go.[68] At the height of the story, when the reader (or listener) anticipates how the events might unfold, there is no climax. The culmination is simply missing, and there is no logical explanation for it. Roza's story does not stop there: the officer goes back to her father and escorts him to the railway station to be executed, Rosa follows them and pleads for the life of her father, and nothing happens—the officer simply lets her go again.[69] After studying scores of similar narratives, I would argue that rape indeed very often did take place, as might be expected. Dubinsky, a survivor of the Smela pogrom who was quoted earlier, said that "cases of rescue from the rape are very rare."[70]

The absence of rape itself from the rape story is often very poorly disguised, to the point of absolute absurdity: a pogrom victim from Kremenchug named Sara Leibkind, aged fifty, tells that she had been assaulted in front of her husband and young sons by groups of Cossacks. They wanted to rape her and hit her with the revolver on the head, so she lost her consciousness and she does not know if she was raped or not.[71] It appears that even formal avoidance of the shameful stigma, even when the truth is obvious, was used as a psychological defense. The stories of miraculous escape from rape became another variation of the "no ending" story. Mirian Gleizer of Kremenchug, aged eight, said that she went hiding with other girls in a shed, and then at the rabbi's home; when the Cossacks came, she held the rabbi very tight, and cried for his children to call her parents. Miriam's parents ran to her rescue, and ransomed her and her twelve-year-old sister.[72] The sheer number of similar stories suggests that more often than not, such stories are stories of rape, and not of miraculous escape.

Another fairly straightforward method of camouflaging the rape is by telling the story about somebody else as a way to convey first-person suffering.

68 Miljakova, *Kniga Pogromov*, 320–21.
69 Ibid., 321.
70 YIVO Archive, file 209, 18797.
71 Ibid., file 208, 18570.
72 Ibid., file 208, 18573.

The most obvious objects of those stories of rape that happened to somebody else were women who died as a result of pogroms. Even then their names were disclosed reluctantly, but as pogroms became more and more violent, and rapes excessively brutal, humiliating, and torturous, the stories of rape were told about refugees, or neighbors, or relatives, even those who survived, but not about oneself. The narrative of rape is being transferred onto those who do not care anymore (the dead) or are less important (from the point of view of the narrator), or somebody at random. It is legitimate to assume that some of the stories told are actually first-person narratives disguised as a story about a third person. In May 1919 in Elisavetgrad, Esther Poddubnaia survived the pogrom, while her husband was murdered along with other Jews in their yard. She related how her younger children miraculously escaped death, and she herself tried to run away with her older daughter. Poddubnaia then continued her evidence with the story of another teenage girl, one Donya Kagan, who had been brutally raped in front of her brother.[73] In late summer in Kremenchug Esfir Zvonitsky, aged forty, emphatically assured an interviewer that their relationship with Cossacks was always very good, so when Cossacks came into her apartment, Esfir offered them tea, which they drank. Then the Cossacks decided to rape all the Jewish women in the building, which included several apartments. Esfir omitted whether she was among those who had been raped, but commented that those who tried to protect their property and stayed behind were raped, while those who ran away were not.[74] She did stay behind, and Cossacks rarely made exceptions.

The traumatic ordeal that shamed rape victims and undermined their dignity was an emotional experience that left an enormous impact on victims' lives. Jewish women who survived gender violence during pogroms did tell their stories, and it is possible to decipher them, despite the fact that Jewish women have never articulated their exact feelings. Jewish women did express their terrible despair and their misery, and they did lament their loss. Jewish women, as a rule, did not describe the minute fluctuations of their fear, anger, and disgust; they did not often analyze their emotions. Jewish men did.

THE RAPE NARRATIVE: MEN

This is Ida Shwartz's story of the Kremenchug pogrom that has been already discussed: "My Christian neighbor told me that Cossacks are coming, but

73 Ibid., file 168, 14363.
74 Ibid., file 208, 18571 reverse.

I couldn't leave because my child was sick with measles. I begged the Cossacks and kissed their hands, but they have raped me anyway, while my father was locked in the next room. When leaving the Cossacks robbed me of 20 thousand rubles."[75] Deichman, an educated Jewish man, described the very same pogrom in his diary: "About midnight we heard desperate screams of people begging for mercy. Soon the sounds became more evident, and turned into [a] continuous wail of hundreds of voices. Women's screams, children's shrieks, dogs barking. Sounds of music and crackle of the rifle shots. Stomping hooves of the galloping horses. A horrible orgy of sounds in the midst of the night bringing horror and insanity. This horrible 'music' was repeated several times during the night. By morning we've learned about the dreadful violence committed against women and children, mass robberies and looting, murders."[76]

Deichman, whose emotional diary is precious evidence of an immediate, unedited response to the unfolding pogrom, communicates in those abrupt, clipped sentences the paralyzing effect of the fear that he experienced after witnessing violence and particularly the rape of Jewish women. In the paragraphs preceding those cited, Deichman describes his wanderings around the town engulfed in the pogrom: he visits various communal organizations, where Jewish men try to produce some substantial reaction to the violence. Any attempts, if there were any—it is unclear from the diary—of organized self-defense had been abandoned long before then. The prominent Jewish citizens of Kremenchug assemble and decide to put out a publication, maybe a newspaper. The purpose of this publication is unclear, and Deichman declines to participate. The leaders of the community looked for a way to communicate to the advancing White Army that they, the Jews of Kremenchug, were not Bolsheviks but loyal subjects of the new power, and should therefore be spared from the pogrom. The plea proved pointless, the pogrom had started, and by the next day Deichman is completely demoralized by what he witnessed. The suffering women's faces haunt his memory and leave him in a state of complete surrender.

Jewish men were the designated audience for the mass rape of Jewish women. They were forced to become voyeurs, to partake in this capacity in the horrible spectacle of rape, and to be utterly degraded by it. Roitbok from Skvira, who witnessed the rape and murder of his sister, and barely escaped death himself, fell asleep on the chair in the ransacked apothecary, because he was absolutely "exhausted"—not physically, but emotionally.[77] So is Deichman,

---

75 Ibid., file 208, 18570.
76 Ibid., file 208, 18560–65.
77 Miljakova, *Kniga Pogromov*, 228.

who experiences a terrible apathy and listlessness, haunted by what he saw: "the faces of women, frightened, in mad agony. At night—screams, shrieks, crying and sobbing; the thundering shots echoing around the city. You sit with your eyes fixed dumbly on nothing. The nerves are so shattered that any steps, any slight sound at all seem like artillery barrage. The apathy is taking over. You are losing the ability to react. It all looks so natural. The destruction, the rape, the abuse, the looting. . . . How can it be otherwise. . . . That's 'the lawful power of the state' for you. . . ."[78]

Thirty years later, the Auschwitz survivor and writer K. Tzetnik (Yehiel Dinur) testified during Adolf Eichmann's trial and talked about "Planet Auschwitz," whose inhabitants even "breathed according to different laws of nature."[79] The perception of the world of violence being a separate universe detached from the rest of the world runs through the testimony of pogrom survivors. The reality of the pogrom universe, when the whole world shrank to the minute-by-minute reality of the unfolding violence inside the borders of one hot, burning locality, compelled submissiveness onto witnesses like Deichman, who became overpowered by the "different laws of nature." Deichman's impotence stands in stark contrast to the literary depiction of a witness of pogrom rape by Lamed Shapiro a decade earlier. In his story "The Cross," a grown son is forced to watch his mother being raped by a number of Cossacks and gets caught up in the world of sadistic violence. In the act of forced voyeurism he sees his mother's naked body with a mixture of disgust, fear, pain, love, and sadistic satisfaction, which translates inside him into violence and aggression, as he becomes a rapist himself.[80]

Violence and impotence are the two sides of the reaction to the traumatic experience, and pogroms of the Civil War elicited mostly the latter, as it was the intended effect of genocidal rape. The relationship between the witness and the trauma are not linear, but the two are interdependent, argues Ana Douglass, and the witness makes the traumatic event real, validating it.[81] The witness is an inextricable part of the trauma; the witness carries the trauma on through

---

78 Ibid., 221.
79 There is an extensive scholastic discussion of K. Tzetnik's testimony in the context of trauma narrative, which does not, unfortunately, fit the framework of the current research. The full video recording of the testimony of K. Tzetnik is available online: "Eichmann Trial—Session No. 68, 69," YouTube, http://www.youtube.com/watch?v=m3-tXyYhd5U.
80 Lamed Shapiro, *Di Yudishe Melukhe: Un Andere Zakhen*. A naye oyfl. ed. (New York: Idish leben, 1929).
81 Ana Douglass and Thomas A. Vogler, *Witness and Memory: The Discourse of Trauma* (London: Routledge, 2012).

time and experiences it over and over, even though the narrative is the most difficult part of the trauma discourse, because it is impossible:[82] How does one describe the indescribable?

DESCRIBING THE INDESCRIBABLE

Galperin, whose evidence was quoted at the beginning of the chapter, struggled to find the right words and the right style to communicate his despair, his pain, and his disgust in the face of the barbarian cruelty, and so did Deichman and many other male pogrom witnesses. Lacking a socially acceptable narrative patterns, an appropriate language, and a means of comprehending the rapidly escalating violence resulted in inconsistency in the narrative style in the male responses to the pogrom inquiries. Jewish men created a narrative of rape that is raw and revealing. The archetypal evidence is provided in the report by one Lifshitz, who survived the pogrom in Pechara in the Podolsky region and later became an inspector for the Kiev Commission of the Jewish Public Committee for Relief to Victims of Pogroms (EVOBSCHESTCOM). His communication to Kiev two years after the pogrom, accompanying the interviews with the pogrom survivors, states the following:

> May 31, 1921.
>
> The pogrom in Pechara took place on June 12, 1919 at five o'clock in the morning. Sokolov's guerrilla army of 500 men has entered Pechara followed by the large convoy of carts loaded with the loot taken from the Jews during the previous pogroms in other places. Once [the gang entered the town] the looting began and in an hour the murders started as well. The local priest went to the gang headquarters, but his pleas to stop the massacre were answered with—"This is the payback to Bolsheviks for the Red Terror." The priest argued that local Jewish population was apolitical, but his reasoning didn't help. Then the priest claimed that he came on behalf of the local Christian population demanding the end of the pogrom. This had a certain effect: following the ataman's signal the massacre stopped. In an hour, at three o'clock in the afternoon, they marched out, accompanied by the local music. The gang was passing through the streets drenched with Jewish blood. The Jewish possessions were left behind for the local

---

82 Ibid., 31–32.

peasant population to loot (except for jewelry and money that bandits took for themselves). With the blood of their sons, with the sacred blood of their infants, with the honor of their daughters have the Pechara Jews paid, as have all the Jews of Ukraine, for the coming bright future.

Signed: Inspector for the Nemirov Region (Pechara refugee) Lifshitz

P.S. Almost all women from thirteen years old up had been raped by the bandits. Children were raped in front of their parents' eyes, some were killed afterwards. [Bandits] raped in the streets in front of giggling onlookers. Many women contracted venereal diseases. There were cases of pregnancy. One woman, whose husband is in America, has learned about her pregnancy five months later and went insane. One of the pogrom victims and survivors, a student named Efim Israelevich Kogan who by an accidental chance had survived the pogrom alive, poisoned himself with arsenic. He was saved in the local hospital. After six months he poisoned himself again, unable to endure the horrors of the pogrom that he witnessed.

Lifshitz[83]

This evidence is quoted here in full because Lifshitz used in his very short piece most of the techniques employed by the male narrators. First of all, Lifshitz does not include the information about mass rapes in the main part of his report summary. Laconic and to the point, the description of the negotiations between the local priest and the bandits is followed by the rather sketchy though powerful account of the bandits leaving Pechara, and the paragraph is concluded with the very differently styled grandiloquent phrase that Jewish suffering is the price for the "bright future." In 1921 "bright future" probably meant the Soviet Republic of Ukraine; however, the rest of the phrase, constructed with borrowed clichés, disguises the enormity of the disaster and the lack of a customary script to narrate this massive escalation of violence, especially gender violence.

Lifshitz described the "proper" history of the Pechara pogrom in a short note, but in the postscript he scrutinized with astonishing precision the mass rape and its implications. He accounted for the magnitude of rape and how it

---

83 Miljakova, *Kniga Pogromov*, 158.

was performed as public spectacle. He also talked about the physical repercussions of rape: venereal diseases and pregnancies, and the moral suffering of victims and witnesses: madness and suicide. The narrative of the postscript is very different from the first part of the letter and is written in short sentences which sound as if whispered. Lifshitz could not neglect those important observations, but he could not fit them into the "official" document either.

Gender violence traumatized all of the Jewish community, including the secondary witnesses who assessed the damage or even merely read about it. The first traumatic experience of this kind is reflected in Bialik's poem "City of Slaughter," in which he described the aftermath of the Kishinev pogrom of 1903, and specifically his first encounter with rape, creating a new vernacular to communicate the traumatic experience.[84] Still, in 1919 and later the unfolding mass rape of Jewish women on an unprecedented scale was shocking, and left witnesses confused and perplexed.

This is the narrative of the immediate visual and emotional experience of a Jewish man, which can be compared to shell shock: the witness is stunned and utterly lost. The narrator is Rekis, a Poalei Zion activist, political immigrant, and Sorbonne graduate,[85] who found himself in the spring of 1919 in his hometown of Rotmistrovka, a small shtetl in the Cherkassy region, where he witnessed a violent pogrom by Grigoriev's guerrilla army. Rekis is absolutely staggered by his experience: on one hand, he is so horrified by the cruelty of what he had witnessed that no adjectives appear to be adequate to communicate the shock which he is nevertheless eager and compelled to describe. On the other hand, he confines himself to the safe framework of social and moral norms: Rekis is extremely concerned that rape is exceedingly shameful for the victim and thus should be concealed as much as possible. "Sixteen-year-old peasants, the monsters, they raped and ravished, inflicting suffering on our best, our most beautiful, most meek and gentle maidens and women. I cannot speak much about this moment, lest I increase the suffering of those martyrs,"[86] he writes.

Like Lifshitz, Rekis removes some of the rape narrative from the main body of his eighty-page account of the pogroms in May 1919. Several para-

84 Sara R. Horowitz, "The Rhetoric of Embodied Memory in the 'City of Slaughter,'" *Prooftexts* 25, no. 1 (2005): 73–85.

85 The biography of Rekis and his activity is currently a work in progress. Very little is known about him. All the biographic information has been gleaned from his personal papers. "World Socialist Union of Jewish Workers—Poalei, Zion," Microfiches 565–73.

86 YIVO Archive, file 183, 15904.

graphs after the quote above, in which the author states how impossible it was for him to describe and how shameful for the victim the rape was, and how it should not be subject of public discussion, Rekis writes in the footnote: "I beg the Editorial Board to promise on their <u>honor</u> [underlined by the author] not to publicize the event I am about to describe to you. Both victims are alive and they will take their own lives were they to recognize <u>the author of this communication</u> [the last four words underlined by the author]. Here is what happened. . . ."[87] Torn by the importance of his communication and the shame he is inflicting, Rekis proceeds to tell the story of two beautiful Jewish sisters, already betrothed, who were searched for and discovered by the gang members while in hiding with their brother. Both girls were brutally raped by groups of soldiers in front of their brother, who was tied up and forced to watch. Rekis also underlines the last phrase of his note, because he unmistakably recognized both the tragically new form of gendered violence and its historical significance.

The idea of the historical significance of the events unfolding during the pogroms compelled witnesses like Rekis, Lifshitz, Galperin, and many others to contribute their stories to the materials collected by the Editorial Board. The tradition of *Khurbn Forshung*, history writing, has been a long-established Jewish response to a catastrophe, and Tcherikower and his collaborators aimed to collect an archive of documents that would represent the history of pogroms in its fullness. They put a call out for the public to come forward with personal narratives of the pogroms, and to contribute to history writing.[88] Those who responded to the call and, like Rekis, did not just contribute their own memoirs, but actively questioned people and encouraged further pogrom writing, recognized their role as writers of history. This notion especially impacted the pogrom narratives of Jewish men, as very few Jewish women actively participated in this effort. Tcherikower names two women among the members of the Editorial Board: Rakhil Faigenberg and his own wife Rivka Tcherikower;[89] and in the archival collection assembled by the Editorial Board, there are very few pogrom stories written by women, but a lot of female responses to the pogrom inquiries.

Detailed analysis of the political situation and historical reasoning as part of the pogrom narrative became integral to most of the evidence provided by

---

87 Ibid., file 183, 15904 reverse.
88 Jockusch, *Collect and Record*, 28–30.
89 Cherikover, *Anṭisemiṭizm*, 8.

the Jewish men. Rekis starts his eighty-page narrative with seventeen pages of historical writing,[90] which is very similar to Tcherikower's own works, where the author aims to determine the historical situation that led to pogroms. Feiga Shamis, on the other hand, does not try to rationalize any of the historical events she was caught in.[91] Rekis builds his narrative as an argument against the most popular rationale for pogrom violence, which was the idea that "all Jews are Bolsheviks," so he feels compelled to justify the Jewish cause and to prove the accusations false. Jewish historical writing[92] that was contemporary to him provided the necessary tools and script to narrate the story. The basic concept accepted by the Jewish historians of the time was that the pogroms were masterminded and organized by the government or other powers, and the political history was considered the only way to explain anti-Jewish violence. Gender violence during pogroms did not fit into historical writing attempted by many male narrators, and so the new kind of pogrom narrative began to surface in the evidence, muddling its structure and style.

Gender narrative of rape is key to understanding how the diverse Jewish community responded to pogroms. In the immediate aftermath of rape, it was important to deal with wounds, diseases, and pregnancies, but when the urgency of action subsided the major question that faced all members of Jewish community was this: How were they to continue living with what had just happened? The Jewish community was left to comprehend, internalize, and learn to live on a daily basis with the traumatic experience that forever branded its survivors. In the chaos of the Civil War and the establishment of the Soviet power, and the growing mobility of Jewish population, the way the Jewish communities had been constituted prior to the revolutionary changes deteriorated rapidly, and even the memory of pogroms were carefully expunged from the official Soviet historiography.[93] The dearth of established sources makes the pogrom narratives with reference to circumstantial evidence the major resource of information on how Jewish people emotionally responded to the trauma of rape.

---

90 YIVO Archive, file 183, 15896–937.
91 Shamis, *Shalom Shalom My Dear Children*, 13.
92 Jockusch, *Collect and Record*, 18.
93 Bemporad, *Legacy of Blood*, chapter on the Jewish "site of memory," by author's permission.

CHAPTER 6

"Wretched Victims of Another Kind": Making Sense of Rape Trauma

Through the boundless spaces, through the dark and terrifying forests and ravines did my poor, numb body stumble farther. In a deep ravine about 12 *verstas* from the shtetl that I had left I stood on the bank of a creek. The supple branches of the old hollowed willows hung close over the water. In the young spring growth of the grass the frogs croaked incessantly and hypnotically, and a powerful, invigorating odor of the recently plowed earth spread over all this and floated over the infinite expanse of the air, infiltrating all the spaces and filling up all the pores of being. The faraway village, fast asleep, shone dimly under the moonlight. Deep repose and peace emanated from this night scene unfolding before my eyes. And here I was—tortured and wounded, half-dead, I stood there and watched the remote glow of the burning shtetl that loomed like a terrifying blemish over the horizon. And I heard the terrifying distant chorus of the poor Jewish shtetl dying a flaming death in the murderers' hands.[1]

Rekis, who wrote this homage to a beautiful Ukrainian night in May 1919, ended up hiding in a ditch next to the road amid the bucolic landscape; he was almost enthralled by its beauty, which was marred only by the glow of his home-town of Rotmistrovka, a small shtetl in the vicinity of Smela and Cherkassy, ablaze after the pogrom. He escaped the bloody pogrom earlier that night after witnessing horrific scenes of torture and rape, and was deeply troubled by two thoughts: How could this barbarity coexist in the world with the European civ-ilization? And how were such horrible acts of decidedly humiliating violence

---

1   YIVO Archive, file 183, 15900 reverse.

possible? Rekis exposed in his writing and in his work the major existential contradiction that horrified him even beyond the visceral violence of the pogrom: how this barbaric and archaic violence related to him, an educated, modern human being. Rekis felt the clash of civilizations in his mind and soul, and was tormented by it almost more than by his near-death experience.

Rekis's evidence is unique and extremely significant for two major reasons. First, Rekis demonstrated acute sensibility and awareness of gender violence, unlike most of his contemporaries, and investigated and assembled materials about the mass rape of Jewish women for the Tcherikower Archive; and in his own writing he pays a lot of attention to the gendered experience of violence, providing unparalleled insight into the problem. Secondly, Rekis conscientiously and meticulously recorded his own emotional reactions to the tragic ordeal, analyzed them, and made it his point to highlight the emotional aspect when interviewing others. As a result, Rekis produced evidence across gender lines that sheds light on the challenge of a secularized individual amid the carnival of violence. Rekis appears to have been haunted by the terrible inadequacy of his personal experience of an educated secularized individual to the beastly and visceral violence of the pogrom, which rebelled against nature itself and had no place in Rekis's world.

The twentieth century is even described as the "age of trauma,"[2] because its history is permeated with the traumatic experiences that impacted societies all over the world for generations to come. Trauma as a historical event is experienced by a community through the private suffering of individuals, as it is endured by those who suffered with them as witnesses, or through them as secondary witnesses or descendants. However, trauma is initially experienced privately by individuals, who experience and internalize it. The notions of private experience, private gaze, and private life belong to modernity and characterize it. According to the Foucauldian theory of gaze, the latter is fully attributed to the onset of modernity: the stare of the crowd is substituted with the scrutiny of the society of individuals.[3] The sociological concept of "individual modernity"[4] describes the transition from traditional society to modernity for every individual as a transition from making life choices based on communal

---

2   Nancy K. Miller and Jason Daniel Tougaw, *Extremities: Trauma, Testimony, and Community* (Urbana-Champaign: University of Illinois Press, 2002), 1–13.

3   Foucault, *Discipline and Punish*.

4   Anthony Giddens has originally introduced the concept of individual modernity. See Anthony Giddens, *Modernity and Self-Identity: Self and Society in the Late Modern Age* (Stanford, CA: Stanford University Press, 1991); Anthony Giddens, *The Consequences of Modernity* (Indianapolis: John Wiley & Sons, 2013).

traditions to making life choices based on personal experience. Modernized individuals share not only common basic moral values, but also a larger set of values instigated by modernization, forming, arguably, new social and emotional communities.[5]

The understanding of modernity as an individual experience allows us to discern how trauma, such as pogrom rape, was internalized and transmitted by different members of the Jewish community. However, this is extremely problematic for two major reasons. First, modernity has been widely discussed in Jewish historiography for decades,[6] but the term itself is not clearly defined and may imply a variety of interpretations in the context of Jewish history. Secondly, the available evidence of the pogrom experience does not provide enough information to produce systematic analysis of the degree of modernization of Jewish communities in Ukraine, and of the response by the traditional community to pogrom violence and rape.

Notwithstanding, among the variety of descriptions of mass rape during pogroms[7] that elude systematization there is one exception: in order to illustrate the devastating effects of rape, respondents would describe the most extreme emotional reactions of rape victims, many of which ended in suicides. With very few exceptions, the narrators of such accounts attributed the most dramatic responses to those victims who had received some kind of secular education. The observations of the well-educated secular Jewish men who constituted the majority of inspectors collecting the information, as well as the narratives of both the male and female pogrom survivors of all ages and educational levels, create a striking picture of the coping strategies of secular-educated Jewish women.

The exact number of Jewish women raped in the first pogrom in Smela, which happened in May 1919, is unknown, though it is reported to have been very high. According to Galperin, whose evidence was discussed earlier,[8] the number of rape victims in the second pogrom, which was in August, was "no fewer than

---

5   Christian Welzel, "Individual Modernity," in *The Oxford Handbook of Political Behavior* (Oxford: Oxford University Press, 2007), 185.

6   To name just a few of many significant works on the subject: Eli Lederhendler, *Jewish Responses to Modernity: New Voices in America and Eastern Europe* (New York: New York University Press, 1997); Gershon David Hundert, *Jews in Poland-Lithuania in the Eighteenth Century: A Genealogy of Modernity* (Berkeley: University of California Press, 2004); and Iris Parush, *Reading Jewish Women: Marginality and Modernization in Nineteenth-Century Eastern European Jewish Society* (Hanover, NH: University Press of New England, 2004).

7   Gendered patterns of elusion have been discussed in the previous chapter.

8   YIVO Archive, Elias Tcherikower Archive 1903–63, Rg 80–89 (Mk 470), file 209, 18800–18803.

four hundred," and in December the number "exceeded one thousand." Doctors and midwives, who treated rape victims,[9] among them Dr. Gandlevsky, who worked in the Smela hospital, responded to one inquiry about a women he had treated in December 1919 as follows:

> Some of the cases [of rape] were followed by terrible nervous upheaval. Victims wanted to take their own lives, and the doctors had to prevail upon them morally [to prevent suicide]. One such case [of suicide] involved an intelligent young woman, a medical student. In most cases, however, victims found their grief bearable: their own anguish [resulting from rape] got lost amidst the multitude of other sufferings. The grief was endured with abject resignation to their fate.

Dr. Polyak, another doctor who treated women in that community, added that "some victims [of rape] currently suffer from severe nervous breakdowns, seizures, tremors etc."[10]

Dr. Gandlevsky was deeply concerned with the extent of his patients' emotional distress and their need for counseling, which he himself could not provide. He even seemed to place their emotional condition above their physical state, reporting on the latter only briefly. At least one of Gandlevsky's patients, unable to cope with the trauma of her rape, committed suicide. Dr. Gandlevsky was concerned about the extreme distress of those rape victims who appeared the most vulnerable and unstable. Dr. Polyak, for her part, noted cases where the distress resulted in neurological reactions, such as seizures and convulsive tics. Doctors in the nearby town of Cherkassy, which suffered a fate similar to neighboring Smela, concurred. Dr. Goldman, a gynecologist in the Cherkassy Jewish Hospital, noted a case of suicide by a twenty-year-old woman named Sambur, which undoubtedly followed the "horrible suffering" caused by the rape. Other rape victims stopped menstruating, not necessarily as a result of pregnancy but because of their nervous condition.[11]

The collected medical inquiries, backed by a large corpus of supporting evidence, suggest that rape victims and rape witnesses suffered tremendously, both physically and emotionally, and displayed a full spectrum of reactions to their ordeal. In other words, the victims' response to trauma was defined

---

9   Smela doctors' evidence regarding physical conditions of their patients was discussed in the previous chapter.

10   YIVO Archive, file 209, 18795–812.

11   Ibid., file 210, 19013–39.

not only by their personality but also by another shared characteristic. Neither Dr. Gandlevsky nor his colleagues precisely define the group of the more vulnerable rape victims who were less capable of coping with rape. Notwithstanding, the doctors as well as other narrators consistently specify, whenever possible, if the victim of rape had received any formal education, linking it strongly with the intensity of post-traumatic stress.

The doctors' impressions of their patients closely align with those expressed by both the pogrom survivors and the inspectors who assessed pogrom damage on behalf of various relief organizations all over pogrom-stricken Ukraine. The quoted evidence displayed one remarkable common feature: it demarcated women by one single factor—their exposure to secular education. Very little else is known about them: their social and (often) marital status is unclear, as is their religious observance. In addition, very little is known about how Jewish traditional communities all over Ukraine responded to the pogrom violence.[12] These lacunae render the application of the concept of "modernity" problematic, since modernity is usually defined in the East European Jewish historiography by multiple processes that position the individual in relation to the traditional, religious community. However, the educational information provided about the victims does at least enable us to differentiate them on the basis of secularism. Glenn Dynner defines secularism as "not the binary opposite of religiosity but rather as the increased privatization of religious belief, its subordination to reason and evidence-based analysis, and in the Jewish case, the search for human-made solutions to the modern Jewish predicament."[13] Long-term sociological research, it should be noted, has established that "no attribute of a person predicts his attitudes, values, and behavior more consistently or more powerfully than the amount of schooling he has received."[14]

The discussion of the exposure to secularism as a factor that impacted how the trauma of rape was experienced should be founded on the careful analysis of how mass rape was described and reported, and specifically how the rape victims were described. Materials assembled by the Editorial Board provide

12 The only exception found so far in the Tcherikower Archive is the letter from the Pavoloch Jewish community to the Kiev community that reported that most of the female population had been raped, and young girls were registered with the local rabbi "according to tradition." YIVO Archive, file 209, 18703.
13 Glenn Dynner, "Replenishing the 'Fountain of Judaism': Traditionalist Jewish Education in Interwar Poland" (forthcoming from *Jewish History*).
14 Alex Inkeles, "The School as a Context for Modernization," *International Journal of Comparative Sociology* 14 (1973): 163–79.

enough statistics to deduce how the reporting of rape evolved and was transformed from cautious references to extensive research in some cases. In the collections about the pogroms of the first half of 1919, which were perpetrated by the Ukrainian National Army and various independent armed bands, the rape of Jewish women was usually mentioned in a cautious and highly reserved manner. Yet there are many descriptions of the most atrocious instances, particularly in Gornostaipol, Gorodische, Vasilkov, Kazatin, Ovruch, Peschanka, and Teplik, to name just a few.[15]

For example, in January 1919 in Ovruch, a town northwest of Kiev with over four thousand Jewish residents, ataman Kozyr-Zyrka unleashed unusually macabre and sadistic violence. His first order on recapturing the town on the last day of December was to round up ten Jewish girls, who were then continuously raped and tortured by him and his soldiers.[16] The description of this episode and others like it focuses on the unprecedented humiliation and violence of the rapes, but tells nothing about the victims themselves. Their identities and responses were not disclosed, and it is not clear whether they survived the ordeal physically and emotionally. Other forms of violence during the same pogrom were reported in greater detail, though here too the fates of many victims remain unclear.

The brutal nature and massive scope of sexual violence are the focus of the report: "All local hospitals are filled with raped women, many of whom die. ... On the shtetl streets lay heaps of rape victims' bodies, their bellies ripped open or swollen as a result of rape."[17] This description from Gorodische (Horodyshche), a shtetl southeast of Kiev, hit by a pogrom in May 1919, is typical of the way that the mass rape of Jewish women was reported: the scale of the disaster (all hospitals are full, bodies lie in heaps), and the gruesomeness of the rape (bellies ripped open and swollen). Some details of the gender violence, such as bodies of the rape victims "lying in streets," emphasize the public aspect of the rapes and their collective, "gang rape" nature. Another description from the shtetl of Dmitrovka, also from May 1919, reveals that thirty women were raped in one night, including a ten-year old girl and seventy-year old women.[18] Here the narrator, Y. Teplitsky, who probably witnessed the rape (since he knew the exact number of victims and most likely knew some of them

---

15 YIVO Archive, files 163–94.
16 Ibid., file 177, 15294–327.
17 Ibid., file 166, 14163–64.
18 Ibid., file 166, 14225.

personally), focused not only on the scale but also the intensity of the violence by reporting the ages of victims, including children and elderly women.

In Elisavetgrad, a large town south of Cherkassy and Smela, a pogrom was carried out in May 1919 by Grigoriev's army. Esther Poddubnaia, who had lost half of her family in it, described the most horrible instances of rape and torture while completely omitting her own experience, though she and her daughters had personally encountered Grigoriev's soldiers. Poddubnaia, an observant Jewish woman who dictated her story without signing it during the Sabbath, recounted the experience of her next-door neighbor, the sixteen-year-old gymnasium student Donya Kagan,[19] who was raped by a group of soldiers in front of her brother. Kagan begged for death but the assailants threw her in the cellar, where she died from her injuries.[20] Poddubnaia, who considered herself lucky because she only lost her husband and some of her children, chose to relate only a few of the painful memories of violence and torture inflicted on the victims. The exceedingly brutal episode with Donya Kagan illustrated the horrors of these pogroms, but it was not the worst. Poddubnaia also revealed other terrible details about gender violence, how rapists tortured some of their other victims by cutting off breasts and ripping open their bellies. Poddubnaia, in choosing the most gruesome and shocking details, included Kagan's pleas for death. She agreed to provide Kagan's name since Donya had died; thus, her reputation could not be harmed. Yet she also chose to emphasize Kagan's gymnasium education by way of a description of her. Poddubnaia's story is valuable because, together with similar accounts of gender violence, it fits precisely in the patterns of how pogroms unfolded and were perceived.

The White Army, as the major pogrom perpetrators from the summer of 1919, were better trained, had more experience, and were more brutally efficient. In addition, the new pogrom perpetrators sought to exceed the prior level of physical and emotional suffering inflicted on Jews. Reports of rape increased respectively. Several factors contributed to their greater detail, among them the resulting epidemic of venereal diseases[21] that increased the need for medical supplies and had therefore to be communicated to relief organizations. At the same time, the scope of gender violence grew out of proportion and could not be easily dismissed. And the sheer exasperation of the survivors and inspectors alike, who did not know how to comprehend and process the horrors of gender

---

19 See the discussion in the previous chapter.
20 YIVO Archive, file 166, 14163.
21 The definition employed by Tcherikower himself: Cherikover, *Antisemitizm.*

violence, compelled them to begin talking about rape despite all the social and moral taboos.

Narratives of the horrors of rape therefore became more detailed and explicit. Borzna, a shtetl to the northeast of Kiev that changed hands nine times between the Bolsheviks and the White Army, suffered a vicious pogrom after the White Army finally took over by the end of August 1919.[22] The Hussars of Death, as the pogrom perpetrators called themselves, stripped young Jewish girls naked before brutally gang raping them in front of their families and other spectators. Jews were publicly murdered, tortured, and humiliated, and by the end of the pogrom only one hundred Jewish families out of three hundred fifty survived. Similar atrocities were reported from almost all pogrom-stricken Jewish communities, from small shtetls to large towns. Some reports and witness narratives included information about the rape victims. In the case of Monastyrische, a narrative highlighted a happy escape from imminent rape: Nesya Fridman, a sixth-grade gymnasium student, pretended to be dead and lay in the street while Cossacks kicked her, regretting that they could not rape "such a good looking *zhidovochka* (kike girl)."[23] Several reports, like the one from the large town of Korsun, named rape victims and described their ordeals but left out the victims' responses and even the conclusion of their story: the fifteen-year-old daughter of one Sigalov was raped many times in front of her wounded parents, who were finally killed after witnessing the torture of their daughter.[24]

A report from Fastov, a large town with a former Jewish population of over ten thousand, begins the account of the September 1919 pogrom with a description of three railway carriages of wounded pogrom victims that arrived in the Kiev hospital bearing rape victims as young as eight years old.[25] Some died soon after. Inspector Rabinovich mentions that over half of the wounded Jews from Fastov were very emotionally distraught and demonstrated symptoms of psychosis, especially rape victims. Similar reports were coming from all over Ukraine. Sometimes, as in Rakitino,[26] the narrator went as far as to name the victims and described what was done to them. In Kremenchug,[27] a pogrom

22 YIVO Archive, file 206, 18272–87.
23 Ibid., file 208, 18649–54.
24 Ibid., file 208, 18536–58.
25 Miljakova, *Kniga Pogromov*, 253.
26 YIVO Archive, file 209, 18762–64.
27 Ibid., file 208, 18559–89.

inspector actually briefly questioned rape victims and their families—the first attempt at this kind of research.

The aforementioned Smela and Cherkassy cases were a part of a conscious effort to compile information about mass rape. At the same time, these reports generally followed the pattern of reporting on the rape phenomenon that swelled out of proportion by the end of 1919. The personal efforts of the pogrom researchers who sought to investigate gender violence enriched the evidence pool, but still described eventualities that were very similar to what was happening all over Ukraine. The emotional responses to the pogroms became a prominent feature of the pogrom reporting. Indicating the educational level of the victims of rape appears to be a widely employed method of description. The way the traumatic experience of rape was recorded suggests that Jewish women exposed to secularism through education responded to their ordeal in a way somewhat different from the other victims.

Exposure to secular education impacted interiority by introducing a common set of intellectual and moral values and imperatives.[28] Secularism, with its emphasis on individualism, is a deeply personal way to experience the world and, while the notion of "modernity" cannot be fully applied here without information about victims' religious adherence, secular education is certainly a key indicator of engagement in the modernization process. Concepts like privacy and personal space further reinforce the enhancement of subjectivity. As feminist scholar Rita Felski argues, "modernity" does not refer simply to "substantive socio-historical phenomena," but to the "experience of temporality and historical consciousness."[29] For secularized Jewish women caught in pogrom gender violence, this set of emotional responses inevitably colored their experiences of trauma. Leitmotifs of predators chasing prey and the predators' unleashing of a metaphorical beast within pervade virtually all narratives of secularized Jewish men and women alike, in contrast to those of other witnesses.

An excerpt from the description of the violence that took place during the pogrom in Smela in December 1919 is indicative of both pogrom reporting and schematization:

> I ran into the dining room, where a Cossack with a crimson face was placing a drawn blade against my sister's throat, demanding money and jewelry.

---

28 Welzel, "Individual Modernity," 185.
29 Rita Felski, *The Gender of Modernity* (Cambridge, MA: Harvard University Press, 2009), 9.

I rushed to her but they pushed me towards my mother's bedroom. I heard her moaning and ran to her bedroom. There one Cossack was fixing a rope to the ceiling light hook and preparing a noose for my brother-in-law. At the time, they were whipping him all over, he was lying almost senseless on the floor by the overturned dresser. I ran to the Cossack and snatched the rope from him. He whipped me in turn and went to another room. In the meantime they started to beat up a boy, my nephew, right on the bed of my sick mother. My niece was sick with typhoid, but they took the blanket off her, and forced some kind of powder into my mother's eyes. All that time anything and everything was being taken out of the house—food, linen—and they were still raping the girls. One of the girls, a student of the University courses, was raped by five Cossacks. Then the sixth [Cossack] was taking her from the study to the kitchen when suddenly he left her there and ran away. Another girl, a fifteen-year-old gymnasium student, was raped by three villains. The poor things tried to hide in the room of the telephone operator, who was renting [a room] from us, but she threw them out. The rest of the girls managed to flee into the garden.[30]

This testimony was provided by Dr. Sara Margolin as part of the research effort by Rekis, who interviewed doctors in Smela and Cherkassy. Dr. Margolin described the pogrom action in her house, where apparently she treated the sick and wounded. This excerpt consists of two stylistically different parts: in the first, she described torture of her male and female relatives; and in the second the rape of a number of women in her house. Significant movement and dynamics distinguish the first part of the story. Dr. Margolin used the verb "to run" three times in a few sentences to portray her own movement around the violent scene. In the second part of the paragraph, however, Dr. Margolin's narrative becomes more sketchy, with obvious gaps in the story. She utilizes motion verbs to describe actions of perpetrators and abettors, while the failed attempt to hide was the only depiction of movement attributed to the rape victims. Similarly, in this paragraph and the previous one, the actions and emotional response to violence are attributed predominantly to the tortured, but not raped, victims, witnesses, and perpetrators. Dr. Margolin's mother watches the beating of her son with "numb despair";[31] the Cossacks are "burning with

---

30   Miljakova, *Kniga Pogromov*, 332–33.
31   Ibid., 331.

hatred"[32] and disgust. Dr. Margolin herself rushes around the house in "mad desperation,"[33] while the victims of rape cry for help or attempt "to resist while being dragged."[34]

Dr. Margolin talks about the victims of rape in the passive voice and refrains from discussing victims' reactions altogether. The narrator, like Tcherikower and his contemporaries, invokes stiff clichés like "screams of the unfortunate,"[35] commonly employed to portray and yet also camouflage the gender violence. Such expressions served to highlight her own despair rather than define the victim's behavior. Dr. Margolin, a secularized and educated Jewish woman herself, did indicate the education level of rape victims, but ultimately refrained from commenting on their emotional state. Secular education may have been a way for the narrator to identify with the victims. She could empathize with the suffering of her patients and relatives, although the experience she described could very well have been her own. Dr. Margolin's story suggests that she was spared from rape, but this should not be taken for granted. As Dr. Margolin employs the strategy of omission in describing her ordeal,[36] circumstantial evidence may provide certain clues to her story.

An anonymous doctor from Cherkassy who left a poignant description of his and his wife's experience during the pogrom in Cherkassy, in August and December 1919,[37] mentioned briefly that his female colleagues and relatives of medical profession were raped, but intentionally omitted any further details. The doctor's evidence suggests that neither belonging to the medical profession nor, judging by the reports from other towns like Borzna[38] and Kremenchug,[39] social status protected Jewish women from rape. Likewise, some female medical workers in Smela were sexually assaulted along with other Jewish women, as Dr. Margolin herself attests.[40] Extrapolation of the contextual evidence in Dr. Margolin's story suggests the narrator herself was a victim of gender violence. Her choice of language is indicative of her experience as a witness or a victim: exceedingly reticent yet needing to communicate the ordeal nonetheless. In addition, Dr. Margolin uses similar emotional

32 Ibid.
33 Ibid., 332.
34 Ibid.
35 Ibid.
36 Discussed in the previous chapter.
37 YIVO Archives, file 210, 19019–26.
38 Ibid., file 206, 18272–87.
39 Ibid., file 208, 18559–89.
40 Miljakova, *Kniga Pogromov*, 333.

language to that of the other secularized narrators, male and female alike. For example, she employs numerous animalistic allegories to reflect her emotional experience. She describes the "wild animals' faces"[41] of pogrom perpetrators, and herself as a "hunted animal."[42] The hunting metaphor is reinforced by the bloodlust of the leading officer: "Suddenly he turned to me [Dr. Margolin] and said that he had already butchered many people and that he was a regular surgeon when it came to severing heads neatly, even better than a real doctor."[43]

The gymnasium student Teitelbaum, who survived the pogrom in Kiev in October 1919, described her encounter with White Army officers and soldiers who ransacked her apartment and abused her family in a similar way. Confronted by the pogrom perpetrators operating under the command of an officer, and not having managed to follow her mother, who escaped, she recalls: "I was so scared to see those furious faces and the revolvers drawn [at me], that I became petrified and stood there stunned, rooted to the spot."[44] Teitelbaum conveys her pogrom experience through descriptions of imminent terror and the miraculous escape of her family members, while seeming to understate her own experience. She admits only to an attempted assault, as the lieutenant grabbed her and tried to drag her somewhere, but maintains that she managed to flee to the attic and hide there.[45] The similarity of the escape pattern in the victims' narratives suggests that Teitelbaum, like Dr. Margolin, may have indeed been sexually assaulted. According to Teitelbaum's version of events, the lieutenant boasted: "I am an intelligent person [belong to the intelligentsia], but when I see Jewish blood I feel moral satisfaction. It's nothing to kill a person [by shooting]; the true pleasure is to stab them."[46] What shocks the young girl is the horrific, visceral aspect of the violence being committed intentionally by this self-proclaimed intelligent person, who treated Jews as slaughter animals and enjoyed behaving like a butcher himself. Both women were appalled by the voluntary degradation of a human to the level of an animal predator, as expressed in his beastly craving for blood, the intense yearning to inflict death by his own hand.

---

41 Ibid., 332.
42 Ibid., 333.
43 Ibid., 332.
44 Ibid., 309.
45 Ibid., 310.
46 Ibid.

"The vicious and wild scenes of tortures, murders, violence, humiliation and rapes were unfolding [in front of us]"[47] is how Rekis describes a pogrom in May 1919, in a manner strikingly similar to the two secularized Jewish women quoted above. Rekis invokes adjectives like "wild," "visceral," "slaughter," and "beastly" to depict pogrom perpetrators who, in his view, did not belong to the world of human beings. He fears that pogrom violence, and the witnessing of it, reduced him as well to the level of an animal. Time after time Rekis compares himself to hunted prey crouching at the bottom of the ravine or to a meager worm crawling in the dark.

Rekis's use of language is also similar to that of an anonymous Jewish doctor from Cherkassy, known only by his initials A. K., whose story of his and his wife's suffering during the two last pogroms in Cherkassy in August and December 1919 is replete with metaphors like "the wild animal face" or "visceral, beastly fear."[48] Forced to hide in the pit behind the garden in August, the doctor watched his pregnant wife, a dentist herself, moving with difficulty through overgrown vegetation, and felt hunted, small, reduced to crouching in a nook, unable to protect himself or his poor wife. He felt his despair like physical pain in his chest, and he wanted to die. He was lost under the enormous sky, eerily alone amid the large blooming town. Frightened to death, he and his wife said their goodbyes, anticipating that the circle of violent screams of tortured people and raped women that grew closer and closer would swallow them.[49] They tried to find shelter in the house of a Russian colleague, but the latter's wife didn't want to protect Jews and risk their own security. The doctor described not only his unwilling hostess's antisemitic rhetoric but also her wild stare and the way she threatened them with a knife,[50] reminiscent of the experience communicated by secularized female survivors.

Rekis utilized the same imagery as the secularized Jewish women, but enhanced it with a portrayal of their emotional experience, which is muted in female narratives. Feeling like prey cornered by wild beasts, Jewish men projected their fear and despair onto natural settings on the one hand and civilization on the other. The Cherkassy doctor looked at the starry night far above him and smelled the fragrant blooming gardens, but felt utterly insignificant and forlorn in the large town that suddenly became "alien"[51] to him. He felt

47 YIVO Archive, file 183, 15904.
48 Ibid., file 210, 19020–21.
49 Ibid., file 210, 19021.
50 Ibid., file 210, 19020.
51 Ibid., file 210, 19020 reverse.

betrayed by the whole world and banished from it, while still acknowledging its powerful beauty. Rekis escaped a bloody pogrom and described the beauty of the nature in stark contrast to his traumatic experience, which was quoted at the beginning of the chapter. Like the Cherkassy doctor who observed the sky from the pit, Rekis experienced the overwhelming dissonance between the pogrom violence and the unadorned beauty of the world. Secularized narrators tended to communicate their emotional experience by juxtaposing pogrom violence against their worldview, which was defined by two powerful markings: the world's natural beauty, on one hand, and civilization as the culmination of the betterment of mankind, on the other. Rekis exposed a horrifying cognitive dissonance that threatened his fundamental values: how this primeval violence could in any way be related to him, an educated, modern human being. Rekis felt the clash with violent barbarity in his mind and his very soul, and was tormented by his near-death experience:

> Faraway, forgotten pictures rose in front of my eyes, as powerful as delirium or feverish fantasies, and enveloped the wild, impossible reality—that I survived: Europe, world cities, full of vigorous activity, science, industry, masses of people engaged in peaceful toil and the commonwealth of agreeing and disagreeing, mutual trust and respect, your life and that of the others being of equal value, and the society being trustworthy, secure, at once your powerful guardian and confessor.[52]

Rekis had returned to Ukraine from France, where he first received his education, and stayed as a political emigrant. His powerful imagery and lively language communicated the shattering effect of barbaric violence that appeared to exist alongside civilization. He was haunted by the inadequacy of his own personal experience, which included his European education and familiarity with technical progress and the comforts of a society composed of people like himself. These tools were insufficient to make sense of the beastly and visceral archaic violence of the pogroms. The barbarity that had been unleashed had no place in Rekis's world, and he had no means to comprehend it. Female narrators similarly conveyed the dramatic rupture in their worldview caused by pogroms. But as a rule, they used subtler metaphors and avoided grand allusions to illustrate the demoralizing transformation of the human into a beast.

The gymnasium student Teitelbaum was also shocked by the existence of the crude barbarity of pogrom violence alongside civilized society. Teitelbaum

---

52   Ibid., file 183, 15901 reverse.

claimed that she escaped the assault by the pogrom perpetrators by running and hiding in the attic with her father. At this point, however, Teitelbaum cut her own story short abruptly, claiming that it is impossible to communicate all the horror of her experience, though in the previous paragraphs she was very detailed. It is probable that she did not want to disclose some parts of her ordeal and focused on the later episode that shocked her the most. In the last paragraph, Teitelbaum quoted the officer who boasted about pleasure of knifing Jews with his own hands.[53] She concluded with an observation that the same group of pogrom perpetrators enjoyed fancy carriage rides and leisurely strolls in a very nonchalant manner.[54] Teitelbaum reiterated this episode in two sentences, word for word, clearly shocked to observe her assailants remaining apparently unconcerned about the atrocities they had committed. She could not comprehend how the visceral violence was possible within the civilized world, and was staggered to see her assailants shamelessly and casually enjoying life as if they had not committed the most brutal, violent acts. Leisurely strolls in public symbolized the achievements of civilization, so elaborately and passionately described by Rekis. The shameless behavior of the officer who prided himself on his bloodthirst was in radical juxtaposition to Teitelbaum's own ethical values, and this incongruity greatly traumatized her.

The drastic disjuncture between anticipated behavior and reality defined Dr. Margolin's narrative as well. Dr. Margolin began with a description of the mounting tension in anticipation of the pogrom; however, when the officers and Cossacks entered her home, they first had tea with her and engaged in rather intelligent conversation. Dr. Margolin specifically mentioned that the officer, who flirted with her two Russian tenants and who joined them for tea, had studied at the Technical University.[55] Education appeared to be a significant marker for the narrator, something that she valued and could relate to. But what was so shocking for Dr. Margolin was that education in no way guaranteed civilized behavior. Once the officer finished his tea, instead of saying "thank you," he ordered his troops to commence the pogrom and proceeded to commit violence in her house. Dr. Margolin observed the officer, in a matter of seconds, become transformed from a gallant, intelligent man into a beast:

> [T]he former Technical University student set about looting in the most earnest fashion. Upon seeing me he showed me that one of his pockets

---

53 Miljakova, *Kniga Pogromov*, 310.
54 Ibid.
55 Ibid., 331.

was full of gold and silver, and he kept taking knickknacks and various items from the dresser and putting them into his pockets. I reminded him of his words when he said that his presence in our house guaranteed us safety both personal and material. He answered: "It's a whole different story now," and proceeded to loot my room, which they had not ransacked yet.[56]

Next, the violence gyrated completely out of any comprehensive boundaries and turned into a nightmare that repeated itself over and over.[57] Dr. Margolin decided to quit her looted and smashed house, which looked "terrible," but she remarked that "we [looked] even more terrible, impacted by our suffering."[58] Following the excruciating night spent by Smela Jews in anticipation of further violence, a Bolshevik avant-garde came into town and brought the wounded to the hospital. Dr. Margolin concluded her story in several clipped sentences. First, she said, many Jews were murdered and tortured to death. Then, she said, in almost all the Jewish homes "were [found] raped girls, women and even children, and their number was huge."[59] Then, on the next day, the main Bolshevik forces entered the "tormented town."[60] Dr. Margolin's evidence, despite being full of gruesome depictions of violence, focused on the unbearable emotional suffering that resulted from the traumatic experience of pogrom. Dr. Margolin's narrative structure and imagery clearly communicated that the brutal rape of Jewish women during pogrom was the ultimate heinous crime and the embodiment of the most wild and ruthless violence. Mass rape was, nevertheless, intentionally employed by pogrom perpetrators as the culmination of the violent carnival. Secularized Jewish women exposed to gender violence personally or as spectators experienced a severe rupture in their worldview, and were singled out by the pogrom reporters because of their dramatic responses to rape.

Although female narrators camouflaged their private experience, secularized men who shared the same ethical values and principles demonstrated an ability to empathize with female suffering and even comprehend it. Rekis conveyed his experience as a pogrom survivor in an eighty-page typed manuscript. With keen sensibility, he expressed his own inner turmoil, and related deeply

---

56 Ibid., 331–32.
57 Ibid., 333.
58 Ibid.
59 Ibid.
60 Ibid.

and sincerely to what was in his eyes the most acute form of wild barbarity, rape. He tried to narrate both his own experience and that of Jewish women. His evidence is unique and extremely significant for two main reasons. First, unlike most of his contemporaries, Rekis demonstrated acute awareness of gender violence, investigating and collecting materials about the mass rape of Jewish women and paying close attention to the gender experience of violence in his own writings, which provided extraordinary insight. Second, Rekis conscientiously and meticulously recorded his own emotional reactions to the tragic ordeal, and made it his goal to highlight emotions when interviewing others. As a result, his evidence crossed gender lines and shed light on the specific challenges of secularized individuals who found themselves in the midst of a carnival of violence.

In attempting to convey the catastrophe caused by rape, Rekis struggled with taboos that made public discussion of sexual violence difficult. His writings reflect his internal conundrum, as he moves some of the rape descriptions to the footnotes and demands secrecy from the Editorial Board.[61] Rekis struggled to express the enormity of the trauma of rape through reference to universally recognized values, such as victims' beauty and prospective marriages. Dr. Shendarevsky, from Cherkassy, similarly underscored the tragedy of rape by noting the beauty of his patients: two young rape victims Shlif, nineteen, and Panorova, eighteen, died from home abortions.[62] As another attempt to communicate the devastating effect of rape on Jewish women, Rekis clearly connects the traumatic experience and suicidal behavior, as do the doctors he interviewed in Cherkassy and Smela.

Harboring suicidal thoughts and begging for death, as well as actual suicide, became the leitmotif of numerous pogrom reports, signaling the extremes of the emotional responses of rape victims. The doctors' inquiries collected by Rekis suggest that the group of women usually defined by their exposure to secular education was thoroughly traumatized yet had fewer coping mechanisms compared to some other victims.[63] The dual nature of secularization, which encompassed both commonly shared ethical values and an extremely private experience of the world, shaped the way in which rape was experienced by secularized Jewish women. Bergoffen argued that "the rapes were calculated to expose and exploit the women's unique vulnerability— the fragility of their

---

61 See full quote in the previous chapter. YIVO Archive, file 183, 15904 reverse.
62 Ibid., 355.
63 Ibid., 342.

honor."[64] As mentioned, mass rape was often the focal point of the pogrom carnival, as in Rossava[65] or in the small shtetl Bobrovitsy, where pogrom perpetrators waited until after the pogrom for the Jewish population to assemble in the cemetery to bury their dead, in order to return and rape the fifteen-year-old daughter of the local *shammes* in front of the crowd.[66] Public spectacle aimed to maximize the shame experienced by the victim and the victimized community, in order to inflict emotional suffering in addition to physical torture.

The politics of shame attaches emotions to the body of the raped, making it an object of disgust, abjection, and hatred. According to Ahmed, disgust marks its subject as being subhuman.[67] Stripping victims of their humanity and reinforcing their subservience is a prime objective of genocidal rape. Physical violation of the female body turns it into a hateful and repulsive object. In the theater of pogrom and amid the spectacle of rape, the raped woman becomes her own spectator and her own tormentor, subjected to the Lacanian gaze[68] that makes the body of the raped disgusting. This positions the raped woman to despise her own body, to neglect it and want to kill it.[69] While shame is a shared encounter,[70] the experience of it became private, all the more so for women who internalized the secularist concept of privacy, an intrinsic and defining quality of modernity.

The internal and solitary experience of self-hatred and revulsion against the backdrop of a shattered sense of the world seems to have led some secularized Jewish women to take their lives. Dr. Gandlevsky of Smela[71] and Dr. Shendarevsky of Cherkassy[72] reported isolated cases of suicide among rape victims, and there are a number of other cases reported across pogrom-stricken Ukraine. Although no comprehensive statistics are available, it is rather clear that the suicides did not represent a widespread response. Nevertheless, references to death as an indication of internal upheaval are widely invoked in the personal narratives and reports. There are multiple accounts of Jewish women

64 Bergoffen, *Contesting the Politics of Genocidal Rape*, 22.
65 YIVO Archive, file 210, 18871.
66 Ibid., file 206, 18233–40.
67 Ahmed, *Cultural Politics of Emotion*, 96–97.
68 Lacan, *The Split between the Eye*.
69 Ahmed, *Cultural Politics of Emotion*, 86.
70 Ibid., 103.
71 Miljakova, *Kniga Pogromov*, 342.
72 Ibid., 354.

begging for death in fear of rape,[73] during rape,[74] or after the rape.[75] Death became a part of everyday life during pogroms. Frequently the bodies of the murdered Jews would be described as lying in "heaps," like in Gorodische, where heaps of raped women with their bellies cut open "lay around."[76] The seemingly endless sequence of pogroms and the commonality of death made the close ending of life to appear to be almost inevitable and preferable to the constant terror and fear of suffering to come. The dread of imminent suffering and death sometimes drove men and women insane. In Krivoe Ozero a Jewish woman, who was not named but referred to by her initials F. K., was hiding from pogrom perpetrators in the cellar with other Jews. In a fit of madness she suffocated her own infant to prevent him being tortured by *pogromschiki* and to protect fellow Jews, who would be discovered if the baby were to cry.[77]

The doctor from Cherkassy wished for death during the August pogrom, and mentioned it twice in the course of two pages. He cursed the predicament of being forced to hide in a pit and envied even a dog, because animals could not experience his excruciating fear and dread of the violence to come. The anticipation was "unbearable," making a swift death an attractive option.[78] When describing the pogrom in December, the doctor mentions his wife also hoping for death twice during their ordeal. While the doctor wished for death in abstract terms, comparing himself to hunted prey, his wife, who had given birth since the August pogrom, expressed her plea in a more concrete way. Twice she begged him for poison in order not to die "in the hands of bandits."[79] Considering the doctor's repeated references to the brutal rape of Jewish women around them, his wife probably feared rape more than death, considering poison to be a preferable alternative.

Secularized Jewish men who were designated to witness the public spectacle of rape responded in a manner quite similar to that of secularized Jewish women. A report by inspector Lifshitz, who assessed the pogrom in Pechara after having survived it himself[80] reflected on the devastating effects of gender violence, concluding his short report with the following episode,

73 YIVO Archive, file 208, 18583.
74 Ibid., file 210, 18871.
75 Ibid., file 183, 15904 reverse.
76 Ibid., file 166, 14121–74.
77 Ibid., file 209, 18590–616.
78 Ibid., file 210, 19020–21.
79 Ibid., file 210, 19025–26.
80 Quoted in full in the previous chapter. Miljakova, *Kniga Pogromov*, 158.

as mentioned earlier: "One of the pogrom victims and survivors, a student named Efim Israelevich Kogan, who by accidental chance survived the pogrom alive, poisoned himself with arsenic. He was revived in the local hospital. After six months he has poisoned himself again, unable to endure the horrors of the pogrom that he witnessed."[81] Jewish men who experienced gender violence as witnesses were also deeply traumatized. The student Kogan from Pechara, like some other patients of the Cherkassy and Smela doctors, unable to cope with the violence he observed, committed suicide.

Secularized Jewish women who did manage to cope with the rape that they experienced, or possibly avoided, did not elaborate on their fear, shame, devastation, and despair, as did the doctor's wife from Cherkassy (her husband did not mention her describing her emotional turmoil in any detail). Some narratives provided by Jewish men who, like Rekis, encountered gender violence can serve as a reference point for the female emotional experience. Emblematic of the effect of mass rape on a Jewish man is the diary of the educated Jewish man P. Deichman, who witnessed the pogrom in Kremenchug in August 1919: "You sit with your eyes fixed dumbly on nothing. The nerves are so shattered that any steps, any slight sound at all seem like an artillery barrage. The apathy is taking over. You are losing the ability to react. It all looks so natural. The destruction, the rape, the abuse, the looting. . . . How can it be otherwise. . . ."[82]

Mass rape experienced by Jewish women during pogroms inflicted tremendous physical and emotional suffering that affirmed the feeling of deterioration and depression described by Deichman. The profoundly solitary experience of the rupturing of one's worldview, the extreme shame and the feeling of violation, and the utter dearth of socially acceptable ways to express one's emotions drove secularized Jewish women to the only available option: to abandon the place of the tragedy, if not their life altogether. For many Jewish women, escape became the ultimate solution to dealing with traumatic experience. Dr. Shendarevskaia, who treated victims of rape in Cherkassy, observed that "the moral state of the victims is still subdued, many of them try to leave the places that are haunted by the horrible memories."[83] After the Civil War, as Ukraine became Soviet, the Jewish population, free from the legal restrictions imposed on them by the Russian Empire, could now move to the larger

81   Ibid.
82   Ibid., 221.
83   Ibid., 355.

towns and cities, strive for a better life, and attempt to leave behind the horrible memories.[84]

Many Jewish women who moved away from the terrible memories nevertheless carried traumatic experiences with them that would impact lives for generations to come. For Jewish women exposed to secular education, the experience of the trauma of gender violence resulted in a special kind of upheaval since, according to Felski, women's experiences of the world and their role in it had undergone a more dramatic transformation as the patriarchal basis of society began to crumble.[85] During the pogroms in Ukraine in 1917–21, Jewish women exposed to secular education responded in a unique way to the barbaric, archaic violence that ruptured their interiority, which had been based on commonly shared ethical values. The individualistic nature of secularization only amplified the suffering among secularized Jewish women and men alike, making them the perfect victims of genocidal rape. When integrating mass rape of Jewish women during the pogroms into the larger picture of twentieth-century genocidal rape,[86] the victims' exposure to secularism should be thus taken as a key factor in the manner in which sexual violence was deployed.

Rekis found his personal redemption in dedicated and thorough research of gender violence during the pogroms and in engagement in the underground work to aid Jewish refugees leaving Ukraine following the pogroms.[87] On the list of Jews murdered during pogroms in May 1919 in the Cherkassy region he wrote: "This list does not include an account of the wretched victims of another kind, the kind that might be even more wretched than those murdered—the raped and tortured women."[88] For many women who were raped during pogroms, and for others who witnessed it, rape was much worse than death, because death ended the suffering, but rape just started it.

---

84 Bemporad, *Legacy of Blood*, with author's permission.
85 Felski, *The Gender of Modernity*, 9.
86 Bergoffen, *Contesting the Politics of Genocidal Rape*; Jeffrey S. Kopstein and Jason Wittenberg, "Intimate Violence: Anti-Jewish Pogroms."
87 "World Socialist Union of Jewish Workers—Poalei, Zion," Microfiches 565–73.
88 YIVO Archive, file 251, 23963.

CONCLUSION

In modern scholarship, a pogrom is recognized as a violent riot that follows a definitive script and is directed at a minority that is not necessarily Jewish.[1] The return of the pogrom to modern history can be traced back to the anti-Jewish violence during the Civil War in Ukraine in 1917–21. During the pogroms in Ukraine, for the first time in history the archaic script of a pogrom became adapted to accommodate genocidal violence and to increase its aggregate damage to the widest extent possible. A pogrom permits its perpetrators an intimate involvement with the victims that enables the assailants to receive gratification and fulfill their agenda, while inflicting disgrace and humiliation on their victims. Ultimately, the pogrom is utilized as a form of genocidal violence that aims to ensure social death along with the physical extermination of the targeted community. Among the dehumanizing pogrom practices, the genocidal rape emerges as the most powerful strategic weapon that inflicts maximum harm onto a community through the spectacle of mass rape and continues to function almost indefinitely, as the traumatic effect is passed from generation to generation.

The disaster of the pogroms of 1917–21 has been overshadowed by the rapid and dramatic social and political developments in interwar Europe, and subsumed within the unprecedented genocide of Jewish people during the Holocaust. The history of pogroms was lost in the chaos of the Russian Civil War, the history of which has been streamlined and canonized by the Soviets,[2] while the official Ukrainian historiography has downplayed the problem,[3] and the pogroms have completely disappeared from the modern legacy of the White movement.[4] The term "pogrom" automatically connected anti-Jewish violence during the Civil War to previous waves of pogroms. The fact that the pogrom

---

1   Ghassem-Fachandi, *Pogrom in Gujarat*.
2   Bemporad, *Legacy of Blood*, with author's permission.
3   Volodymyr Serhiichuk, *Pohromy v Ukraïni, 1914–1920: Vid Shtuchnykh Stereotypiv do Hirkoï Pravdy, Prykhovuvanoï v Radiañskykh Arkhivakh* (Kiev: Vyd-vo im. O. Telihy, 1998); Yekelchyk, *Ukraine: Birth of a Modern Nation*.
4   V. Tsvetkov, "Beloe Dvizhenie v Rossii. 1917–1920 gody," *Voprosy Istorii* (2000).

rationale, employed by various and often opposing groups of pogrom perpetrators, was unequivocally political and branded Jews as Bolsheviks, also clouded the understanding of pogrom violence for a long time. Not only does the high death toll of the pogroms distinguish them from previous waves of pogroms in 1881–83 and 1903 and 1905, but also the "new" pogroms are defined by the genocidal strategy of anti-Jewish violence. It would never be possible to account for all of the victims of rape during the pogroms with any degree of accuracy, as shame silences rape victims and witnesses alike. However, the essence of genocidal rape is that it victimizes the whole community without any exceptions: every woman who was raped, every woman who miraculously escaped rape, and every member of the Jewish community of Ukraine who saw rape or even heard of it became its victims.

What distinguishes the Jewish community of Ukraine that suffered pogrom violence during the Civil War from other victimized communities that experienced genocidal rape during the other conflicts of twentieth century is that the Jews of Ukraine, who survived the turbulent years of the Civil War, have stopped being the Jewish community of Ukraine. When pogroms broke out in Ukraine, it was a country that struggled to gain independence from the former Russian Empire and to build a new democratic state that would guarantee and respect the rights of minorities. Pogroms surged tremendously during 1919, and by the beginning of 1920 the pogrom wave began to slowly subside. The Red Army forced its enemies to the south and to the west, growing in numbers as it moved. Many former soldiers of the White Army, the Ukrainian National Army, and various gangs chose to join the winning side, but they did not change their attitudes or practices. From 1920 and through 1922 anti-Jewish violence in Ukraine began to slow down notwithstanding that during those years violent pogroms had sprung up all over Ukraine, carried out by regiments of the Red Army, now supplemented with former pogrom perpetrators. However, the Red Army, in accordance with the Soviet principles of internationalism and equality, continued to prosecute pogrom instigators and perpetrators, and gradually the pogroms abated. What remained of Ukrainian Jewry, which had already lost a significant part of its population to pogroms, was reduced to extreme poverty. Many shtetls were destroyed, never to be rebuilt. A lot of Jews left their pogrom-stricken homes and tried to escape to other countries. A refugee crisis overwhelmed border areas. Many Jewish political activists, political parties, and relief organizations struggled to help the desperate refugees by all means possible: Rekis, the valiant activist of Poalei Zion who contributed significantly to the Editorial Board's archival effort, personally helped scores of Jewish refugees cross the border into Romania.[5] Many Jews moved to Kiev and other larger cities in Ukraine, while others, especially the younger generation, moved to large cities in Russia, since there were no more restrictions on migration. Young educated Jews flocked to the capitals to start a new life, and overall they succeeded in this.[6] Moreover, the country itself was now different. Ukraine became the Ukrainian Socialist Republic, the first one to join Russia in the newly formed Union of the Soviet Socialist Republics, established at the very end of 1922. There was no longer any place for traditional Jewish community within the socialist state. Aggressive antireligious propaganda and Yiddish-language socialist education and cultural policies created a new entity—Soviet Jewry.[7] This new Soviet Jewry in the making demonstrated remarkable upward mobility, which was promoted, on the one hand, by the abundance of opportunities that were previously unavailable, and on the other hand, by the very strong impulse to leave behind the terrible tragedy of pogroms.[8] The Jews, spurred by the haunting memories, made every possible conscious effort to break from the past. This was the crucible in which the new identity of the Soviet Jews was forged.

Even though there was no Jewish community, in the traditional understanding of this word, left to experience the social death triggered by the pogroms, and specifically by genocidal rape, the traumatic effect of rape did not evaporate. The emerging rich and diverse historiography that discusses the identity of the Soviet Jewry[9] establishes the lost continuity between rape trauma and its reflections in the history of the Soviet Jews.[10] As Jews became increasingly mobile in the Soviet Union, there were a lot of intermarriages

5 "World Socialist Union of Jewish Workers—Poalei Zion."
6 Anna Shternshis, *When Sonia Met Boris: An Oral History of Jewish Life under Stalin* (Oxford: Oxford University Press, 2017); Yuri Slezkine, *The Jewish Century* (Princeton, NJ: Princeton University Press, 2004).
7 Anna Shternshis, *Soviet and Kosher: Jewish Popular Culture in the Soviet Union, 1923–1939* (Bloomington: Indiana University Press, 2006), 182.
8 On pogroms and the making of Soviet Jewry, see the first chapter of the book by Bemporad, *Legacy of Blood*, with author's permission.
9 New research into history of Soviet Jewry bridges the gap and allows a connection to be established between pogrom rape trauma and Soviet Jewish Identity: Shternshis, *When Sonia Met Boris*; Shternshis, *Soviet and Kosher*; Anna Shternshis, "Between Life and Death: Why Some Soviet Jews Decided to Leave and Others to Stay in 1941," *Kritika: Explorations in Russian and Eurasian History* 15, no. 3 (2014); Jeffrey Veidlinger, *In the Shadow of the Shtetl: Small-Town Jewish Life in Soviet Ukraine* (Bloomington: Indiana University Press, 2013); and Olga Gershenson and David Shneer, "Soviet Jewishness and Cultural Studies," *Journal of Jewish Identities* 4, no. 1 (2011).
10 Although special research would be crucial to study this connection.

between Jews from different communities of the former Pale, as Jews largely preferred to marry Jews,[11] and so the trauma of pogrom rape spread wide and lay silently at the foundation of Soviet Jewry.

Archival materials provide some insight into the post-traumatic behavior of pogrom survivors. Jewish women who escaped the pogrom-stricken or completely destroyed shtetls had only one option for dealing with trauma: concealing it, and they moved far away to find the solace of concealment. For many Jewish women, especially educated ones, escape became the ultimate solution to deal with the traumatic experience. Dr. Shendarevskaia, who treated victims of rape in Cherkassy, observed a direct connection: "[The] moral condition of the victims is still subdued, many of them try to leave the places haunted by the horrible memories."[12] In the materials collected by the Kiev Regional Commission for Relief to Victims of Pogroms for the report to the Genoa Conference on damages caused by the pogroms, there are questionnaires filled out by young Jewish women who escaped from the pogroms to Kiev. None of those young educated Jewish women, at that time living in deplorable conditions and in dire need of basic clothing and other necessities, admitted to being victims of rape, although all of them survived one or more pogroms, and more probably than not were victims of gender violence.[13] Jewish women and men alike tried to move on to new life, but Jewish men sometimes endeavored to describe their emotional state, to record how human psyche created protective barriers over the abyss of despair. Yakov Smelyansky, who survived the Cherkassy pogrom, described in his letter to his brother the scenes of carnage in the pogrom-stricken city, and the miserable state in which he found himself and his family. He concluded the description as following: "but people are brutal and despicable beasts; they put up with anything, they get used to everything; and we are amongst them."[14]

Although it appears that Soviet Jewry has succeeded in putting the trauma of rape behind it, in reality the trauma was never gone and has guided both the everyday and the life-changing decisions that Soviet Jews made. In her latest book about Soviet Jewish life, Anna Shternshis analyzes the story of a woman who was born in Uman, Ukraine in 1914. In 1919 Uman experienced a number of violent pogroms, leaving many Jews dead, many wounded, and many women raped. Although rape had never been brought up during the

---

11 Shternshis, *When Sonia Met Boris*, Part II.
12 Miljakova, *Kniga Pogromov*, 355.
13 Jewish Pogroms in Ukraine, 1918–24, File 266.
14 YIVO Archive, file 210, 19032.

interview, the respondent volunteered the story that from the time she was a young girl, unlike her brothers, she was not allowed to stay out late and was severely punished if she broke the rule. The girl's mother explained that "a man is like a glass. It can get dirty and then you clean it, and you don't know if it was dirty. A woman is like a piece of cloth, it gets dirty, it will be stained forever."[15] It is not remarkable that there were no references to the pogroms and rape during the interview: pogroms and victimhood were not part of the life story of a Soviet Jew. By itself, the story about the glass and the cloth might sound as an admonishment from a mother to a daughter about the fragility of female honor. However, when read in context of the very recent pogroms, the mother's worries and the severity of punishment clearly translate into the post-traumatic behavior of a parent terrified by the prospect of rape. The severity of reaction to an arguably minor transgression as well as overprotective parenting have been named among symptoms of enduring pogrom and rape trauma.[16] In the narratives of the Soviet Jews, references to pogroms surfaced directly when crucial decisions had to be made. During the Second World War the choice of whether to flee the hometown before the German troops would come in or stay was based on pogrom experience: a mother of two daughters who survived the pogroms when she was young chose to leave.[17] Considering that nothing was known about German policies toward Jews at the time, this decision resulted from the firm conviction that once unconstrained by the Soviet laws, the neighbors would harm the Jews and the girls would be raped. Further direct research into behavior patterns and decision-making of the Soviet Jewry would, I believe, uncover further traces of pogrom rape trauma. To test this hypothesis, I have conducted an impromptu public opinion research while writing this book: I have asked Jewish women between the age of thirty and seventy if they knew about rape during the pogroms. Although no implications were made whatsoever about the family histories of the respondents, I have received just two types of answers: either emphatic and definitive denial of the mere possibility that any of their family could ever have been a rape victim, or a family narrative of a lucky escape from rape during a pogrom by hiding in a cellar or chest, etc. This anecdotal evidence alone suggests that rape trauma has been passed on through the generations and should be thoroughly studied.

---

15 Shternshis, *When Sonia Met Boris*, 25–26.
16 Mildred Antonelli, "Intergenerational Impact of the Trauma of a Pogrom," *Journal of Loss and Trauma* 17, no. 4 (2012): 388–401; Judith L. Alpert, "Enduring Mothers, Enduring Knowledge: On Rape and History," *Contemporary Psychoanalysis* 51, no. 2 (2015): 296–311.
17 Shternshis, "Between Life and Death."

Rape trauma is transmitted not collectively but privately and silently, at the family level. Those Jews, particularly those Jewish women who fled the pogroms, had been as a rule more exposed to modernity and suffered more from the pogroms. They were the Jews who survived and succeeded in the Soviet Union, and contributed to the making of Soviet Jewry. The modernized members of the Jewish community proved to have responded more acutely to the barbaric, archaic violence than the Jews who were not exposed to modernity, because a modernized individual had to experience the rape and the spectacle of rape alone, deprived of the support mechanisms available to the community. The individualistic nature of modernization amplified the suffering among modernized Jewish women and men, making them the perfect victims of genocidal rape. When contextualizing the mass rape of Jewish women during the pogroms within the larger picture of genocidal rape during conflicts of the twentieth century,[18] the exposure to modernity of the victimized community should be considered as another factor in how sexual violence was strategically employed in those conflicts. Current research suggests that the ultimate efficiency of genocidal rape is dramatically increased by, if not based on, the modernized individuals within the victimized community, who are exceedingly susceptive of the humiliation and disgrace of mass rape, and thus fulfill the mass rape objective to the fullest. This puts forward the question of violence in its most archaic, visceral, and disgracing form of mass rape becoming a strategic weapon in modern history, because it is singularly efficient against modern humankind.

This research endeavored to place genocidal rape during the pogroms of the Civil War in Ukraine in 1917–21 into the context of global studies of gender violence and genocidal violence, and it not only expands the understanding and research of the pogroms from the perspective of Jewish history but enriches global gender and violence studies as well.

---

18 Bergoffen, *Contesting the Politics of Genocidal Rape*; Jeffrey S. Kopstein and Jason Wittenberg, "Intimate Violence: Why Do Pogroms Occur in Some Localities and Not Others?" unpublished version (2011): 6–23.

BIBLIOGRAPHY

Sources

Jewish Pogroms in Ukraine, 1918–24. "Documents of the Kiev Oblast' Commission for Relief to Victims of Pogroms (Obshetskom) (Fond 3050)." Years covered by document are 1918–21.

Miljakova, L. V., ed. *Kniga Pogromov: Pogromy na Ukraine, v Belorussii i Evropejskoj Chasti Rossii v Period Grazhdanskoj Vojny 1918–1922 gg. Sbornik Dokumentov*: ROSSPĖN, 2007.

Shamis, Feiga Mirel. *Shalom Shalom My Dear Children*. Johannesburg, 1998.

Shammas, Feyge Mirel. *The Memoir*. n/a.

World Socialist Union of Jewish Workers—Poalei Zion. "Rossiiskii tsentr khraneniia i izucheniia dokumentov noveishei istorii:" [Poalei Zion archive]: [on microfiche] IDC, Harvard Library, 1998.

YIVO Archive, Elias Tcherikower Archive 1903–1963, Rg 80–89 (Mk 470).

Bibliography

Abramson, Henry. *A Prayer for the Government: Ukrainians and Jews in Revolutionary Times, 1917–1920*. Cambridge, MA: Harvard University Press, 1999.

Ahmed, Sara. "Collective Feelings: Or, the Impressions Left by Others." *Theory, Culture & Society* 21, no. 2 (2004): 25–42.

———. *Cultural Politics of Emotion*. Edinburgh: Edinburgh University Press, 2014.

Allen, Beverly. *Rape Warfare: The Hidden Genocide in Bosnia-Herzegovina and Croatia*. Minneapolis: University of Minnesota Press, 1996.

Alpert, Judith L. "Enduring Mothers, Enduring Knowledge: On Rape and History." *Contemporary Psychoanalysis* 51, no. 2 (2015): 296–311.

Altshuler, Mordechai. "Russia and Her Jews—the Impact of the 1914 War." *The Wiener Library Bulletin* 1973/74, no. 30/31 (1973): 12–16.

———. "Ukrainian Jewish Relations in the Soviet Milieu in the Interwar Period." In *Ukrainian-Jewish Relations in Historical Perspective*. Edmonton, AB: Canadian Institute for Ukrainian Studies, University of Alberta, 1990: 281–305.

Ansky, Salomon, and Joachim Neugroschel. *The Enemy at His Pleasure: A Journey through the Jewish Pale of Settlement during World War I*. New York: Macmillan, 2002.

Antonelli, Mildred. "Intergenerational Impact of the Trauma of a Pogrom." *Journal of Loss and Trauma* 17, no. 4 (2012): 388–401.

Armer, Michael, and Allan Schnaiberg. "Measuring Individual Modernity: A Near Myth." *American Sociological Review* 37, no. 3 (1972): 301–16.

Aronson, Irwin Michael. *Troubled Waters: The Origins of the 1881 Anti-Jewish Pogroms in Russia.* Pittsburgh, PA: University of Pittsburgh Press, 1990.

Avrutin, Eugene M. "Pogroms in Russian History." *Kritika: Explorations in Russian and Eurasian History* 14, no. 3 (2013): 585–98.

Babel, Isaac, Carol J. Avins, and Harry Taylor Willetts. *1920 Diary.* New Haven, CT: Yale University Press, 2002.

Baer, Elizabeth Roberts, and Myrna Goldenberg. *Experience and Expression: Women, the Nazis, and the Holocaust.* Detroit: Wayne State University Press, 2003.

Baker, Katharine K. "Sex, Rape, and Shame." *DePaul J. Health Care L.* 8 (2004): 179.

Barkow, Jerome H., Leda Cosmides, and John Tooby. *The Adapted Mind: Evolutionary Psychology and the Generation of Culture.* Oxford: Oxford University Press, 1995.

Baskin, Judith Reesa. *Jewish Women in Historical Perspective.* Detroit: Wayne State University Press, 1998.

Beer, Daniel. "Morality and Subjectivity, 1860s–1920s." In *The Oxford Handbook of Modern Russian History.* Oxford: Oxford University Press, http://www.oxfordhandbooks.com/ view/10.1093/oxfordhb/9780199236701.001.0001/oxfordhb-9780199236701-e-018.

Beletskaia, E. M. *Kazachestvo v Narodnom Tvorchestve i v Russkoi Literature XIX veka: Monografiia.* Tver': Zolotaia bukva, 2004.

Benavot, Aaron. "Education, Gender, and Economic Development: A Cross-National Study." *Sociology of Education* 62, no. 1 (1989): 14–32.

Bergoffen, Debra B. *Contesting the Politics of Genocidal Rape: Affirming the Dignity of the Vulnerable Body.* London: Routledge, 2013.

Berk, Stephen M. *Year of Crisis, Year of Hope: Russian Jewry and the Pogroms of 1881–1882.* Westport, CT: Greenwood Press, 1985.

Berliner, Lucy, and Mary Kay Barbieri. "The Testimony of the Child Victim of Sexual Assault." *Journal of Social Issues* 40, no. 2 (1984): 125–37.

Block, Alan P. "Rape Trauma Syndrome as Scientific Expert Testimony." *Archives of Sexual Behavior* 19, no. 4 (1990): 309–23.

Bohachevsky-Chomiak, Martha. *Feminists Despite Themselves: Women in Ukrainian Community Life, 1884–1939.* Edmonton, AB: Canadian Institute for Ukrainian Studies, University of Alberta, 1988.

Brass, Paul R. *Riots and Pogroms.* New York: New York University Press, 1996.

Brown, Michelle. *The Culture of Punishment Prison, Society, and Spectacle.* New York: New York University Press, 2009.

Brownmiller, Susan. *Against Our Will: Men, Women, and Rape.* New York: Simon and Schuster, 1975.

―――. "Making Female Bodies the Battlefield." *Newsweek,* January 4 (1993): 37.

Budnitskii, Oleg. "Shots in the Back: On the Origin of the Anti-Jewish Pogroms of 1918–1921." In *Jews in the East European Borderlands. Essays in Honor of John D. Klier*, edited by Eugene M. Avrutin and Harriet Murav, 187–201. Boston: Academic Studies Press, 2012.

Budnitskii, Oleg V. *Rossijskie Evrei Mezhdu Krasnymi i Belymi (1917–1920)*. ROSSPĖN, 2005.

————. "Jews, Pogroms, and the White Movement: A Historiographical Critique." *Kritika: Explorations in Russian and Eurasian History* 2, no. 4 (2001): 1–23.

————. *Russian Jews between the Reds and the Whites, 1917–1920*. 1st ed. Philadelphia: University of Pennsylvania Press, 2012.

Budnitsky, Oleg, and Alexandra Polyan. *Russko-Evreiskij Berlin (1920–1941)*. Moscow: Novoe Literaturnoe Obozrenie, 2015.

Burgess, Ann Wolbert. "Rape Trauma Syndrome." *Behavioral Sciences & the Law* 1, no. 3 (1983): 97–113.

Burgess, Ann Wolbert, and Lynda Lytle Holmstrom. "Rape Trauma Syndrome." *American Journal of Psychiatry* 131, no. 9 (1974): 981–86.

Buss, Doris E. "Rethinking 'Rape as a Weapon of War.'" *Feminist Legal Studies* 17, no. 2 (2009): 145–63.

Cacho, Lisa Marie. *Social Death: Racialized Rightlessness and the Criminalization of the Unprotected*. New York: New York University Press, 2012.

Cahill, Ann J. "Foucault, Rape, and the Construction of the Feminine Body." *Hypatia* 15, no. 1 (2000): 43–63.

Cantor, Aviva. *Jewish Women/Jewish Men: The Legacy of Patriarchy in Jewish Life*. Harper: San Francisco, 1995.

Card, Claudia. "Addendum to "Rape as a Weapon of War"." *Hypatia* 12, no. 2 (1997): 216–18.

————. *The Atrocity Paradigm: A Theory of Evil*. Oxford: Oxford University Press, 2002.

————. "Genocide and Social Death." *Hypatia* 18, no. 1 (2003): 63–79.

————. "Rape as a Weapon of War." *Hypatia* 11, no. 4 (1996): 5–18.

Carpenter, R. Charli. "Surfacing Children: Limitations of Genocidal Rape Discourse." *Human Rights Quarterly* 22, no. 2 (2000): 428–77.

Caruth, Cathy. *Unclaimed Experience: Trauma, Narrative, and History*. Baltimore: Johns Hopkins University Press, 2016.

Chalk, Frank. "Refining Genocide." In *Genocide: Conceptual and Historical Dimensions*, edited by George J. Andreopoulos, 47–63. Philadelphia: University of Pennsylvania Press, 1994.

Chang, Iris. *The Rape of Nanking: The Forgotten Holocaust of World War II*. New York: Basic Books, 2012.

Cherikover, I. "Antisemitizm i Pogromy na Ukraine, 1917–1918 gg." *K istorii ukrainsko-evreiskikh otnoshenii* (1923).

————. *Anṭisemiṭizm un Pogromen in Uḵraine, 1917–1918: Tsu der Geshikhṭe fun Uḵrainish-Yidishe Batsihungen*, edited by Archiv Ostjüdisches historisches, Geshikhṭe fun der Pogrom-Baỵegung in Uḵraine, 1917–1921. Berlin: Mizreḥ-Yidishn hisṭorishn arkhiỵ, 1923.

————. *Di Uḵrainer Pogramen*. Pogroms in the Ukraine in 1919. New York: Yidisher Ỵisenshaflecher Institut, 1965.

Chouliaraki, Lilie. *The Spectatorship of Suffering*. Thousand Oaks, CA: Pine Forge Press, 2006.

Cohen, Julie E. "Privacy, Visibility, Transparency, and Exposure." *The University of Chicago Law Review* 75, no. 1 (2008): 181–201.

Copelon, Rhonda. "Gendered War Crimes: Reconceptualizing Rape in Time of War." In *Women's Rights, Human Rights: International Feminist Perspectives*, edited by Julie Peters and Andrea Wolper, 197–214. London: Routledge, 199.

Das, Veena, Arthur Kleinman, Margaret M. Lock, Mamphela Ramphele, and Pamela Reynolds. *Remaking a World: Violence, Social Suffering, and Recovery*. Berkeley: University of California Press, 2001.

Dekel-Chen, Jonathan L. *Anti-Jewish Violence: Rethinking the Pogrom in East European History*. Bloomington: Indiana University Press, 2011.

Denikine, Anton Ivanovich. *Ocherki Russkoj Smuty*. Vol. 3. Moscow: Ajris, 2006.

Douglass, Ana, and Thomas A. Vogler. *Witness and Memory: The Discourse of Trauma*. London: Routledge, 2012.

Draitser, Emil. *Making War, Not Love: Gender and Sexuality in Russian Humor*. New York: Macmillan, 1999.

Du Toit, Louise. *A Philosophical Investigation of Rape: The Making and Unmaking of the Feminine Self*. London: Routledge, 2009.

———. "Rape Understood as Torture: What Is the Responsibility of Men?" *Rape: Rethinking Male Responsibility* (2003): 36–67.

Dynner, Glenn. "The Hasidic Tale as a Historical Source: Historiography and Methodology." *Religion Compass* 3, no. 4 (2009): 655–75.

———. "Replenishing the 'Fountain of Judaism': Traditionalist Jewish Education in Interwar Poland" (forthcoming from *Jewish History*).

Economou, Nicole Rosenberg. "Defense Expert Testimony on Rape Trauma Syndrome: Implications for the Stoic Victim." *Hastings LJ* 42 (1990): 1143.

Enders, Jody. "The Spectacle of the Scaffolding: Rape and the Violent Foundations of Medieval Theatre Studies." *Theatre Journal* 56, no. 2 (2004): 163–81.

Engel, Barbara Alpern. *Women in Russia: 1700–2000*. Cambridge: Cambridge University Press, 2004.

Engel, David. *Lwów, 1918: The Transmutation of a Symbol and Its Legacy in the Holocaust*. n/a, 2003.

———. *The Assassination of Symon Petliura and the Trial of Scholem Schwarzbard 1926–1927: A Selection of Documents*. Gottingen: Vandenhoeck & Ruprecht GmbH & Co, 2016.

———. "What's in a Pogrom? European Jews in the Age of Violence." In *Anti-Jewish Violence: Rethinking the Pogrom in East European History*, edited by Jonathan Dekel-Chen, 19–37. Bloomington: Indiana University Press, 2010.

Engelstein, Laura. *The Keys to Happiness: Sex and the Search for Modernity in Fin-De-Siecle Russia*. Ithaca, NY: Cornell University Press, 1992.

Faber, Marion, and Alexandra Stiglmayer. *Mass Rape: The War against Women in Bosnia-Herzegovina*. Lincoln: University of Nebraska Press, 1994.

Farwell, Nancy. "War Rape: New Conceptualizations and Responses." *Affilia* 19, no. 4 (2004): 389–403.

Felman, Shoshana, and Dori Laub. *Testimony: Crises of Witnessing in Literature, Psychoanalysis, and History*. Oxford: Taylor & Francis, 1992.

Felski, Rita. *The Gender of Modernity*. Cambridge, MA: Harvard University Press, 2009.

Finkel, Evgeny. *Ordinary Jews: Choice and Survival during the Holocaust*. Princeton, NJ: Princeton University Press, 2017.

Fitzpatrick, Sheila, and Yuri Slezkine. *In the Shadow of Revolution: Life Stories of Russian Women from 1917 to the Second World War*. Princeton, NJ: Princeton University Press, 2000.

Foucault, Michel. *Discipline and Punish: The Birth of the Prison*. [In translation of "Surveiller et punir."] New York: Vintage Books, 1995.

Frankel, Jonathan. *Crisis, Revolution, and Russian Jews*. Cambridge: Cambridge University Press, 2009.

———. "The Dilemmas of Jewish National Autonomism: The Case of Ukraine 1917–1920." *Ukrainian-Jewish Relations in Historical Perspective* (1990): 263–79.

Freeze, ChaeRan Y. *Jewish Marriage and Divorce in Imperial Russia*. Hanover: University Press of New England for Brandeis University Press, 2002.

———. "Lilith's Midwives: Jewish Newborn Child Murder in Nineteenth-Century Vilna." *Jewish Social Studies* 16, no. 2 (2010): 1–27.

Freidberg, A. "The Mobilized and Virtual Gaze in Modernity." With introductions by N. Mirzoeff, 253–78. London: Routledge, 1998.

Friedrichs, Christopher R. "Politics or Pogrom? The Fettmilch Uprising in German and Jewish History." *Central European History* 19, no. 2 (1986): 186–228.

Gadzhieva, Leila. "Mir Kazachestva v Izobrazhenii N.V. Gogolya, L.N. Tolstogo, M.A. Sholokhova." Ph.D. diss., Moscow: Moscow State University of Humanities, 2007.

Gershenson, Olga, and David Shneer. "Soviet Jewishness and Cultural Studies." *Journal of Jewish Identities* 4, no. 1 (2011): 129–46.

Ghassem-Fachandi, Parvis. *Pogrom in Gujarat: Hindu Nationalism and Anti-Muslim Violence in India*. Princeton, NJ: Princeton University Press, 2012.

Giddens, Anthony. *The Consequences of Modernity*. Indianapolis: John Wiley & Sons, 2013.

———. *Modernity and Self-Identity: Self and Society in the Late Modern Age*. Stanford, CA: Stanford University Press, 1991.

Gilley, Christopher. "Beyond Petliura: The Ukrainian National Movement and the 1919 Pogroms." *East European Jewish Affairs* 47, no. 1 (2017): 45–61.

Gluzman, Michael. "Pogrom and Gender: On Bialik's Unheimlich." *Prooftexts* 25, nos. 1–2 (2005): 39–59.

Goldstone, Richard J. "Prosecuting Rape as a War Crime." *Case W. Res. J. Int'l L.* 34 (2002): 277.

Goldin, Semion. "Deportation of Jews by the Russian Military Command, 1914–1915." *Jews in Eastern Europe* 41, no. 1 (2000): 40–73.

Goodwin, Jeff, James M. Jasper, and Francesca Polletta, eds. *Passionate Politics: Emotions and Social Movements*. Chicago: University of Chicago Press, 2009.

Grishchenko, A. N., and A. V. Lazarev. "Konstantin Konstantinovich Mamantov." *Voprosy Istorii*, no. 1 (2012): 47–66.

Gusev-Orenburgskiy, S. I. *Bagrovaya Kniga. Pogromy 1919–20 gg. na Ukraine*. New York: Ladoga, 1983.

Gutting, Gary. *The Cambridge Companion to Foucault*. Cambridge: Cambridge University Press, 2005.

Hagen, William W. *Germans, Poles, and Jews: The Nationality Conflict in the Prussian East, 1772–1914*. Chicago: University of Chicago Press, 1980.

––––––. "The Moral Economy of Ethnic Violence: The Pogrom in Lwow, November 1918." *Geschichte und Gesellschaft* 31, no. 2 (2005): 203–26.

––––––. "Murder in the East: German-Jewish Liberal Reactions to Anti-Jewish Violence in Poland and Other East European Lands, 1918–1920." *Central European History* 34, no. 1 (2001): 1–30.

Hareli, Shlomo, and Brian Parkinson. "What's Social about Social Emotions?" *Journal for the Theory of Social Behaviour* 38, no. 2 (2008): 131–56.

Henke, Suzette A. *Shattered Subjects: Trauma and Testimony in Women's Life-Writing*. New York: Macmillan, 2000.

Henry, Jim. "System Intervention Trauma to Child Sexual Abuse Victims Following Disclosure." *Journal of Interpersonal Violence* 12, no. 4 (1997): 499–512.

Herbeck, Ulrich. "National Antisemitism in Russia during the 'Years of Crisis,' 1914–1922." *Studies in Ethnicity and Nationalism* 7, no. 3 (2007): 171–84.

Herman, Judith Lewis. *Trauma and Recovery*. Vol. 551. New York: Basic Books, 1997.

Himka, John-Paul. "The Lviv Pogrom of 1941: The Germans, Ukrainian Nationalists, and the Carnival Crowd." *Canadian Slavonic Papers* 53, nos. 2–4 (2011): 209–43.

––––––. "Ukrainian Collaboration in the Extermination of the Jews during the Second World War: Sorting out the Long-Term and Conjunctural Factors." *The Fate of the European Jews* 1945 (1997): 170–89.

Hirsch, Marianne, and Leo Spitzer. "The Witness in the Archive: Holocaust Studies/Memory Studies." *Memory Studies* 2, no. 2 (2009): 151–70.

Hoffmann, Christhard, and Werner Bergmann. *Exclusionary Violence: Antisemitic Riots in Modern German History*. Ann Arbor: University of Michigan Press, 2002.

Horeck, Tanya. *Public Rape: Representing Violation in Fiction and Film*. London: Routledge, 2013.

Horowitz, Sara R. "The Rhetoric of Embodied Memory in the 'City of Slaughter.'" *Prooftexts* 25, no. 1 (2005): 73–85.

Hron, Madeline. "Intimate Enemy: Images and Voices of the Rwandan Genocide." *African Studies Quarterly* 10, no. 2–3 (2008).

Hundert, Gershon David. *Jews in Poland-Lithuania in the Eighteenth Century: A Genealogy of Modernity*. Berkeley: University of California Press, 2004.

Hyman, Paula E. *Gender and Assimilation in Modern Jewish History: The Roles and Representation of Women*. Seattle: University of Washington Press, 1995.

Inkeles, Alex. "Making Men Modern: On the Causes and Consequences of Individual Change in Six Developing Countries." *American Journal of Sociology* 75, no. 2 (1969): 208–25.

———. "The School as a Context for Modernization." *International Journal of Comparative Sociology* 14 (1973): 163–79.

Janoff-Bulman, Ronnie. *Shattered Assumptions*. New York: Simon and Schuster, 2010.

Jewish Women in Eastern Europe. Edited by ChaeRan Y. Freeze, Paula Hyman, Antony Polonsky, in Volume 18 of *Polin: Studies in Polish Jewry*. Oxford: Basil Blackwell for the Institute for Polish-Jewish Studies, 2005.

Jockusch, Laura. *Collect and Record! Jewish Holocaust Documentation in Early Postwar Europe*. Oxford: Oxford University Press, 2012.

Kahn, Arnold S., Virginia Andreoli Mathie, and Cyndee Torgler. "Rape Scripts and Rape Acknowledgment." *Psychology of Women Quarterly* 18, no. 1 (1994): 53–66.

Kakar, Sudhir. *The Colors of Violence: Cultural Identities, Religion, and Conflict*. Chicago: University of Chicago Press, 1996.

Kalman, Mihaly. "A Pogromless City: Jewish Paramilitaries in Civil War Odessa." Presentation at New Directions in Russian Jewish Studies: A Scholars Workshop at Brandeis University on April 3, 2016.

Karlip, Joshua M. "Between Martyrology and Historiography: Elias Tcherikower and the Making of a Pogrom Historian." *East European Jewish Affairs* 38, no. 3 (2008): 257–80.

———. *The Tragedy of a Generation*. Cambridge, MA: Harvard University Press, 2013.

Karpenko, Sergei. "Vrangel Petr Nikolaevich (1878–1928)." *Novyi Istoricheskii Vestnik*, no. 3 (2001): 177–85.

Kauffman, Jeffrey. *Loss of the Assumptive World: A Theory of Traumatic Loss*. London: Routledge, 2013.

Kenez, Peter. *Civil War in South Russia, 1918: The First Year of the Volunteer Army*. Berkeley: University of California Press, 1971.

———. *Civil War in South Russia, 1919–1920: The Defeat of the Whites*. Vol. 2. Berkeley: University of California Press, 1977.

———. "The Ideology of the White Movement." *Europe-Asia Studies* 32, no. 1 (1980): 58–83.

———. "Pogroms and White Ideology in the Russian Civil War." *Pogroms: Anti-Jewish Violence in Modern Russian History* (1992): 293–311.

Kennedy, Dennis. *The Spectator and the Spectacle*. Cambridge: Cambridge University Press, 2009.

Khushalani, Yougindra. *The Dignity and Honour of Women as Basic and Fundamental Human Rights*. Leiden: Martinus Nijhoff Publishers, 1982.

Klier, John. *Russians, Jews, and the Pogroms of 1881–1882*. Cambridge: Cambridge University Press, 2011.

———. *Imperial Russia's Jewish Question, 1855–1881*. Vol. 96. Cambridge: Cambridge University Press, 2005.

———. "The Pogrom Paradigm in Russian History." In *Pogroms: Anti-Jewish Violence in Modern Russian History*, edited by John Klier and Shlomo Lambroza, 13–38. Cambridge: Cambridge University Press, 1992.

Klier, John, and Shlomo Lambroza. *Pogroms: Anti-Jewish Violence in Modern Russian History.* Cambridge: Cambridge University Press, 1992.

Kopstein, Jeffrey S., and Jason Wittenberg. "Anti-Jewish Pogroms in Northeastern Poland, Summer 1941." (2011): 1–26.

———. "Deadly Communities: Local Political Milieus and the Persecution of Jews in Occupied Poland." *Comparative Political Studies* 44, no. 3 (2011): 259–83.

———. "Intimate Violence: Anti-Jewish Pogroms in the Shadow of the Holocaust," unpublished version (2013): 6–23.

———. "Intimate Violence: Why Do Pogroms Occur in Some Localities and Not Others?" unpublished version (2011): 6–23.

Lacan, Jacques. *The Split between the Eye and the Gaze.* In *The Four Fundamental Concepts of Psycho-Analysis.* Vol. 11. New York: W. W. Norton & Company, 1998.

LaCapra, Dominick. *Writing History, Writing Trauma.* Baltimore: Johns Hopkins University Press, 2014.

Landis, Erik-C. "A Civil War Episode: General Mamontov in Tambov, August 1919." *The Carl Beck Papers in Russian and East European Studies,* no. 1601 (2002): 39.

Laub, Dori. "An Event without a Witness: Truth, Testimony and Survival." *Testimony: Crises of Witnessing in Literature, Psychoanalysis, and History* (1992): 75–92.

———. "Truth and Testimony: The Process and the Struggle." *Trauma: Explorations in Memory* 63 (1995).

Lederhendler, Eli. *Jewish Responses to Modernity: New Voices in America and Eastern Europe.* New York: New York University Press, 1997.

Lemkin, Raphael, and Donna-Lee Frieze. *Totally Unofficial: The Autobiography of Raphael Lemkin.* New Haven, CT: Yale University Press, 2013.

Levi, Primo. *Survival in Auschwitz.* New York: Simon and Schuster, 1996.

Leys, Ruth. *Trauma: A Genealogy.* Chicago: University of Chicago Press, 2010.

Litvak, Olga. "Khave and Her Sisters: Sholem-Aleichem and the Lost Girls of 1905." *Jewish Social Studies* 15, no. 3 (2009): 1–38.

Liulevicius, Vejas Gabriel. *War Land on the Eastern Front Culture, National Identity, and German Occupation in World War I.* Cambridge: Cambridge University Press, 2000.

Lohr, Eric. *Nationalizing the Russian Empire: The Campaign against Enemy Aliens during World War I.* Vol. 94. Cambridge, MA: Harvard University Press, 2003.

———. "The Russian Army and the Jews: Mass Deportation, Hostages, and Violence during World War I." *The Russian Review* 60, no. 3 (2001): 404–19.

MacDonogh, Giles. *After the Reich: The Brutal History of the Allied Occupation.* New York: Basic Books, 2009.

MacKinnon, Catherine A. "Ictr's Legacy on Sexual Violence, The." *New Eng. J. Int'l & Comp. L.* 14 (2007): 211.

———. "Rape, Genocide, and Women's Human Rights." *Harv. Women's LJ* 17 (1994): 5.

Massaro, Toni M. "Experts, Psychology, Credibility, and Rape: The Rape Trauma Syndrome Issue and Its Implications for Expert Psychological Testimony." *Minn. L. Rev.* 69 (1984): 395.

McCord, David. "The Admissibility of Expert Testimony Regarding Rape Trauma Syndrome in Rape Prosecutions." *BCL Rev.* 26 (1984): 1143.

McGlynn, Clare. "Rape as 'Torture'? Catharine Mackinnon and Questions of Feminist Strategy." *Feminist Legal Studies* 16, no. 1 (2008): 71–85.

McKeon, Michael. *The Secret History of Domesticity: Public, Private, and the Division of Knowledge.* Baltimore: Johns Hopkins University Press, 2009.

McMeekin, Sean. *The Russian Origins of the First World War.* Cambridge, MA: Harvard University Press, 2011.

Merback, Mitchell B. *Pilgrimage and Pogrom: Violence, Memory, and Visual Culture at the Host-Miracle Shrines of Germany and Austria.* Chicago: University of Chicago Press, 2012.

Meron, Theodor. "Rape as a Crime under International Humanitarian Law." *The American Journal of International Law* 87, no. 3 (1993): 424–28.

Merridale, Catherine. *Ivan's War: Life and Death in the Red Army, 1939–1945.* New York: Macmillan, 2006.

Miller, Alexandra A. "From the International Criminal Tribunal for Rwanda to the International Criminal Court: Expanding the Definition of Genocide to Include Rape." *Penn St. L. Rev.* 108 (2003): 349.

Miller, Nancy K., and Jason Daniel Tougaw. *Extremities: Trauma, Testimony, and Community* Urbana-Champaign: University of Illinois Press, 2002.

Minow, Martha. *Between Vengeance and Forgiveness: Facing History after Genocide and Mass Violence.* Boston: Beacon Press, 1998.

Mogilner, Marina. "Toward a History of Russian Jewish 'Medical Materialism': Russian Jewish Physicians and the Politics of Jewish Biological Normalization." *Jewish Social Studies* 19, no. 1 (2012): 70–106.

Moore, Alison M. "History, Memory and Trauma in Photography of the Tondues: Visuality of the Vichy Past through the Silent Image of Women." *Gender & History* 17, no. 3 (2005): 657–81.

Moss, Kenneth B. "At Home in Late Imperial Russian Modernity—Except When They Weren't: New Histories of Russian and East European Jews, 1881–1914." *The Journal of Modern History* 84, no. 2 (2012): 401–52.

Motzkin, Leo. *Les Pogromes en Ukraine sous les Gouvernements Ukrainiens, 1917–1920.* Pogromes en Ukraine, 1917–1920. Cœuvres-et-Valsery: Ressouvenances, 2010.

Mulvey, Laura. "Visual Pleasure and Narrative Cinema." In *Visual and Other Pleasures,* 14–26. New York: Springer, 1989.

Nagel, Joane. *Race, Ethnicity, and Sexuality: Intimate Intersections, Forbidden Frontiers.* New York: Oxford University Press, 2003.

Nathans, Benjamin. *Beyond the Pale: The Jewish Encounter with Late Imperial Russia.* Vol. 45. Berkeley: University of California Press, 2004.

Neill, Elizabeth. *Rites of Privacy and the Privacy Trade: On the Limits of Protection for the Self.* Kingston: McGill-Queen's Press, 2001.

Nirenberg, David. *Communities of Violence: Persecution of Minorities in the Middle Ages.* Princeton, NJ: Princeton University Press, 1998.

Ostrovskii, Z. S. *Evreiskie Pogromy, 1918–1921.* Moscow, 1926.

Owens, Peter, Yang Su, and David Snow. "Social Scientific Inquiry into Genocide and Mass Killing: From Unitary Outcome to Complex Processes." *Annual Review of Sociology* 39 (2013): 69.

Pajaczkowska, Claire, and Ivan Ward. *Shame and Sexuality: Psychoanalysis and Visual Culture.* London: Routledge, 2014.

Parush, Iris. *Reading Jewish Women: Marginality and Modernization in Nineteenth-Century Eastern European Jewish Society.* Hanover, NH: Brandeis University Press, 2004.

Paust, Jordan J. "Human Dignity as a Constitutional Right: A Jurisprudentially Based Inquiry into Criteria and Content." *Howard LJ* 27 (1984): 145.

Peto, Andrea. "Memory and the Narrative of Rape in Budapest and Vienna in 1945." In *Life after Death: Approaches to a Cultural and Social History of Europe during the 1940s and 1950s,* edited by Richard Bessel and Dirk Schumann. Cambridge: Cambridge University Press, 2003.

————. "From Visibility to Analysis: Gender and History." *Paths to Gender* (2009): 1.

Phillips, Kathy. "Mass Nakedness in the Imaginary of the Nazis." *War, Literature & the Arts: An International Journal of the Humanities* 27 (2015): 1–19.

Pinker, Steven. *The Better Angels of Our Nature: Why Violence Has Declined.* New York: Viking, 2011.

Pipes, Richard. *Russia under the Bolshevik Regime.* New York: Vintage, 2011.

Rabinovitch, Simon. *Jewish Rights, National Rites: Nationalism and Autonomy in Late Imperial and Revolutionary Russia.* Stanford, CA: Stanford University Press, 2014.

————. "Jewish-Soviet-Ukrainian Relations during the Civil War and the Second Thoughts of a Minister for Jewish Affairs." *Studies in Ethnicity and Nationalism* vol. 17, no. 3 (2017). (Forthcoming.)

Revusky, Abraham. *Wrenching Times in Ukraine: Memoir of a Jewish Minister.* Edited by Sam Revusky and Moishe Kantorowitz. St. John, NL: Yksuver Pub., 1998.

Rosen, Michael. *Dignity: Its History and Meaning.* Cambridge, MA: Harvard University Press, 2012.

Rosenwein, Barbara H. "Worrying about Emotions in History." *The American Historical Review* 107, no. 3 (2002).

————. "Problems and Methods in the History of Emotions." *Passions in Context* 1, no. 1 (2010).

Roth, John K. *Genocide and Human Rights.* New York: Springer, 2005.

Russell-Brown, Sherrie L. "Rape as an Act of Genocide." *Berkeley J. Int'l L.* 21 (2003): 350.

Sartre, Jean-Paul. *The Look.* n/a, 1956.

Scarry, Elaine. *The Body in Pain: The Making and Unmaking of the World.* Oxford: Oxford University Press, 1985.

Schechtman, Joseph B., Naum Iulievich Gergel', and I. M. Cherikover. *Pogromy Dobrovol'cheskoi Armii na Ukraine: K Istorii Antisemitizma na Ukraine v 1919–1920 gg.* Ostjüdisches Historisches Archiv, 1932.

Scheff, Thomas J. "Shame and the Social Bond: A Sociological Theory." *Sociological Theory* 18, no. 1 (2000): 84–99.

————. "Shame in Self and Society." *Symbolic Interaction* 26, no. 2 (2003): 239–62.

Semujanga, Josias. *Origins of Rwandan Genocide*. Amherst, NY: Humanity Books, 2003.

Serhiichuk, Volodymyr. *Pohromy v Ukraïni, 1914–1920: Vid Shtuchnykh Stereotypiv do Hirkoï Pravdy, Prykhovuvanoï v Radians'kykh Arkhivakh*. Kiev, 1998.

Shapiro, Lamed. *The Cross and Other Jewish Stories*. New Haven, CT: Yale University Press, 2007.

————. *Un Andere Zakhen*. A naye oyfl. ed. New York: Idish leben, 1929.

Sharlach, Lisa. "Rape as Genocide: Bangladesh, the Former Yugoslavia, and Rwanda." *New Political Science* 22, no. 1 (2000): 89–102.

Short, Damien. *Redefining Genocide: Settler Colonialism, Social Death and Ecocide*. London: Zed Books Ltd., 2016.

Shternshis, Anna. "Between Life and Death: Why Some Soviet Jews Decided to Leave and Others to Stay in 1941." *Kritika: Explorations in Russian and Eurasian History* 15, no. 3 (2014): 477–504.

————. "Gender and Identity in Oral Histories of Elderly Russian Jewish Migrants in the United States and Canada." *A Companion to Diaspora and Transnationalism*: 277–92.

————. "Humor and Russian Jewish Identity." In *A Club of Their Own: Jewish Humorists and the Contemporary World*, edited by Eli Lederhendler and Gabriel N Finder, 101–13. Oxford: Oxford University Press, 2016.

————. *Soviet and Kosher: Jewish Popular Culture in the Soviet Union, 1923–1939*. Bloomington: Indiana University Press, 2006.

————. *When Sonia Met Boris: An Oral History of Jewish Life under Stalin*. Oxford: Oxford University Press, 2017.

————. "White Piano in a Shtetl: Material Culture and Ethnic Identity in the Post-Soviet Jewish Urban Community." *Jewish Social Studies* 16, no. 2 (2010): 111–26.

Shtif, Nokhem. "Pogromen in Ukreyne: Di Tsayt fun der Frayviliger Armey." Berlin: Vostock, 1923.

Skjelsbaek, Inger. "Victim and Survivor: Narrated Social Identities of Women Who Experienced Rape during the War in Bosnia-Herzegovina." *Feminism & Psychology* 16, no. 4 (2006): 373–403.

Slezkine, Yuri. *The Jewish Century*. Princeton, NJ: Princeton University Press, 2004.

Smith, David Horton, and Alex Inkeles. "The Om Scale: A Comparative Socio-Psychological Measure of Individual Modernity." *Sociometry* 29, no. 4 (1966): 353–77.

Smith, Helmut Walser. *The Butcher's Tale: Murder and Antisemitism in a German Town*. New York: W. W. Norton & Company, 2002.

————. *The Continuities of German History: Nation, Religion, and Race across the Long Nineteenth Century*. Cambridge: Cambridge University Press, 2008.

————. "German Nationalism and Religious Conflict Culture, Ideology, Politics, 1870–1914." Princeton, NJ: Princeton University Press, 2014.

Snyder, Timothy. *Bloodlands: Europe between Hitler and Stalin*. New York: Basic Books, 2012.

Sontag, Susan. *Regarding the Pain of Others*. New York: Farrar, Straus and Giroux, 2003.

Staliūnas, Darius. "Enemies for a Day Antisemitism and Anti-Jewish Violence in Lithuania under the Tsars." New York: Central European University Press, 2014.

Stampfer, Shaul. "What Actually Happened to the Jews of Ukraine in 1648?" *Jewish History* 17, no. 2 (2003): 207–27.

Sturken, Marita, and Lisa Cartwright. *Practices of Looking*. Oxford: Oxford University Press, 2003.

Szobel, Ilana. *A Poetics of Trauma: The Work of Dahlia Ravikovitch*. Hanover, NH: University Press of New England, 2013.

Tananbaum, Susan L. "From Local to International: Cape Town's Jewish Orphanage." *Jewish Historical Studies* 46 (2014): 75–105.

Thistle, Susan. "The Trouble with Modernity: Gender and the Remaking of Social Theory." *Sociological Theory* 18, no. 2 (2000): 275–88.

Thompson, Edward P. "The Moral Economy of the English Crowd in the Eighteenth Century." *Past & Present*, no. 50 (1971): 76–136.

Tsuker, A., ed. *Intelligentsiia Poet Blatnye Pesni, Iskusstvo XX veka*. Nizhnii Novgorod, 2004.

Tsvetkov, V. "Beloe Dvizhenie v Rossii. 1917–1920 gody." *Voprosy Istorii* (2000).

Veidlinger, Jeffrey. "A Forgotten Genocide: The Pogroms in Ukraine, 1918–1919." Presented at YIVO Institute for Jewish Research, 2016.

———. *Going to the People: Jews and the Ethnographic Impulse*. Bloomington: Indiana University Press, 2016.

———. "The Historical and Ethnographic Construction of Russian Jewry." *Ab Imperio*, no. 4 (2003): 165–84.

———. *In the Shadow of the Shtetl: Small-Town Jewish Life in Soviet Ukraine*. Bloomington: Indiana University Press, 2013.

Vrangel', Petr N. *Zapiski: (Nojabr' 1916 g.–Nojabr' 1920 g.)*. Kosmos, 1991.

Weinberg, Robert. "Visualizing Pogroms in Russian History." *Jewish History* 12, no. 2 (1998): 71–92.

Weine, Stevan. *Testimony after Catastrophe: Narrating the Traumas of Political Violence*. Chicago: Northwestern University Press, 2006.

Weine, Stevan, and Dori Laub. "Narrative Constructions of Historical Realities in Testimony with Bosnian Survivors of "Ethnic Cleansing." *Psychiatry* 58, no. 3 (1995): 246–60.

Weiss, Karen G. "Too Ashamed to Report: Deconstructing the Shame of Sexual Victimization." *Feminist Criminology* 5, no. 3 (2010): 286–310.

Welzel, Christian. "Individual Modernity." In *The Oxford Handbook of Political Behavior*, 185–205. Oxford: Oxford University Press, 2007.

Wilson, John P., Boris Droždek, and Silvana Turkovic. "Posttraumatic Shame and Guilt." *Trauma, Violence, & Abuse* 7, no. 2 (2006): 122–41.

Yekelchyk, Serhy. "Cossack Gold: History, Myth, and the Dream of Prosperity in the Age of Post-Soviet Transition." *Canadian Slavonic Papers* 40, nos. 3–4 (1998): 311–25.

———. *Ukraine: Birth of a Modern Nation*. Oxford: Oxford University Press, 2007.

Zarankin, Andrés, and Melisa Salerno. "The Engineering of Genocide: An Archaeology of Dictatorship in Argentina." In *Archaeologies of Internment*, 207–27. New York: Springer, 2011.

Zimbardo, Philip G. *Lucifer Effect*. Indianapolis: Wiley Online Library, 2007.

Index

Note: Page numbers followed by 'n' denotes notes

CPSIA information can be obtained
at www.ICGtesting.com
Printed in the USA
LVHW081232050622
720536LV00004B/115